PEOPLE AND THEIR ENVIRONMENT

Series editor: Neil Punnett

Settlement and Population

Peter Webber

Oxford University Press

Pupil Profile Sheets

A Pupil Profile base sheet is provided which can be copied to provide sheets for each pupil. It is intended that each pupil should receive a profile sheet at the end of each Study Unit in this book.

At the end of each Study Unit is an Assessment Unit. The second page of the Assessment Unit contains a box in which the details for the Pupil Profile Sheets are listed. The teacher can transfer the details to the base sheet.

The profile will be completed following discussion between the teacher and pupil. It will therefore provide an agreed record of achievement throughout the course. It is hoped that the profile will help to enhance the learning of pupils, increase motivation and provide diagnostic information for the teacher.

Contents

Unit 1 Where people live 4
1.1 Needs 4
1.2 The village and its site 6
1.3 Fieldwork methods 8
1.4 Village change 10
1.5 Change in Grasmere: fieldwork 12
1.6 The town and its functions 14
1.7 Cities and conurbations 16
1.8 The sphere of influence: fieldwork 18
    Assessment 20

Unit 2 Urban settlement patterns 22
2.1 Settlement patterns: the hierarchy 22
2.2 Patterns in the urban area: distributions 24
2.3 Shopping 26
2.4 Fast food: location 28
2.5 Out-of-town shopping 30
2.6 The urban transect 32
2.7 Housing types: maps 34
2.8 Housing quality: fieldwork 36
2.9 Changing school patterns 38
    Assessment 40

Unit 3 Transport and industry 42
3.1 Traffic in towns 42
3.2 Building a by-pass 44
3.3 Travelling by road 46
3.4 Travelling between cities: London to Belfast 48
3.5 Industry in towns: preservation 50
3.6 The industrial estate 52
    Assessment 54

Unit 4 Urban organization 56
4.1 Inside an urban area: land use 56
4.2 Inside an urban area: racism and vandalism 58
4.3 Social areas in a town: 1 60
4.4 Social areas in a town: 2 62
4.5 Urban growth: models 64
4.6 Inner city problems 66
4.7 Inner city renewal 68
4.8 New towns 70
4.9 Planning the urban area 72
    Assessment 74

Unit 5 The developing world 76
5.1 Urban growth in the developing world 76
5.2 Hong Kong: coping with growth 78
5.3 Living in a self-help city 80
5.4 Living in a poverty trap 82
5.5 Urban growth in Brazil 84
5.6 Villages in Tanzania: ujamaa 86
    Assessment 88

Unit 6 Population trends 90
6.1 Explaining population 90
6.2 How long a life? 92
6.3 World distribution of population 94
6.4 Population patterns explained 96
    Assessment 98

Unit 7 Contrasts 100
7.1 Urban/rural population 100
7.2 Mapping from the census 102
7.3 Rich world/poor world: farming 104
7.4 Measuring standards of living 106
7.5 People moving: migration 108
7.6 International migration 110
7.7 Fewer people: population planning 112
7.8 Population patterns: employment 114
7.9 Population patterns: conflicts 116
7.10 Population inequalities: South Africa 118
7.11 Towards a single world: sport and culture 120
    Assessment 122

Index 125
Acknowledgements 126
Photocopiable Pupil Profile base sheet 128

1.1 Needs

Unit 1: Where people live

What are the basic needs of people? Think about what a person needs in order to live and survive. Think back to the earliest people who were living in the British Isles. These Old Stone Age (Paleolithic) people were hunters and gatherers. Think also about the New Stone Age (Neolithic) villagers who had become farmers by planting crops and domesticating animals. The basic needs of these prehistoric people were the same as ours today:

> food, water, shelter, warmth and security.

Study the two photographs of settlements in very harsh environments. Both the photographs show present-day settlement. The Inuit settlement (Figure A), is *permanent* and depends on fishing. The settlement shown in Figure B is only *temporary*. The people are *nomadic*, which means they move around with their animals. Both these settlements are very small and the economies of the communities are simple. Of course these are both rare examples of settlements nowadays. Modern people throughout the world lead a much more sophisticated life. Even the poorest countries have complex village systems and large towns and cities.

Villages to cities

It is worth considering before reading any further, how people's needs have become so advanced. The earliest farmers in the world lived in present-day Iran and Iraq. Farming began about 10 000 BC. The goat was domesticated and wheat and barley were developed from wild grasses.

Figure A An Inuit settlement in Greenland

Once a farming village has a *food surplus* then people can be freed from farming. Some can make ploughs and farm tools, others can become shopkeepers. Trade can develop with other people who produce different goods. Transport systems grow and there are links with people in different environments, mountain people meet with lowlands and coastal people.

Some villages will become bigger. Special skills and services will expand. When a village grows larger and no longer depends on the farmland, it becomes a town. The earliest towns or *urban* settlements were quite small. Catal Huyuk in Turkey is one of the first towns, dating from 6500 BC. One of the earliest cities was Ur, which was flourishing beside the river Euphrates in southern Iraq by 2500 BC. At the same time the pyramids were being built in Egypt, near present-day Cairo. Advanced urban societies had begun and there was time for the development of art, writing and monumental buildings.

Some 4500 years later, today's cities contain some of the world's greatest artistic achievments. Writing has progressed so fast that modern laser printing machines print millions of sheets of paper in the time it took to write one sheet of Egyptian papyrus. The pyramid at Khufu, 138 metres high, was the tallest structure in the world for 4000 years. It is now dwarfed by buildings like the World Trade centre in New York, which is 412 metres high.

But, despite these advances, people always have basic needs which must be met. Not everyone in the modern world enjoys a high quality of life. Settlements and communities are often divided into the 'haves' and 'have-nots'. The poor still struggle to satisfy their basic needs.

Figure B Nomadic tribesmen in the Gobi Desert in Mongolia

Figure C A makeshift home (see question 3)

QUESTIONS

1. Study Figure A.
   a) What do you think the Inuit people who live in this area need?
   b) Write one sentence about each of the following: the landscape, the houses, the exact location of the houses.
2. Study Figure B. How do the needs of the people living in the desert area differ from those living in the arctic area?
3. In no more than 50 words describe the homes and the environment shown in Figure C.
4. When and where did farming begin?
5. Why did the first cities develop much later than the farming villages?
5. Look at Figure C. Where do you think this is? Can you think of other people in the world who struggle to meet their basic needs?

1.2 The village and its site

In some areas people live in *isolated farms* which are scattered in the countryside. Usually people have chosen to live in groups to give themselves a feeling of security. A *hamlet* is a small group of houses and farms. A *village* is a larger settlement of farms, houses and services. Most settlements in Britain were once villages and today's towns often started as small villages. The exact locations of hamlets and villages were carefully chosen by the original settlers.

In the fifth and sixth centuries the Anglo-Saxons settled in England. Two centuries later the Danes raided and settled in England. These new settlers established new farming villages in a very wooded countryside. If you look at any map of England except the south west you will find examples of Anglo-Saxon and Scandinavian place names. Some examples of common place-name elements are given below.

Figure A Three village sites

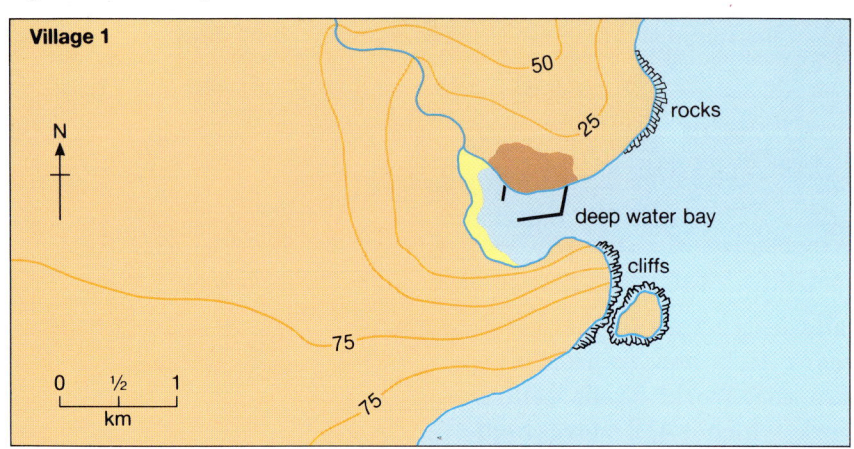

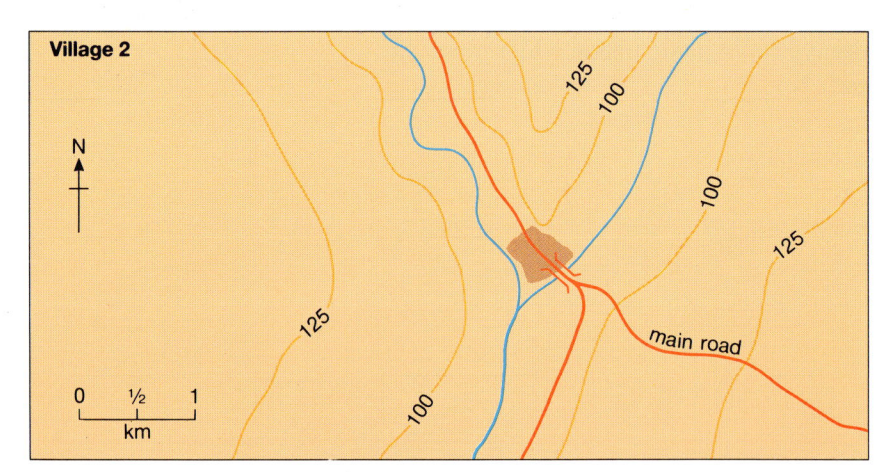

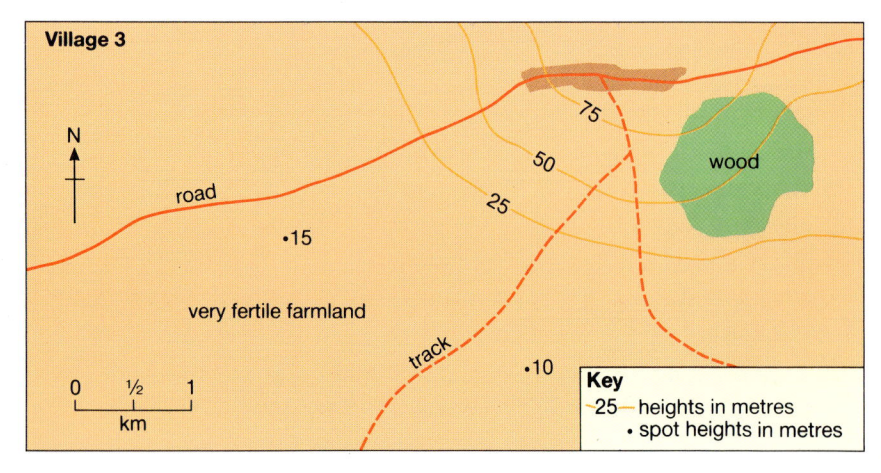

Common place-name elements and their meanings

Element	Meaning
Anglo-Saxon	
-ing	territory of . . .
-ham	homestead
-ton	enclosure
-borough, bury, burgh	fortified place
-field	clearing in a wood
-ley	clearing
-stead	place
-wick	outlying hut
-den	pasture
-hurst, hirst	wood or copse
-weald, wold	wood
-ey	island
Scandinavian	
-by	homestead
-garth	enclosure
-thorpe	daughter settlement
-thwaite	clearing
-force, foss	waterfall
-gill	ravine
-beck	stream
-dale	valley

Figure B Village 2 (see Figure A)

Key
- wooded ridge
- light soils
- heavy soils
- very wet, liable to flood
- marsh

Figure C Possible village sites

Village shape

The buildings in most villages have been built close together. Such villages are called *nucleated*. Sometimes a village will be built along a road and will be *linear* in shape. The villages 1 and 2 in Figure A are nucleated and village 3 is linear. There are many reasons for the siting of a settlement. The checklist below lists some of them.

Checklist for village siting

Water seeking – river, spring
Water avoiding – away from flood or marsh
Good soils, variety of soils
Defence – hill top
Avoiding first class farmland
Bridging point
Shelter – away from exposed places
Specialized sites:
a) harbour – for fishing
b) forestry village – near a forest around a coalmine
c) on a transport route – cross-roads

QUESTIONS

1 Make a list of any settlements you know which include the 25 place-name elements in the table on page 6.

2 **Choosing village sites.** You are a member of a group of Saxons which has arrived in the area shown in Figure C. You know nothing about the area but you want to find sites for two villages. Your group has sent scouting parties to look for places to settle. The scouting parties have found seven possible sites which are labelled K to Q.
a) Which two of the sites would you pick? Working in small groups, list the advantages and disadvantages of each site. Then describe which two sites to choose, and state clearly why you chose them.
b) Now compare your choice with the other groups in your class.

3 Now study Figure A. For each village write down why the village site was chosen.

4 Study the photograph (Figure B). Describe the site and write down why you think it was chosen.

5 Draw your own maps of village sites using the following descriptions.
a) The village lies to the west of a large meandering river. It is sited on slightly higher land away from the land which can flood. A small road runs north/south through the village. To the west of the village the land is forested.
b) The village is sited on top of a small hill (a knoll). All round the site there is marshland which has been criss-crossed with drainage ditches. A trackway leads away from the village towards the south east.

6 Write down the reasons for the siting of each of the villages you have drawn. Look back at the checklist.

1.3 Fieldwork methods

Geographers obtain much of their information from *secondary sources*, for example from maps, atlases, books, graphs, statistics and photographs. But for first hand information, *primary sources* must be used. This involves *fieldwork* and you must approach your fieldwork in an organized way.

Aim. Start with a *general aim*. One example of rural settlement fieldwork is "to investigate the range of shops and services found in villages".

Hypothesis. Then choose an *idea* or *hypothesis* which can be tested by collecting information or *data*. The hypothesis should be simple and cover a specific subject. One example of a hypothesis for a village is "the bigger the village, the more types of shops and services will be found".

Data collecting. You must then decide how you are going to *collect the data* you need to *test* your hypothesis. You want to collect enough information to be able to agree or disagree with your hypothesis. You have to prove or disprove it. One method which could be used for the hypothesis quoted above would be to choose three villages in a nearby area. Then visit the villages and note down all the shops and services. It sounds easy but you must be accurate. You must also find out the village populations.

The data collected for three English villages is shown in the table below.

Presenting the results

You must *present* your fieldwork results clearly and accurately. You must use a variety of methods . . . writing, tables or lists, graphs, maps, sketches or drawings, diagrams and photographs. Your write-up should also include how you collected the data and any difficulties you encountered.

Figures A–C show one student's presentation of the data.

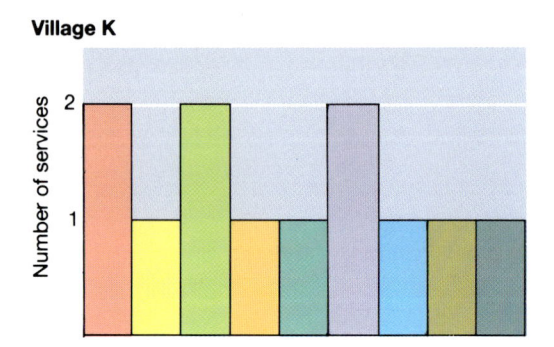

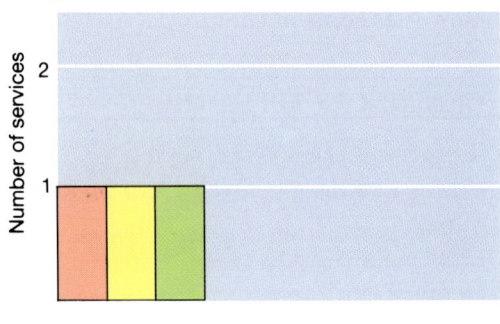

Services in three English villages

Village K population 1600	Village L population 1121	Village M population 403
two public houses	public house	public house
post office	post office	post office
two general stores	general store	general store
newsagents	primary school	
garage (petrol)	newsagents	
garage (service)	garage (petrol)	
butcher		
grocer		
hardware store		

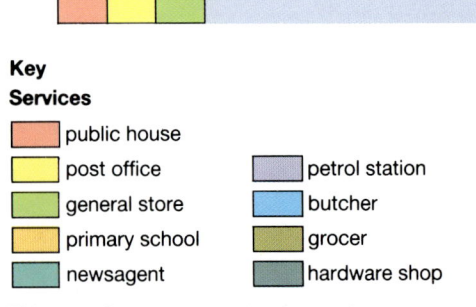

Figure A Graphs of the village services

Figure B (*left*) Sketch map to show the location of the three villages

Explaining the results

When the results have been presented you must *explain* them. State whether you have *proved* or *disproved* your hypothesis. In the case of the village services the hypothesis has been proved. The largest village has nine types of shops or services, and the smallest village has only three types. This can be explained. More people need more services and the larger village serves a bigger area. It probably also serves the smallest village M. People in village M would go to village K for some services, for example petrol. To prove this, more fieldwork would be necessary. People in the villages could be *interviewed* to find out where they go for services.

You can see that this fieldwork could lead to more fieldwork. It would require the setting out of a new general aim and the stating of a new hypothesis. A carefully worded *questionnaire* would have to be used.

Figure C (*left*) Scattergraph showing the relationship between village population and number of services

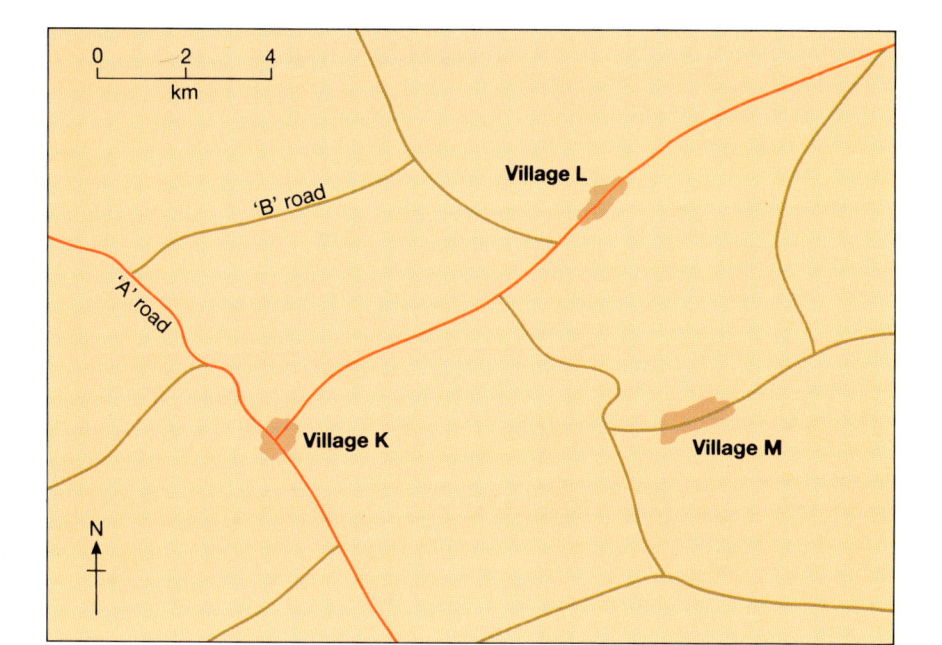

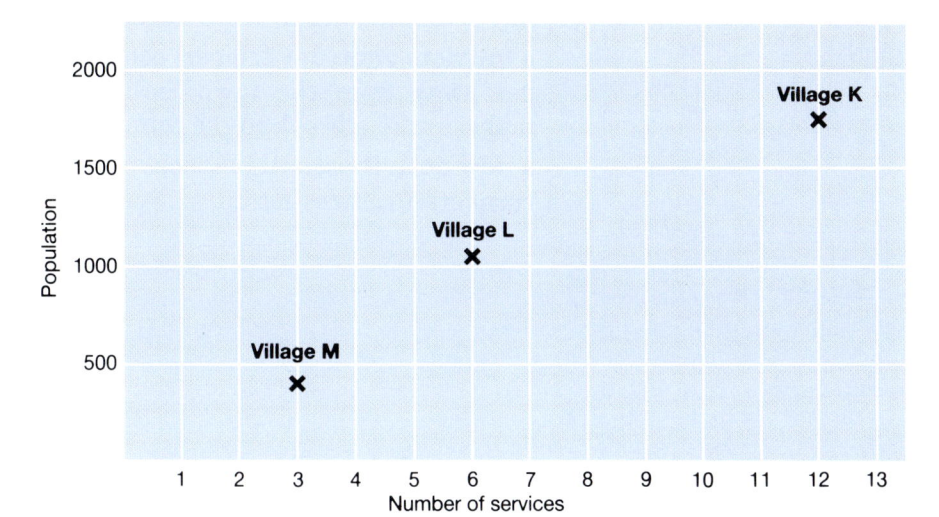

Figure D A rural post office

QUESTIONS

1. Write down a checklist for fieldwork. Use the words in italic type. If you get stuck the fieldwork enquiry route on spread 1.8 will help.
2. Study the presentation of the fieldwork, Figures A – C.
   a) Suggest how the map could have been improved.
   b) How would data from three other villages help this fieldwork?
3. Draw a graph similar to the three shown to show the services in a fourth nearby village, village N (population: 806, public house, general store, newsagents, post office and primary school). Does this village continue to prove the hypothesis?
4. Write out a fieldwork plan to test one of the following hypotheses:
   a) "The village has less services today than twenty years ago."
   b) "The village has more houses today than twenty years ago."
5. **Further work** You can carry out fieldwork in your local area to test a simple hypothesis. Follow each stage of the fieldwork carefully.

1.4 Village change

Some villages have lost population this century. Why do you think this is? Many other villages have increased their population. What reasons can you think of for this?

As well as the decline of population in villages there has been a decline of village services. But many other changes have taken place in villages.

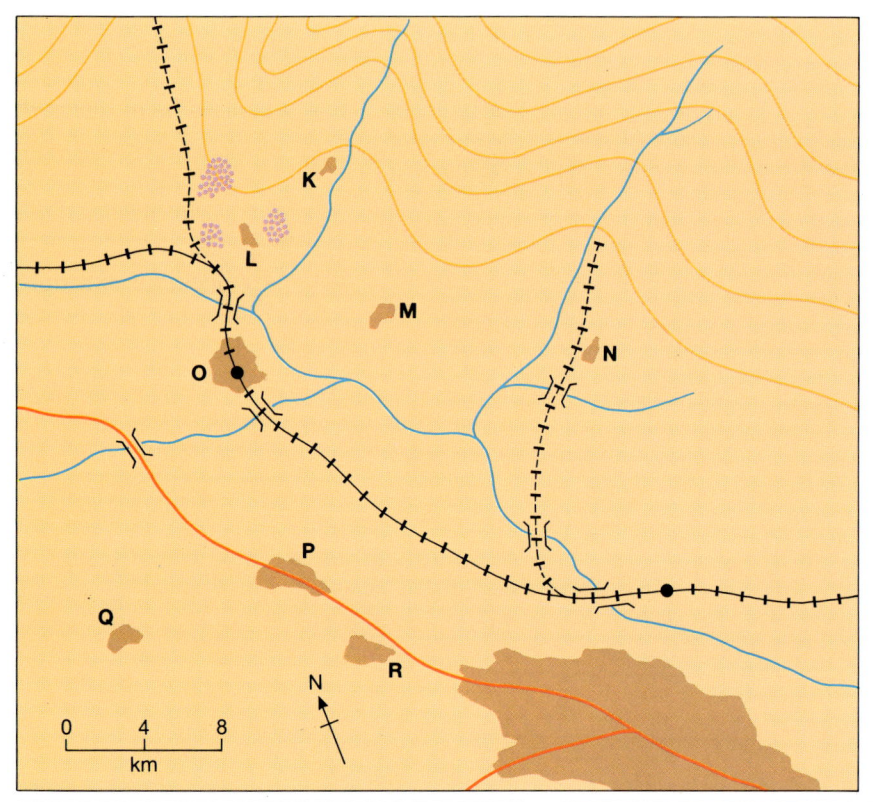

Changes in villages

- **population declines:** farms do not need so many workers; young people move away to the towns.
- **services close down:** village school shuts; post office closes; small shops close, e.g. butcher, baker.
- **public transport reduced:** bus services cut; railway station closes.
- **cost of living rises:** prices in rural shops are higher; villagers use expensive petrol to travel to essential services.
- **new people arrive:** village housing is bought by retired people; people move in and commute to work in nearby towns; people from the urban areas buy second homes in the village.
- **tourists visit:** day trippers come to get away from the town; holidaymakers take a break in the country.
- **new activities:** antique shops open; rural craft centres set up.

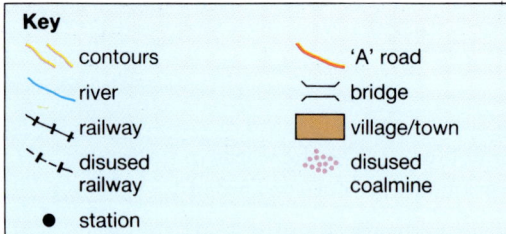

Key
- contours
- river
- railway
- disused railway
- station
- 'A' road
- bridge
- village/town
- disused coalmine

Figure A Locations of eight villages

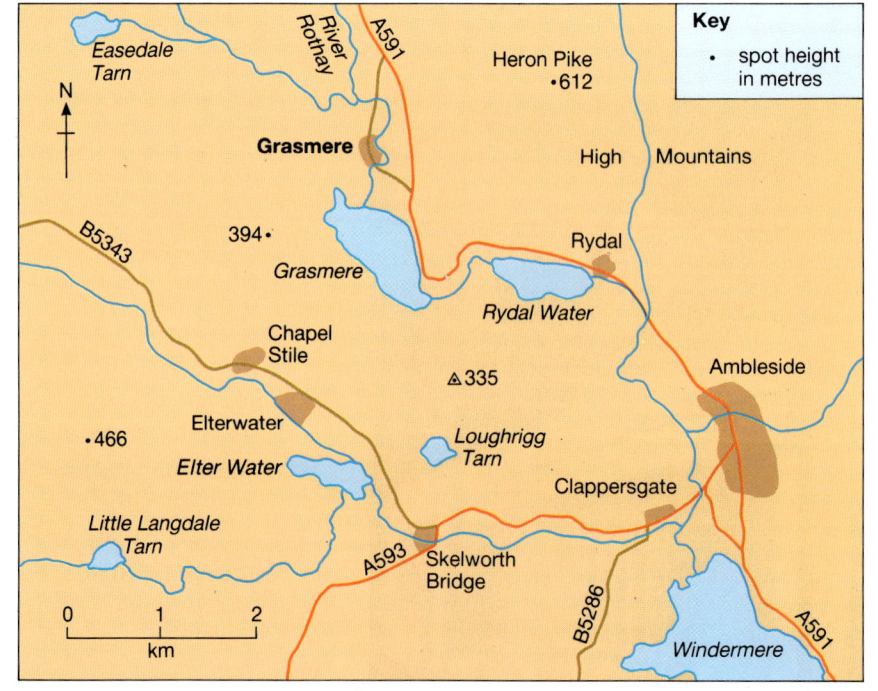

Figure B The situation of Grasmere village

Figure C Grasmere village and its surroundings, looking north

Grasmere

The village of Grasmere is *situated* north of Lake Grasmere in the central Lake District, north west of the town of Ambleside (see Figure B). Note the use of the word situation; it refers to the *position* of the village – where it is in relation to other places. The nucleated village is sited on flat land above the flood level of the lake. The height of the village is about 65 metres above sea level. Surrounding the village are high mountains, some of which rise to over 600 metres.

QUESTIONS

1. Look at Figure A.
   a) Three of the villages shown on the map have lost population in recent years. Decide which three of the villages lettered K to R might have lost population and give reasons for your choices.
   b) Three of the villages have increased their population very rapidly in recent years. Decide which three of the villages might have increased their population fast and give reasons for your choices.

2. You are an old age pensioner and you have lived in a village all your life. Write a letter to a friend explaining how the village has changed.

3. In 1986 the Church of England produced a report on the problems in rural areas. What do you think is meant by the following quotations from the report?
   a) Many small villages 'have no services of any sort and elderly residents are trapped at a considerable distance from shops, social services, doctors and banks'.
   b) 'The sharp decline in the availability of public transport in rural areas (and the cost of what remains) is one of the principle features of deprivation in rural areas.'

4. Draw a labelled sketch from the photograph. Only draw simple lines for your sketch to show the lake, village and the mountains. With the help of Figure B and the text, label the main road and the reasons for its site.

1.5 Change in Grasmere: fieldwork

Some students had been discussing changes in villages and wanted to do some fieldwork in a village. They were going to the Lake District for a long weekend and decided to test the following hypothesis, 'Grasmere is now a tourist village'.

They obtained population figures for this century (Figure C) from the Archives Department of Cumbria County Council. They discovered an old 6 inches to 1 mile Ordnance Survey map dated 1919 (Figure A). They made enlarged copies of this map and obtained a sketch map of the village by writing to the Grasmere Tourist Information Centre.

Using the 1919 map, the group mapped every change they could find in Grasmere. They also marked in everything that was connected with tourists. It was more difficult than they thought! Most of their data is shown in Figure B. On the 1986 map, find the places shown in the two photographs.

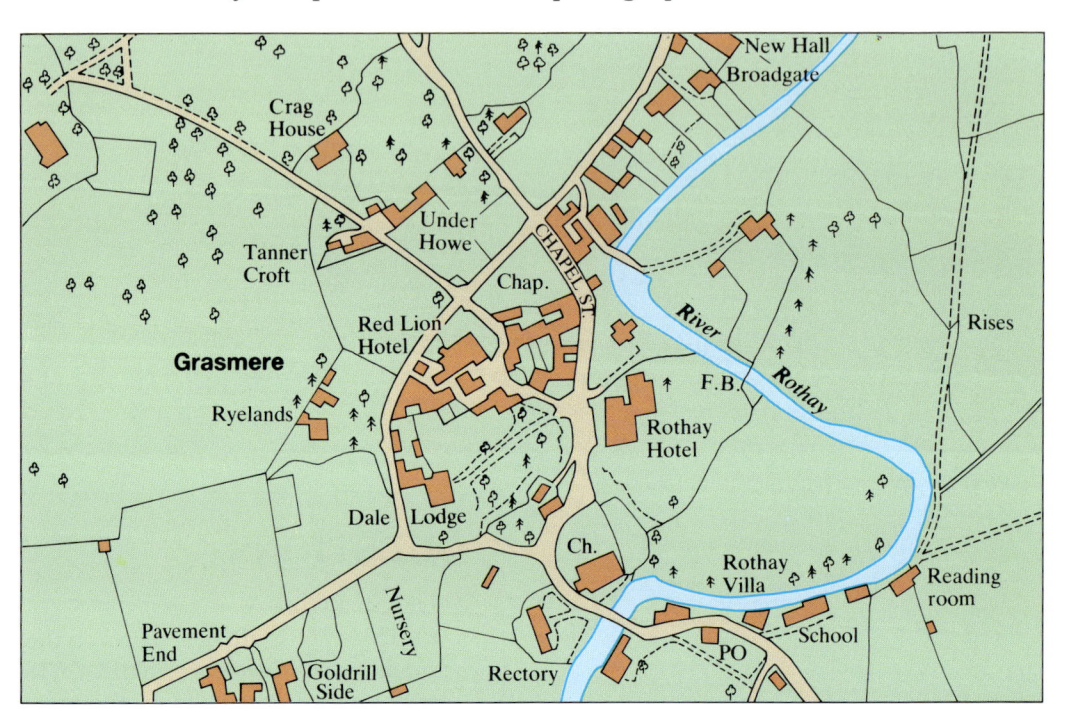

Figure A Grasmere in 1919

Figure B Grasmere in 1986 redrawn neatly from the students' fieldwork notebook

Key
1. Shops
   (a) Gifts
   (b) Bank
   (c) Walking/Climbing shop
   (d) Jewellers/Fine china
2. New shops
   (a) Knitwear
   (b) Tweeds
   (c) Restaurant
   (d) Old Post Office now Greek restaurant

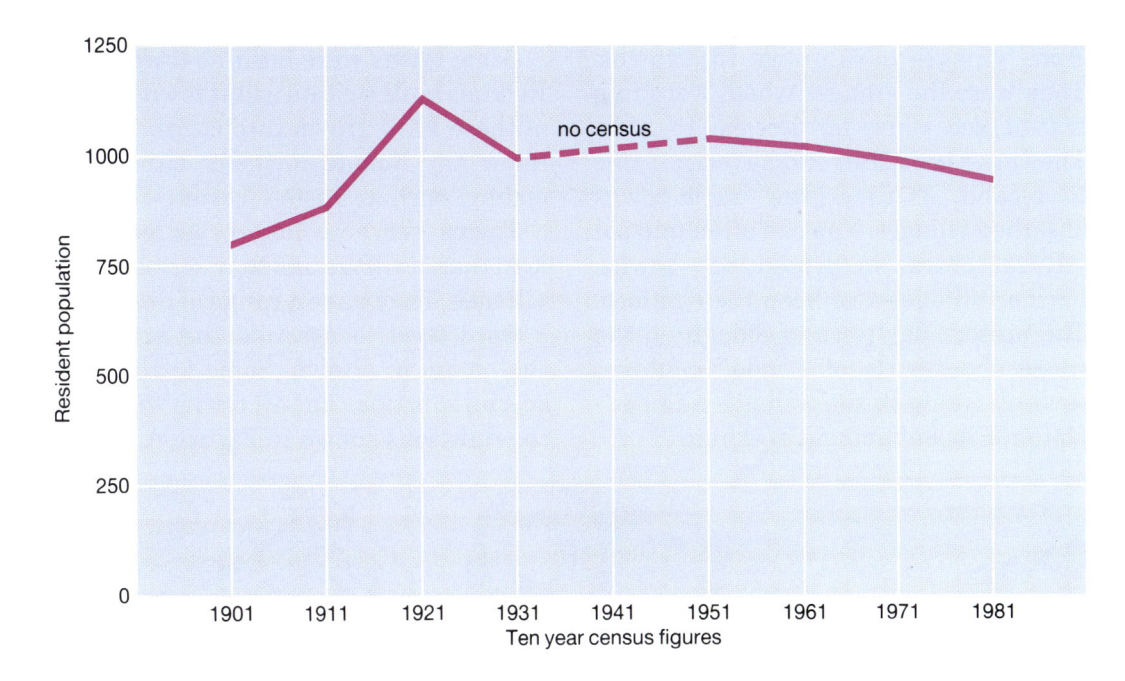

Figure C Population of Grasmere from 1901 to 1981. The Record Office told students that sometimes the number of people holidaying in Grasmere was double the resident population

QUESTIONS

1. Study the 1919 and the 1986 maps of Grasmere.
    a) What was the Wordsworth Hotel called in 1919?
    b) Which hotel has been extended since 1919?
    c) Name two old houses which are now hotels.
    d) Find the Reading Room on the 1919 map. What was it in 1986?
    e) How many hotels were there in 1986?
    f) How many shops and services were there in 1986 at Numbers 1 and 2? Which one of these services would you expect to be used by local (residents) people?
    g) How is the lake used by tourists?
2. What evidence is there on the 1986 map that Grasmere caters for different types of tourists?
3. How has the increase in tourism used up land at Grasmere?
4. What surprises you about the amount of new housing in Grasmere?
5. William Wordsworth is buried in Grasmere churchyard – who was he?
6. The general store to the north of the village centre sells a wide range of food and provisions. Which shops and services do you think would have been in Grasmere in 1919?
7. Why do you think that the population of Grasmere has not declined very quickly since 1931 (Figure C)?
8. Write down a list of how the students set up their Grasmere fieldwork. Did they prove their hypothesis?
9. **Further work** If you have access to a village, you can set up your own fieldwork to investigate change in the village. Do not forget to talk to people in the village if you want to find out details. Old people who have lived in a village for a long time are a living data bank. But remember you have to be *polite* and ask the right questions.

Figure D Two views of Grasmere

1.6 The town and its functions

Some villages have grown into towns. They were the villages which were in a *central place* where farmers met to trade. They have good sites and have been able to expand. As they grew, some towns absorbed villages. You can often find old village centres in present-day towns. Former villages also keep their names. The present day town of Slough on the western outskirts of London contains several Anglo-Saxon village names – Upton, Cippenham and Wexham.

Some towns were built as towns. The Romans built Britain's first towns. Some of these have grown into cities. Do you know any Roman towns or cities with endings such as -caster, -cester, -chester?

Towns serve a larger surrounding area than a village and they serve nearby villages. They have a range of *functions*, a word used to describe the activities that go on in a town. Some towns have special functions but all towns will have the functions shown in Figure A.

Figure A Important functions of a town

Larger towns will have more functions than smaller ones. Some functions will not be able to survive with a small number of customers. The minimum population (number of customers) that will support a function is the *threshold* population. A supermarket chain will not open in a town unless it knows there are enough customers. Each company will have a policy to decide where it can locate.

Five services in five nearby settlements in Wales

Shops and services	Settlements (population)				
	A (15000)	B (8500)	C (5000)	D (1300)	E (990)
chain store	2	1	–	–	–
dentist	5	3	1	–	–
optician	4	2	1	–	–
chemist	4	2	1	–	–
hairdresser	19	13	2	2	1
total	34				

Some of the functions of a British market town

town hall
swimming pool
plastics factory
hairdressers
gym and fitness centre
solicitors
supermarket
district planning office
old peoples' club
railway station
primary school
electrical shop
cinema
furniture store
bus station
Citizens Advice Bureau
public house
restaurant
doctor
insurance agency
comprehensive school
film manufacturers
cattle market
college
take-away
health centre

QUESTIONS

1 Some of the functions of one small market town are shown on the left. Group the town's functions under the following categories: headings:
   Administration
   Social services and health
   Education
   Industry
   Communication
   Retailing (shopping)
   Finance

2 Copy the table above and complete the **total** line.
   a) What is the total number of all the services listed for Settlement B?
   b) Which settlement has only one chain store?
   c) What is the threshold population of the chain store in the area?
   d) What is the threshold population of an optician in the area?

3 Suggest five other shops or services that Settlement A is likely to have.

4 Suggest reasons why the shop referred to in the newspaper article below might have closed down.

> **SHUT DOWN!** Dixons the camera and electrical giant have pulled out of a northern town. A spokesperson for the company said that the reason for

5 Have any shops in your area closed down recently? If so, why do you think it happened?

6 **Further work** Select a small town or a part of a larger urban area. Test the hypothesis "there are several functions in each of the seven function categories in an urban area".
   Note down every function you find in your chosen area. Then group the functions in the categories listed in Question 1. You can make slight changes to the categories if you wish.
   Remember to set out your study as described in spread 1.3, pages 8 and 9.

1.7 Cities and conurbations

A *city* is a large built-up area which serves an area bigger than a town. In the past, a city was a large town with a cathedral. Today this definition is not very useful. Some central places are called cities but are smaller than other places called towns. For example, Ely in Cambridgeshire has a population of only 10 200 and yet it is a city because of its cathedral. A different example is Wolverhampton which has a population of 252 000; it has no cathedral and is not called a city.

A *conurbation* is a built-up area larger than a city: it is several towns or cities that have joined up. Study Figure A. What other large built-up areas and cities can you add to the map?

The *inner city* refers to the central area of a conurbation or city. It is an area of rebuilding and change. There have been problems in these areas, such as dereliction, poor housing, unemployment, crime, racial discrimination, racial disadvantage, and tensions between the people and the police.

Figure B shows the opinions about cities and conurbations that were given by students in various parts of Britain.

Figure A (*far right*) Cities in the United Kingdom

Figure B Students' viewpoints

Rural students

- IT WOULD BE GREAT TO LIVE IN A CITY. THIS PLACE HASN'T GOT A THING! EVERYTIME I WANT TO GO TO TOWN I HAVE TO GET A LIFT FROM MY PARENTS OR FRIENDS.
- I DON'T KNOW IF I COULD COPE WITH CITY LIFE – IT IS SO DIRTY THERE.

Small city students

- I SOMETIMES WISH I LIVED IN A BIGGER CITY. THERE IS A LOT TO DO HERE BUT IT IS NOT LIKE LONDON.
- I OFTEN WISH THE CITY WASN'T SO BIG AND I COULD TRAVEL AROUND MORE SAFELY ON MY BIKE.

Small town students

- IT'S OK HERE, BUT THERE WOULD BE SO MUCH MORE TO DO IN A CITY.
- WHERE WOULD I KEEP MY HORSE IN ONE OF THOSE BIG PLACES?

Inner city students

- IT'S A GOOD LIVING HERE. THERE IS NEVER A DULL MOMENT. THERE ARE CAFES, CINEMAS, SHOPS AND PARKS.
- THIS PLACE IS GETTING SO NOISY AND OUR STREET IS IN A REAL MESS. A SMALLER PLACE NEARER THE COUNTRYSIDE WOULD SUIT ME BETTER.

Key
- • major city
- □ new city
- conurbation

Prejudiced viewpoints

The word *prejudice* means pre-judged. A viewpoint made without any real knowledge would be prejudiced. Some of the viewpoints expressed by the students are prejudiced. One said 'It's so dirty there'. Many cities are probably cleaner than the countryside area around the student's home. Did the student really know that cities are dirty? Be careful when you are working with viewpoints. Are your viewpoints about the city based on real knowledge or are they prejudiced?

Policeman: I SUPPOSE WE GET A LOT OF CRIME HERE BUT NOTHING LIKE THE AMOUNT IN THE CITIES.

Farmer: MY LIFE HAS ALWAYS BEEN ON THE LAND. THOSE CITY PEOPLE DON'T UNDERSTAND US FARMERS. THEY COME OUT HERE AND HAVE NO RESPECT FOR THE COUNTRYSIDE.

Community worker: THERE IS SO MUCH TALENT AND SKILL IN THIS CITY BUT NOT MUCH OF IT IS BEING PROPERLY USED.

Factory worker: THE CITY IS MY WORKPLACE AND I LIVE NEAR MY WORK.

Figure C Workers' viewpoints

QUESTIONS

1 Copy and complete the table below – in the middle column are the statements in favour of the city. In the right hand column are the statements against the city.

City life—good or bad?

Student's home area	Advantages of the city	Disadvantages of the city
rural	– easy access to places of interest – no lifts needed	
small town		
small city		– a bit too big – not safe for cycling
inner city		

2 Look again at the viewpoints of the student from the small town.
   a) What do you think this student would find to do in the city that is not possible in the small town?
   b) What other reasons do you think this student would give for staying in the small town?

3 What type of interest do you think each young person in the small town has?

4 Write in your own words what the people in Figure C think about the city.

5 Write a possible viewpoint about the city for each of the following people.
   A. A person who has left the city to retire in the countryside.
   B. An old lady living alone in the inner city.
   C. An office worker who travels daily to work in the city.

6 What are your views about the city? Write down *five* of your viewpoints.

7 Write down two prejudiced viewpoints of the city that rural people might have.

8 Write down one of your own viewpoints about the city which you know to be prejudiced.

1.8 The sphere of influence: fieldwork

The *sphere of influence* of a school or shop is the area served by that school or shop. Sometimes the term *catchment area* is used to refer to the sphere of influence. On a larger scale a town or city has a sphere of influence. Sometimes the term *hinterland* is used to refer to the area served by a town or a port.

Calculating the sphere of influence of an activity is an interesting piece of fieldwork. It enables you to use the *fieldwork enquiry route* (Figure A).

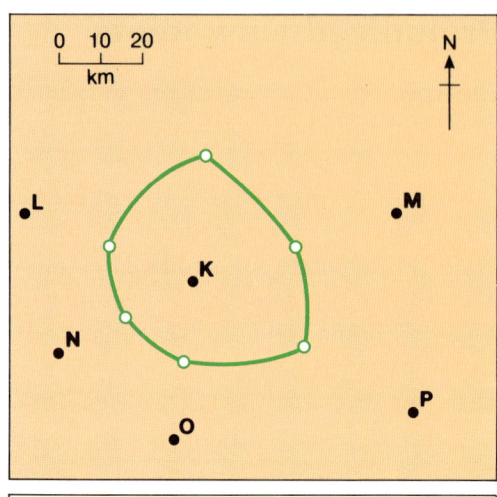

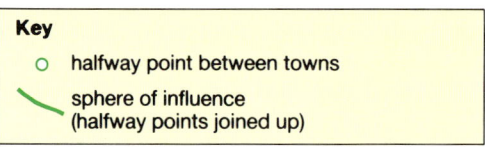

Figure B Probable sphere of influence of Town K

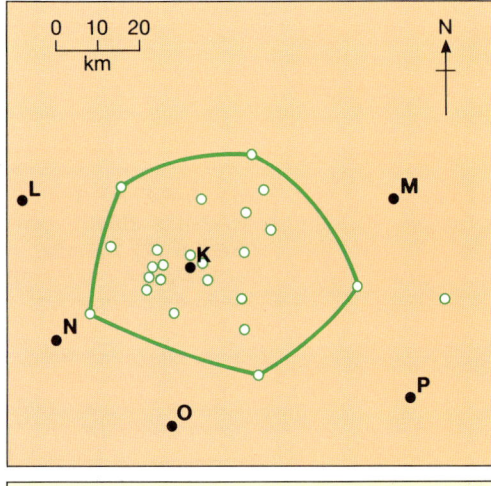

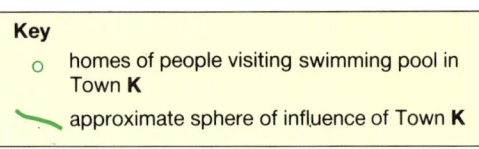

Key
○ halfway point between towns
— sphere of influence (halfway points joined up)

Figure C Sphere of influence of swimming pool in town K

Key
○ homes of people visiting swimming pool in Town **K**
— approximate sphere of influence of Town **K**

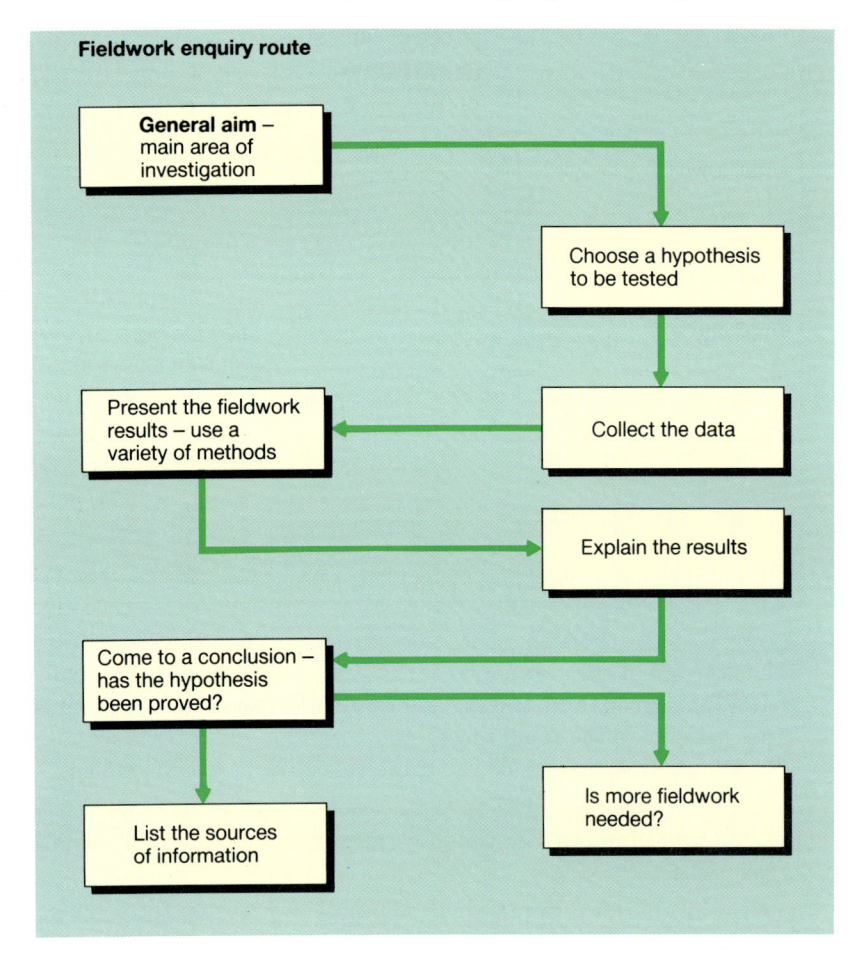

Figure A The fieldwork enquiry route. This is the route you should follow when you carry out your fieldwork

The sphere of influence of a small town

The general aim is to find out about the sphere of influence of a small town K (Figure B). The hypothesis to be tested is 'people travel to the town's swimming pool from no further away than half-way to the next town.'

Figure C shows the results of a survey taken at the swimming pool on *one* afternoon. Nearly all the people using the swimming pool lived within the distance shown on Figure B. The sphere of influence of the swimming pool was drawn around the town – see Figure C.

The explanation of this result is that the nearby towns L, M, and N also have swimming pools.

The hypothesis has been proved. But more fieldwork is necessary if the sphere of influence of the town is going to be measured more accurately. The data in Figure D refers to another activity in the town – a superstore.

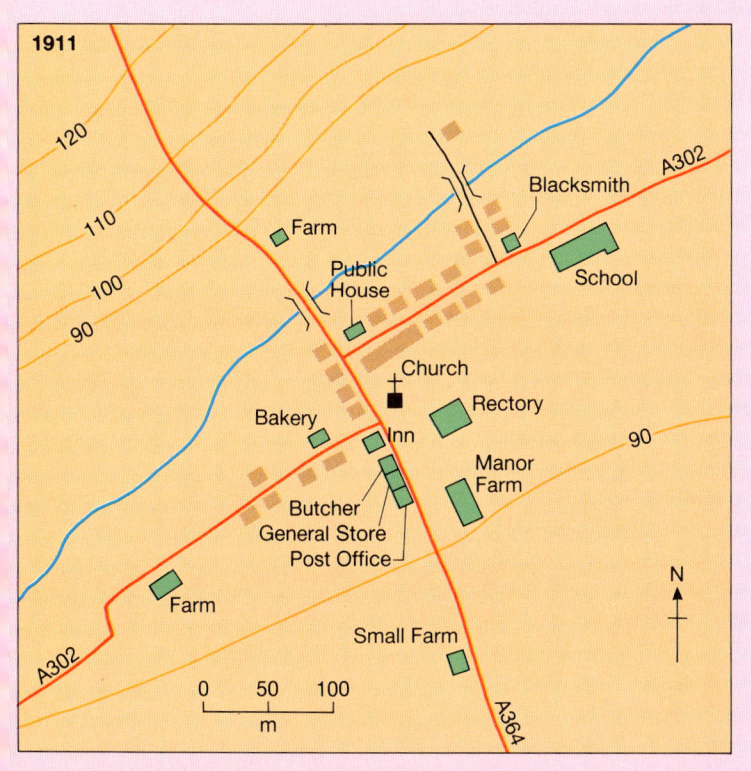

Figure C Village map (1911)
Population in 1911: 620 (village and parish area)

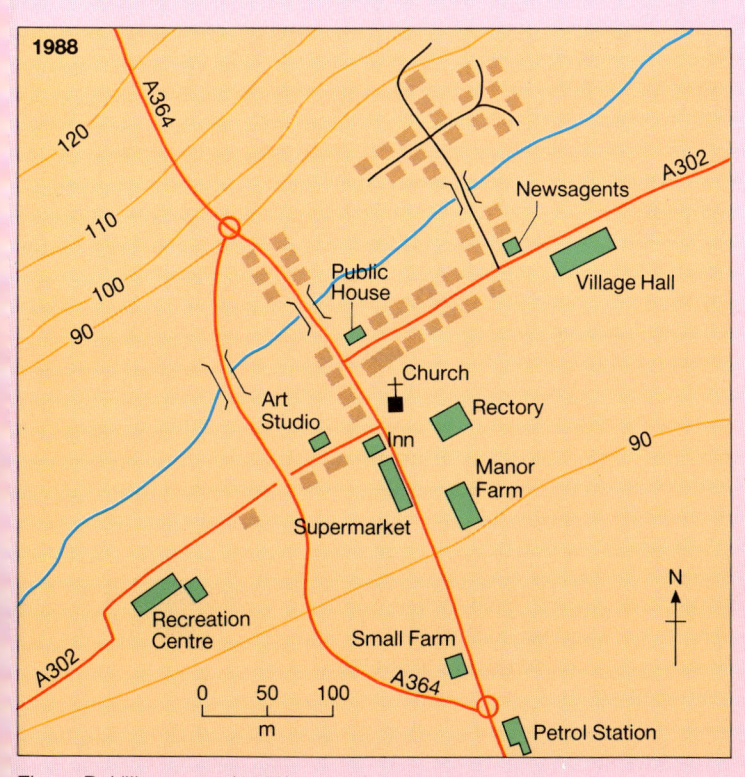

Figure D Village map (1988)
Population in 1988: approx. 400 (village and parish area)

Details for pupil profile sheets Unit 1

Knowledge and understanding

1. People's basic needs
2. Early development of settlements
3. Place names
4. Village sites
5. Fieldwork methods, including a hypothesis
6. Changing villages
7. The functions of a town
8. Threshold population
9. Conurbations
10. Inner city areas
11. Spheres of influence

Skills

1. Deciding on village sites
2. Drawing site maps
3. Using presented fieldwork data
4. Drawing a bar graph
5. Planning fieldwork using a hypothesis
6. Reading information from a map
7. Comparing old and new maps
8. Grouping functions
9. Using sphere of influence data
10. Using a transect diagram

Values

1. Awareness of the harshness of people's environments
2. Understanding that village decline affects services – rural deprivation
3. Realizing that people have different viewpoints about cities
4. Understanding prejudiced viewpoints

2.1 Settlement patterns: the hierarchy

Unit 2: Unit 2 Urban settlement pattern

Look at Figure A which shows where a family from the village does its shopping, then answer Questions 1 to 3 on page 23.

Settlements are arranged in a *hierarchy*. The hierarchy is similar to a pyramid (Figure B). Each activity, shopping, leisure, and education, has a progression.

The *low order centre*, the village, has local activities which are not specialized. The *higher order centre*, the town, has more specialized activities. The *highest order centre*, the city, has the most specialized activities.

Figure A The shopping heirarchy

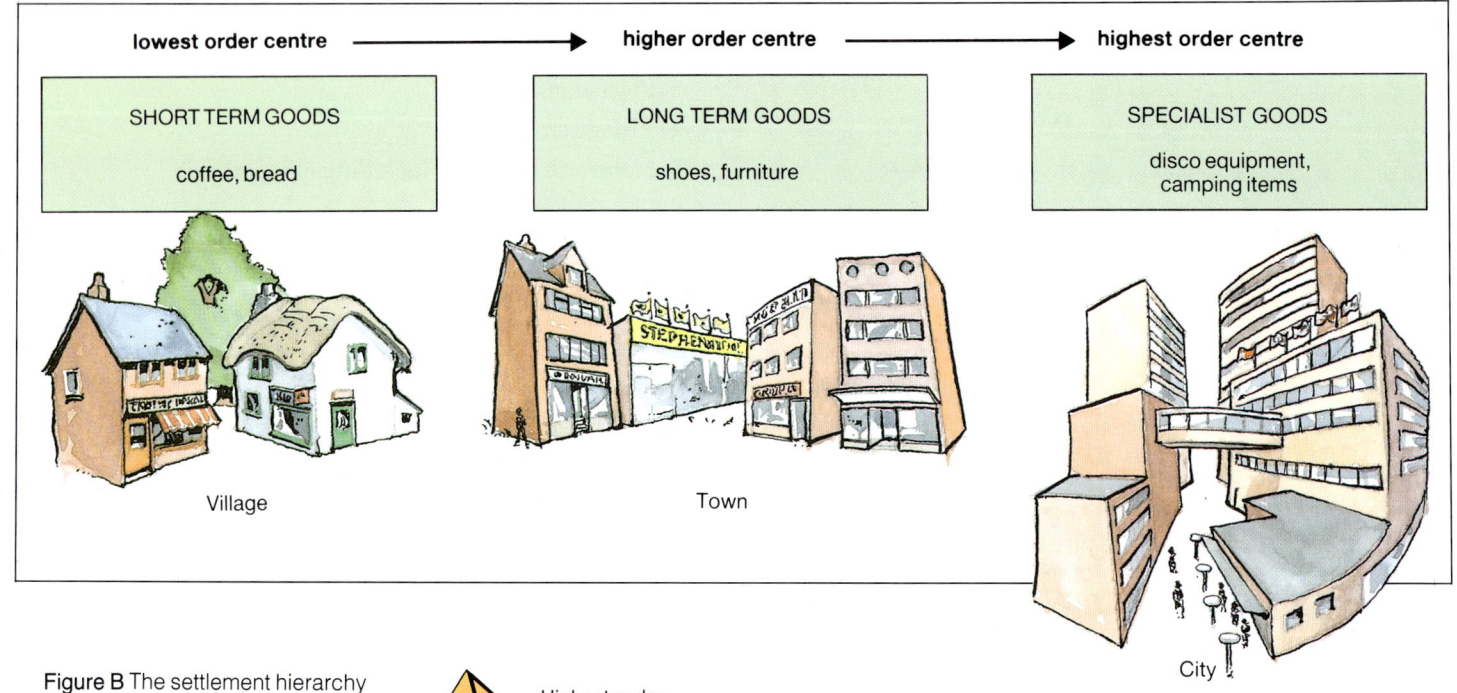

lowest order centre → higher order centre → highest order centre

SHORT TERM GOODS	LONG TERM GOODS	SPECIALIST GOODS
coffee, bread	shoes, furniture	disco equipment, camping items

Village — Town — City

Figure B The settlement hierarchy

Highest order central place — Capital — Cities — Towns — Villages — Lowest order central place

London – the capital

The settlement at the very top of the hierarchy is the dominant city. Sometimes, like London, it is the capital city. London dominates the British settlement hierarchy. It is much larger than the second city, Birmingham. London has more specialized functions than other British cities. Figure C shows some of its highest order functions. These are of national importance.

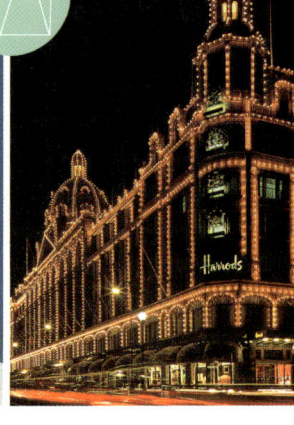

London's national functions

Function	Example from figure	Another example	Your example
Government/Public Services	Houses of Parliament	Buckingham Palace	
Museums/Art Galleries	Victoria and **Albert Museum**	Science Museum	Tate Gallery
Sport		Crystal Palace (athletics)	
Entertainment	Theatres		
Shopping		Hamleys (toy shop)	
Business/Industry		Newspaper publishing	
Trade/Finance	Stock Exchange		
Communications		Rail terminals	
Famous landmarks		Nelson's Column	

QUESTIONS

1 Name two other goods the family probably purchases in each of the village, the town and the city.

2 Draw a similar diagram to show where the family spends its leisure time.

   Members of the family regularly use the local park and church youth club. They support the town football club and swimming pool. They visit the theatre in the city once a year and watch the athletic championships in the city stadium.

   You may label the types of leisure frequently/weekly; weekly/monthly; infrequently/yearly.

3 Draw another diagram to show the family's education.

   Paula (age 10) attends the village primary school. Wayne (age 14) goes to the comprehensive school in the town. Lucy (age 18) has just started at the city polytechnic.

   You may label the levels of education primary; secondary; tertiary.

4 The table above groups some of London's functions. Copy and complete the table.

5 Work out the settlement hierarchy in your local area.

Figure C London's specialized functions

2.2 Patterns in the urban area: distributions

- Where is the nearest fish and chip shop please?
- Is there a Chinese restaurant around here?
- Please direct me to the nearest department store?
- Where is the nearest garage?

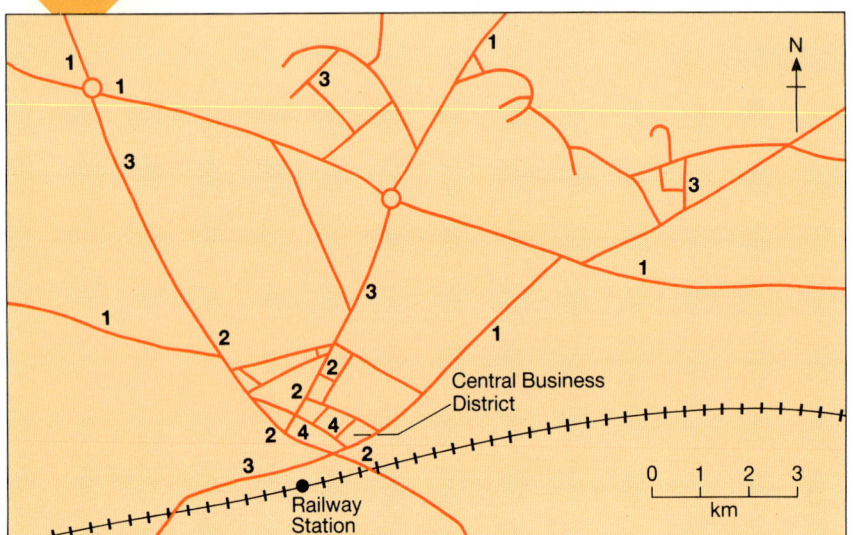

If you visit any urban area and ask these questions you will get a quick answer. Shops and services are well-known urban landmarks and local people know where they are. All urban areas have such services and their locations have distinct patterns.

Look at Figure A and then answer Question 1.

The services shown are: **1** – garages, **2** – Chinese restaurants, **3** – fish and chip shops and **4** – department stores. Can you see the distinct location pattern for each type of service? Now continue to answer all the questions on this spread.

Figure A (*right*) Location patterns for different services

Figure B (*below*) Post Office locations in part of London

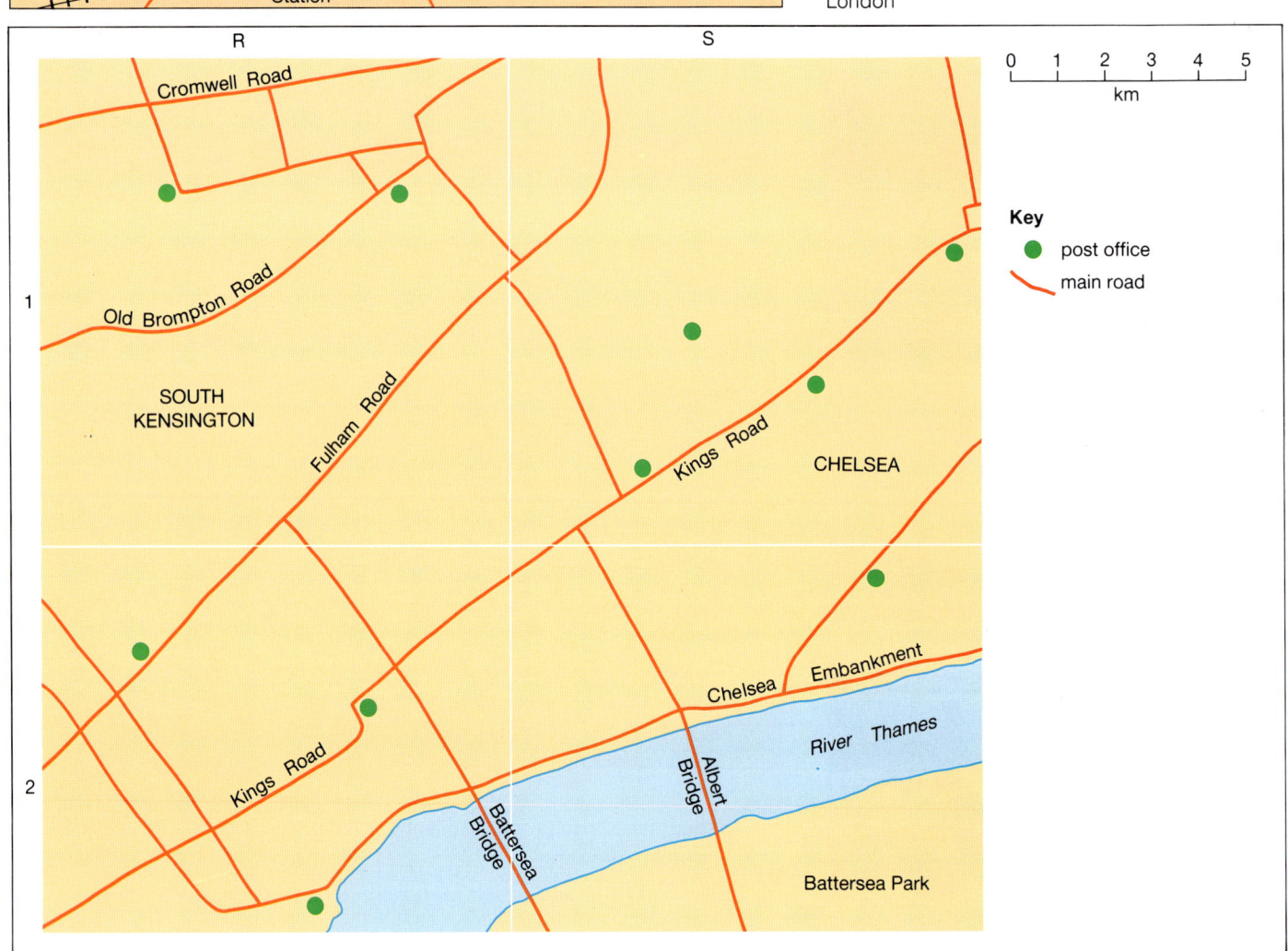

QUESTIONS

1. Look at the map (Figure A) of a large town. Which services do you think are shown by the numbers **1, 2, 3, 4**.
   - fish and chip shops
   - department stores
   - Chinese restaurants
   - garages selling petrol

2. For each of the services **1** to **4** try to explain their location.

3. If you live in an urban area write down where your nearest fish and chip shop is. Is it within walking distance of where you live? Is it in a good location to serve a community?

4. For the urban area where you live, or for one you know, write down where some of the Chinese restaurants are. Do they surround the busiest part of the town like they do in Figure A.

5. Study Figure B. Which square has i) the most post offices and ii) the least post offices?

6. What can you say about the siting of post offices?

7. a) How far apart are the post offices along the Kings Road in square S1?
   b) Measure the shortest distance between two post offices.

8. Square S2 is 10 kilometres × 10 kilometres. It is therefore 100 square kilometres. There are four post offices. The post office density is therefore one post office per 25 square kilometres.
   i) What is the post office density for square R1?
   ii) What is the density for R2 (which is 80 square kilometres)?

9. Recently many smaller urban post offices have been closed.
   a) Suggest why the Post Office has done this.
   b) What effect does shutting a post office have on a community?
   c) Where is your nearest post office?
   d) What would your family feel if this post office was shut down?

10. **Fieldwork: patterns** On a large scale map of a part of an urban area locate one of the following shops or services:
    - newsagents
    - betting shops
    - dry cleaners
    - second hand shops
    - libraries

    You are looking for patterns. Describe the pattern you have mapped and try to explain it.

11. On an even larger scale map of your neighbourhood you could map other services or amenities. Choose one or two of the following:
    - post boxes
    - public shelters
    - telephones
    - litter bins
    - bus shelters

    Try to describe and explain the pattern you find.

12. **Fieldwork: provisions** When you have completed your mapping you should comment on the *provisions* of the service. Read this example to give you an idea of what you have to do.

    Two students had studied the distribution of public seats in their neighbourhood.

    'We found that in the newer housing areas there are more seats. This is an area of semi-detached houses and open spaces. In the older areas there are almost no seats. This situation seems wrong because more old people live in the older area. The old people need public seats more than the families who live in the newer housing areas.'

Figure C Familiar services

2.3 Shopping

The large scale map, Figure A, shows an old shopping centre where there are rows of shops and services along a street. The photograph, Figure B, was taken looking east from the arrow along Wood Street. The Goddard Arms Hotel can be seen at the end of the street. Use this information to answer Questions 1–4.

Figure A An old shopping centre (Scale 1:1250)

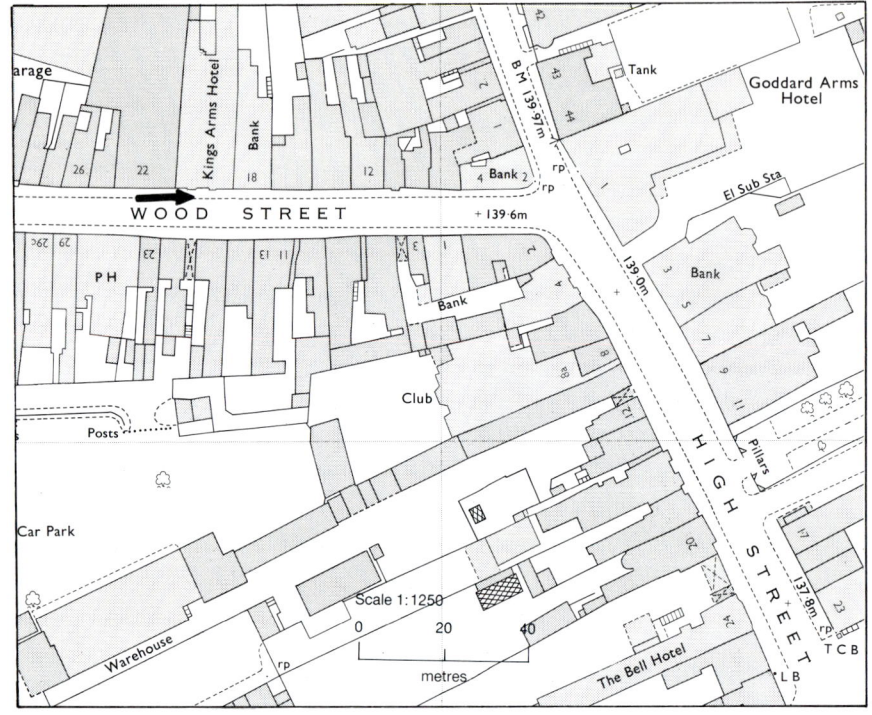

Figure B View eastward along Wood Street

How to group shops

A large scale map like Figure A can be enlarged for use in fieldwork. The types of shops can be marked on the map. There are several ways of grouping types of shops and services. Look at Figure C and answer Questions 5 to 9.

You can see that in the larger centre there are more specialized shops and services. Only five shops are convenience stores or *daily shops*. Pie graphs X and Y, Figure E, show the proportion of convenience shops in the two centres. Pie graph Z shows another shopping centre.

Figure C Layout of a town's shopping centre

Classification of shops and services

1 Convenience stores
newsagent
butcher
chemist
baker

2 Shopper's goods
clothes
shoes
TV rental
electrical

3 Specialist stores
furniture
records
toys

4 Car sales
petrol station
car showroom

5 Food services
café

6 Legal and financial
bank
building society
estate agent
solicitor

7 General services
hairdresser
travel agent

8 Entertainment
cinema

9 Department and chain stores
Woolworth's
WH Smith

High Street (north side, left to right): newsagent, butcher, café, hairdresser, Woolworth's, toys, TV rental, records, travel agent, petrol station, car showroom, electrical goods

High Street (south side, left to right): chemist, newsagent, clothes, clothes, shoes, clothes, travel agent, cinema, baker, WH Smith, furniture

Queens Road (top to bottom): bank, building society, bank, solicitor, estate agent, estate agent, bank

How to grade shopping centres

As you see, shopping centres vary in size. If you use the following grading you can find out about the *hierarchy* of shopping centres in an urban area.

Shopping centre grades

Grade 1 A department store and at least seven shops of the following types: large chain stores, clothes shops, furniture shops, banks

Grade 2 No department store. At least three of the types of shops listed in grade 1

Grade 3 Over 20 shops

Grade 4 Between 10 and 20 shops

Grade 5 Less than 10 shops

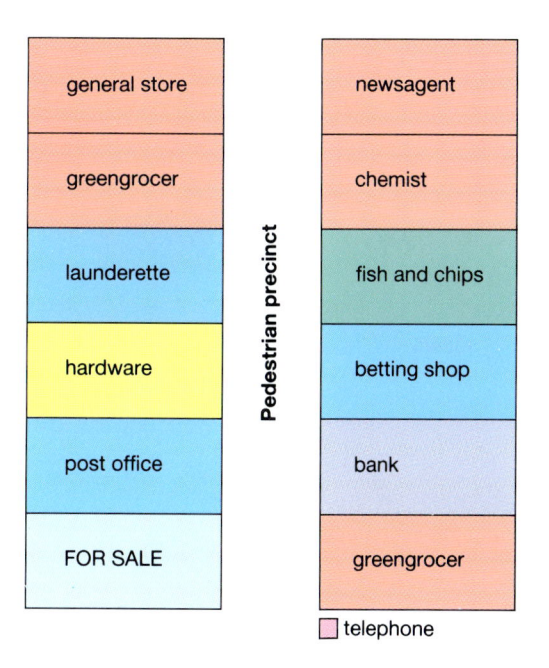

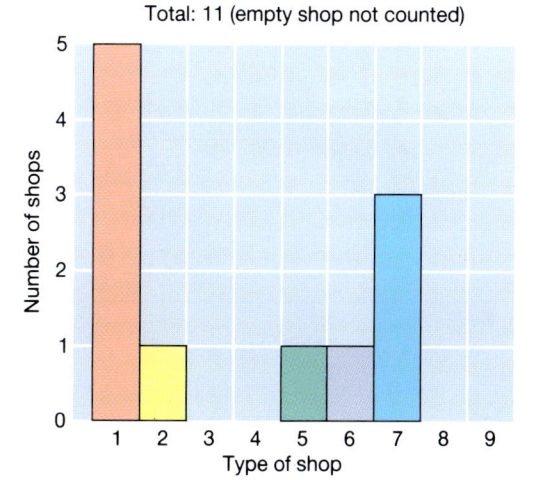

Figure E Comparison of three shopping centres

Figure D Shops in a neighbourhood shopping centre (using the same colour codes as Figure C)

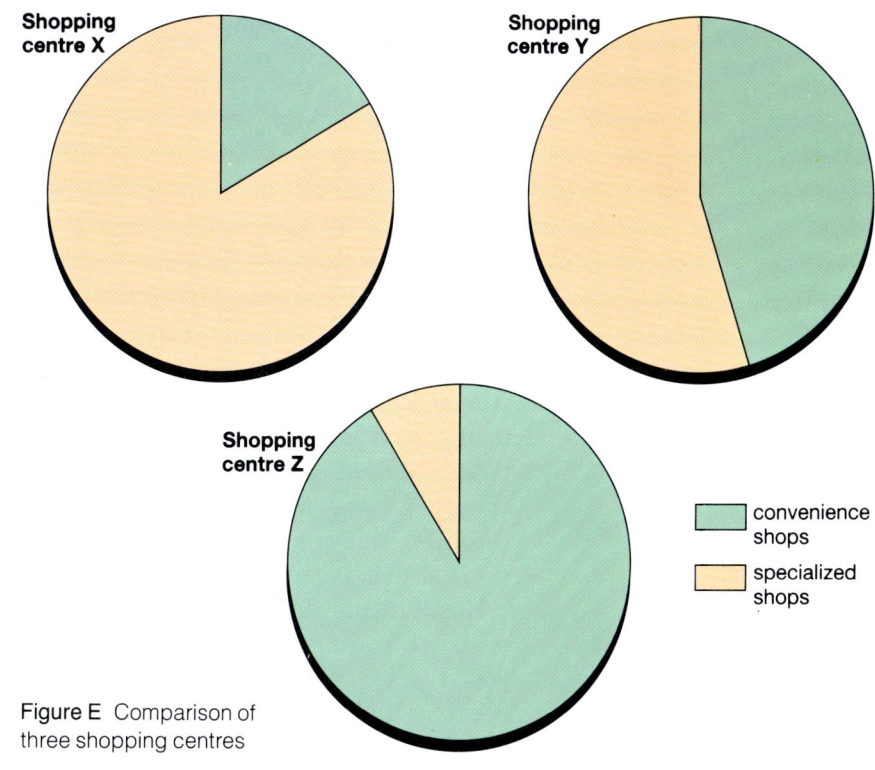

QUESTIONS

1. How many banks are there in this part of the shopping centre?
2. What number Wood Street is the King's Arms Hotel?
3. Describe the shape of the shops.
4. Why are older shopping centres like this not very convenient for the shopper?
5. Redraw Figure C, and colour code it using the nine groups given in the classification key.
6. Draw a bar graph to show the types of shops and services in this shopping centre.
7. What is the total number of shops in this shopping centre?
8. How many shops are in group 1 (convenience stores)?
9. Study Figure D. It has been colour coded and grouped in the same way as the shopping centre in Figure C.
   How many shops are in group 1 in this smaller centre?
10. Suggest the size of the shopping centre referred to in pie graph Z (Figure E).
11. What grade centre is:
    a) the town shopping centre (Figure C)?
    b) the neighbourhood centre (Figure D)?
12. What grade of centre is the shopping centre nearest your home?
13. **Further work** If you live in an urban area you should grade the shopping centres known to you. Then draw a map to show the hierarchy of shopping centres. The symbols for each grade must vary in size.
    Describe the hierarchy and try to explain it.

2.4 Fast food: location

The growth of McDonald's restaurants (Figure A) in Britain has been quick. At the end of 1977 there were only 10 McDonald's 'fast food' restaurants. At the end of 1986 there were 230.

Figure B shows the location of McDonald's restaurants in 1980, 1984 and the new ones built in 1985. The American based company has chosen town centre sites where there is a large *pedestrian flow* (people passing by). A site next to a chain store or busy department store is favoured. Towns with a population of at least 100 000 were chosen for the first McDonald's. More recently, McDonald's have been built in smaller urban centres.

Restaurants have about nine metres of street frontage. Some, like the Liverpool restaurant (Figure A), are bigger because they occupy corner sites. They open from 9am to 11pm, 364 days a year. The busiest restaurants attract up to 30 000 customers a week! Most of the trade is in sit down meals but 'takeaways' are offered.

McDonald's is one of several fast food companies operating in Britain. Eventually they want a restaurant in every large community in the country.

Figure A McDonald's, Liverpool

Key
- McDonald's restaurants in 1980
- new McDonald's restaurants in 1985

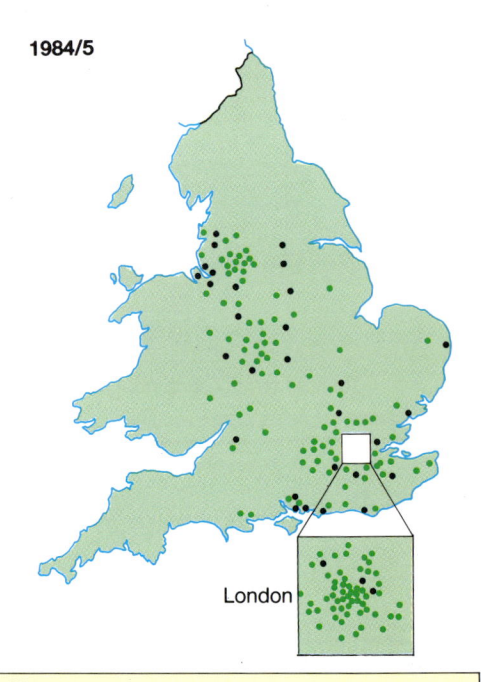

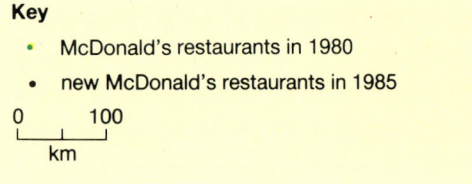

Figure B McDonald's spread throughout England and Wales

Locating a McDonald's restaurant: fieldwork

Where would you locate a new McDonald's restaurant? If you live in an area which already has a McDonald's try to locate another one.

The important locational point to remember is that McDonald's likes to be in a town centre or a high street. The best place is where there is a high pedestrian flow.

Method

A Write down three locations in the town centre where you think the pedestrian flow is highest.

B Count the number of people passing your chosen location for 15 minutes. You must count people who pass you from all directions.

C Multiply your total by 4 to find the *flow per hour*. The highest flow is your busiest place in town.

D Choose the exact site for your new McDonald's as near to the busiest site as possible. Remember you want at least nine metres of street frontage.

E Draw a map of the shopping centre around your chosen site.

Figure C shows the results of a pedestrian flow count outside three town centre shops. The map, Figure D, shows the chosen site for the new McDonald's restaurant.

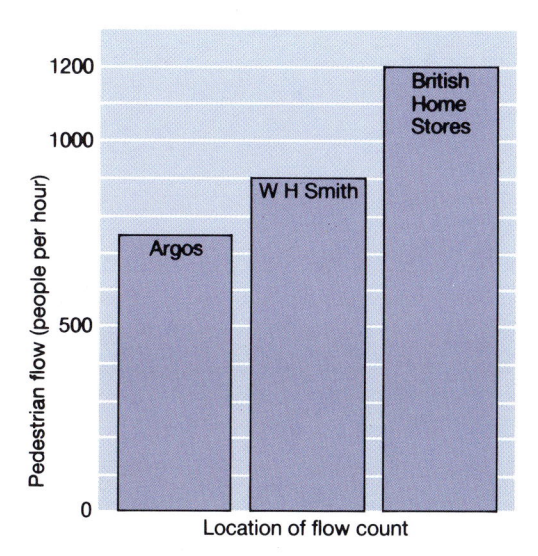

Figure C Pedestrian flow per hour (count taken at midday in large town centre)

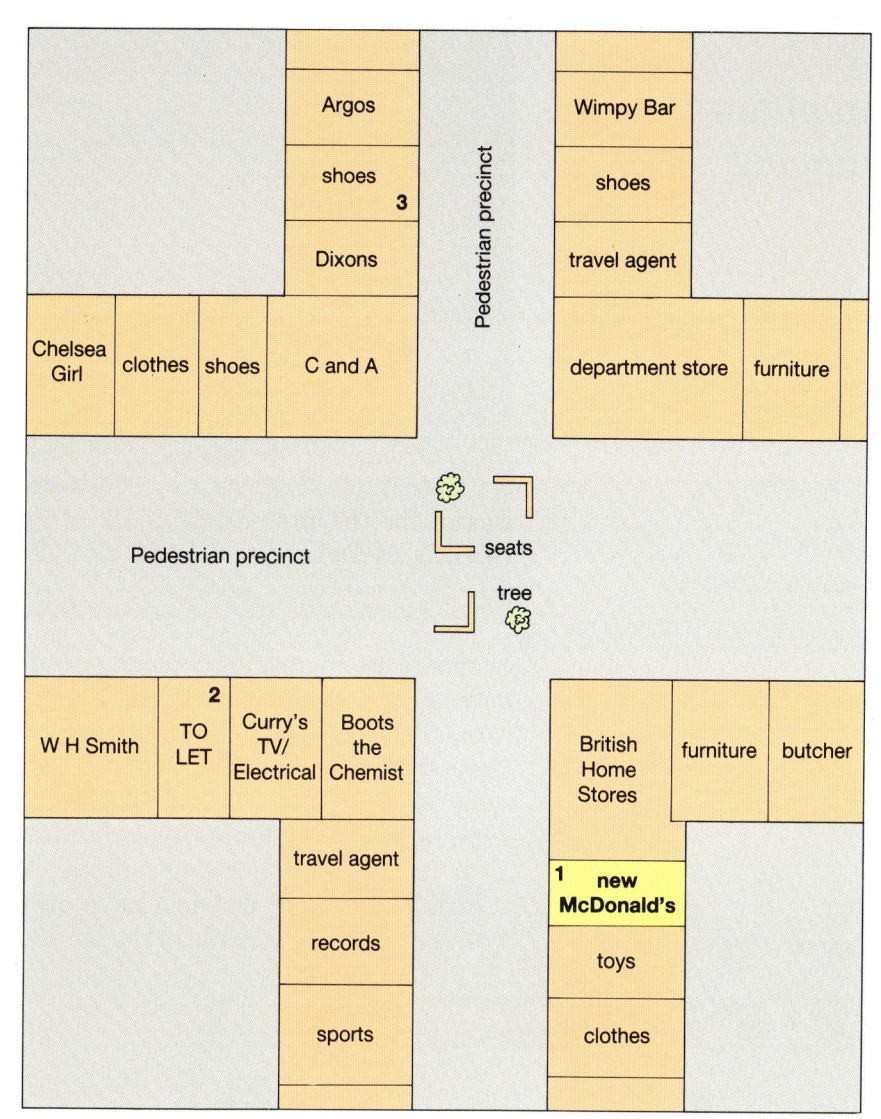

Figure D Location of a new McDonald's

QUESTIONS

1. Why do you think there has been a quick growth of McDonald's 'fast food' restaurants in Britain?
2. Most of the early McDonald's were in London. Why do you think this was so?
3. In which regions of the country did McDonald's open up between 1980 and 1984?
4. Study the map which shows the stores which opened in 1985. Name three towns or cities where new stores opened in 1985.
5. Which major regions of Britain have no McDonald's?
6. Study Figures C and D. The shop sites 1, 2, 3 were all available for a new fast food restaurant. Why do you think site 1 was chosen? Give reasons why sites 2 and 3 were not chosen.
7. You meet an old man who tells you fast food restaurants should be discouraged. How will you argue that they are good for a town centre and that they are here to stay?

2.5 Out-of-town shopping

Figure A Asda at High Wycombe

Figure B Sheffield superstores

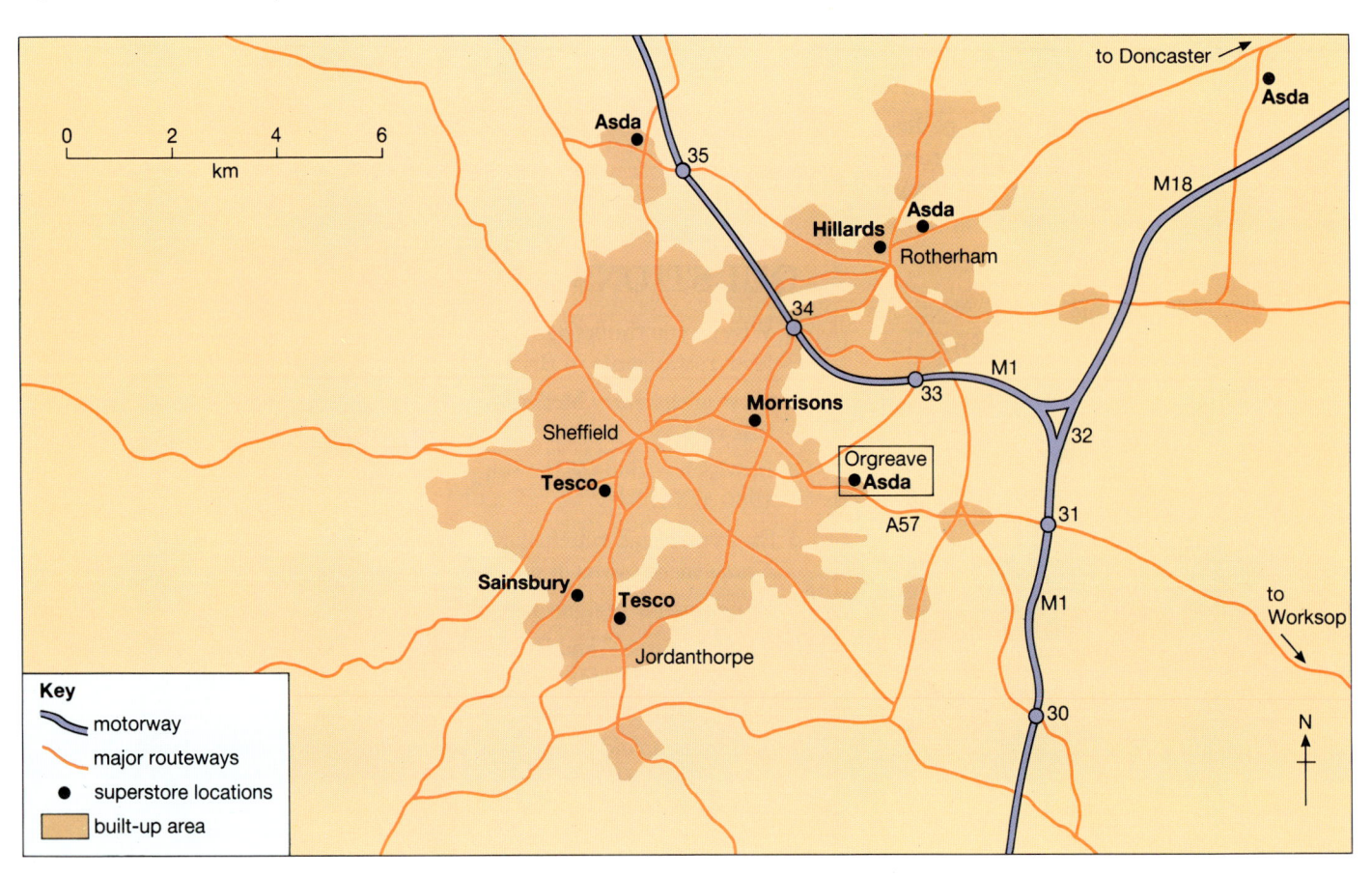

Shoppers are increasingly using *out-of-town* shopping facilities. Texas Homecare, Smiths DO-IT-ALL, MFI, Allied Carpets, Gateway, and Asda are just some of the names. They have built *superstores* or even larger *hypermarkets* away from the old shopping centres.

Asda (Associated Dairies) have over 100 stores and superstores in the United Kingdom. The company serves over two million shoppers each week. It employs over 30 000 people. The superstores have a large sales area and carry 30 000 product lines. There is free parking for over 600 cars and free bus services are available for half the stores. Since 1965 Asda have opened, on average, a new superstore every ten and a half weeks!

Key
- motorway
- major routeways
- • superstore locations
- built-up area

30

Asda

Asda at Orgreave

The Asda superstore at Orgreave near Sheffield was originally built in 1968 but was re-vamped in 1985. To give you an idea of its great size, it has 30 checkouts and parking for over 1000 cars. Figure B shows its location and the location of competing stores. On the map, Figure D, the homes of a sample of shoppers are marked. Note the area of Jordanthorpe. This is a large council housing area to the south of Sheffield. Asda has arranged buses to transport shoppers from this estate to Orgreave.

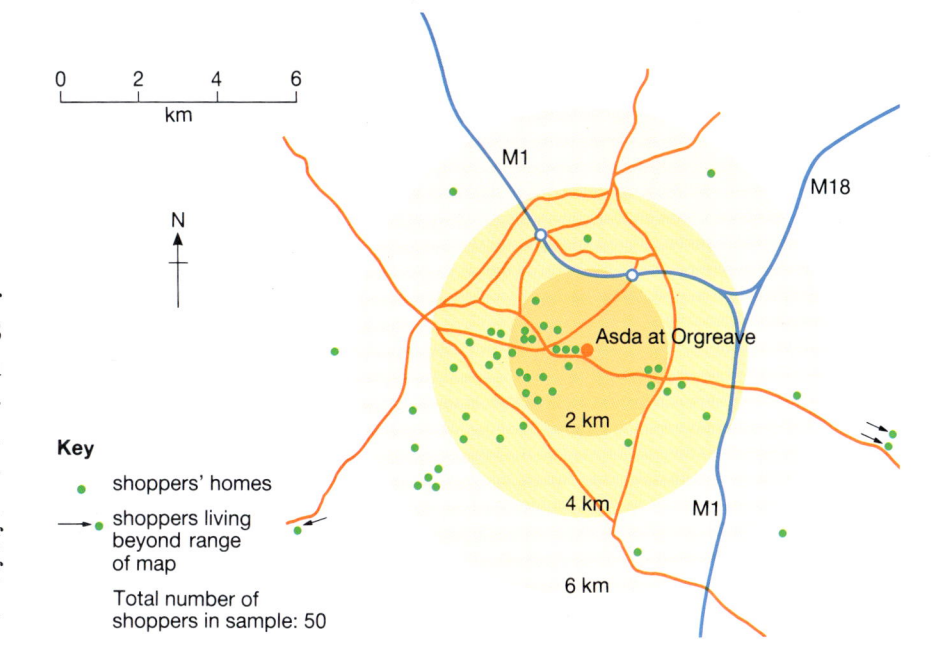

Figure D Where Orgreave's Asda shoppers come from

Figure C Shoppers' opinions

Speech bubbles:
- IT'S ALL SO CRAMPED
- SUCH A LONG WAY FROM THE CAR PARK
- THERE'S A FREE BUS
- WE GET THERE QUICKER – NO TRAFFIC SNARL-UPS.
- ERE IS NOT SO ICH CHOICE
- THERE IS A LOT OF ROOM IN THE SHOPS
- PLENTY OF CAR PARKING
- S SO EXPENSIVE TTING TO TOWN ESE DAYS

QUESTIONS

1. What is a superstore? Why do you think that superstores have been so successful in the last 25 years?

2. Look at these key facts for building an Asda superstore and arrange them as a diagram around the Asda logo.
   a) Population of over 100 000 within 10 minutes driving time
   b) Good road communications
   c) Large area of land for the building and for car parking
   d) Not too many competing stores
   e) Quick planning permission

3. Name an out-of-town superstore near you. What does it specialize in? Why was it sited there?

4. An out-of-town superstore has several advantages over a town centre supermarket. See if you can place the viewpoints of the people on the left into two columns headed 'town centre supermarket' and 'out-of-town superstore'. Work out which store they are referring to.

5. From your point of view write about which type of shopping you prefer – in town or out-of-town?

6. Twenty shoppers interviewed came from within 2 kilometres of the superstore. We can show this as a *percentage*:

   $$\text{Percentage of shoppers living within 2 km} = \frac{\text{number of shoppers living within 2 km}}{\text{total number of shoppers interviewed}} \times 100$$

   $$= \frac{20}{50} \times 100 = 40 \text{ per cent}$$

   Work out the percentage of shoppers living between 2 and 4 kilometres from the superstore.

7. Suggest why 40 per cent of the shoppers come from within 2 kilometres of the superstore.

8. Suggest why some shoppers visit Asda at Orgreave even when there is a superstore nearer to where they live.

2.6 The urban transect

If you draw a cross-section or *transect* across any British city you will reveal a similar skyline. Buildings are generally low rise on the outskirts of the built-up area. In the centre there is high rise development. In some cities the *central business district (CBD)* is very distinctive and there are towering office blocks rising above the main shopping and business streets.

Why are city centres so tightly packed with buildings? Why are the highest buildings usually in these centres? The CBD is the most accessible place in the city. Shops and offices want their premises there because more customers will visit the area. Therefore, profits will be higher in the CBD. And because there is a big demand for sites in the CBD, the land values are high.

The graph (Figure A) shows how land values decline away from the city centre. As you can see, the curve is not always smooth. The land value sometimes rises in neighbourhood centres in the suburbs.

Figure A Land values in the city

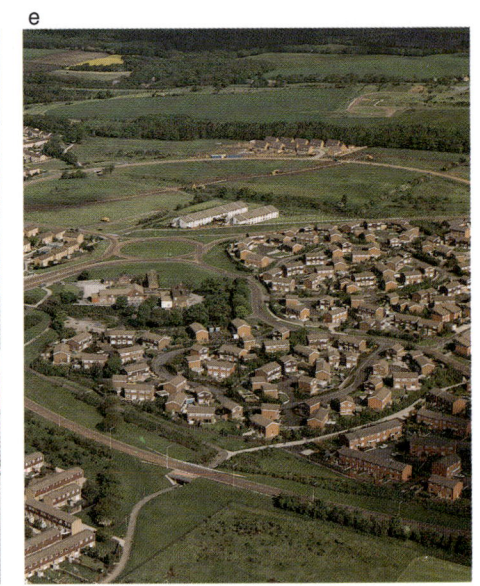

Figure B Transect across a city

Central Business District

Key
- industry
- housing
- offices
- shopping
- transport
- old city core

INDUSTRY AND BUSINESS

Labels on transect (left to right):
- new industry (1)
- old industry
- old city buildings cathedral, castle
- new office and shopping complex
- main railway station
- bus station
- new industry in old housing area
- neighbourhood shopping centre
- new industry planned on edge of urban area

Bottom labels (1–8):
1
2 — new low density housing
3 — old terraced housing
4
5 — very few houses, some flats, near city centre offices
— new high rise development
6 — old housing being cleared
7
8 — new high rise housing
— new housing

HOUSING AND SHOPPING

f

g

h

QUESTIONS

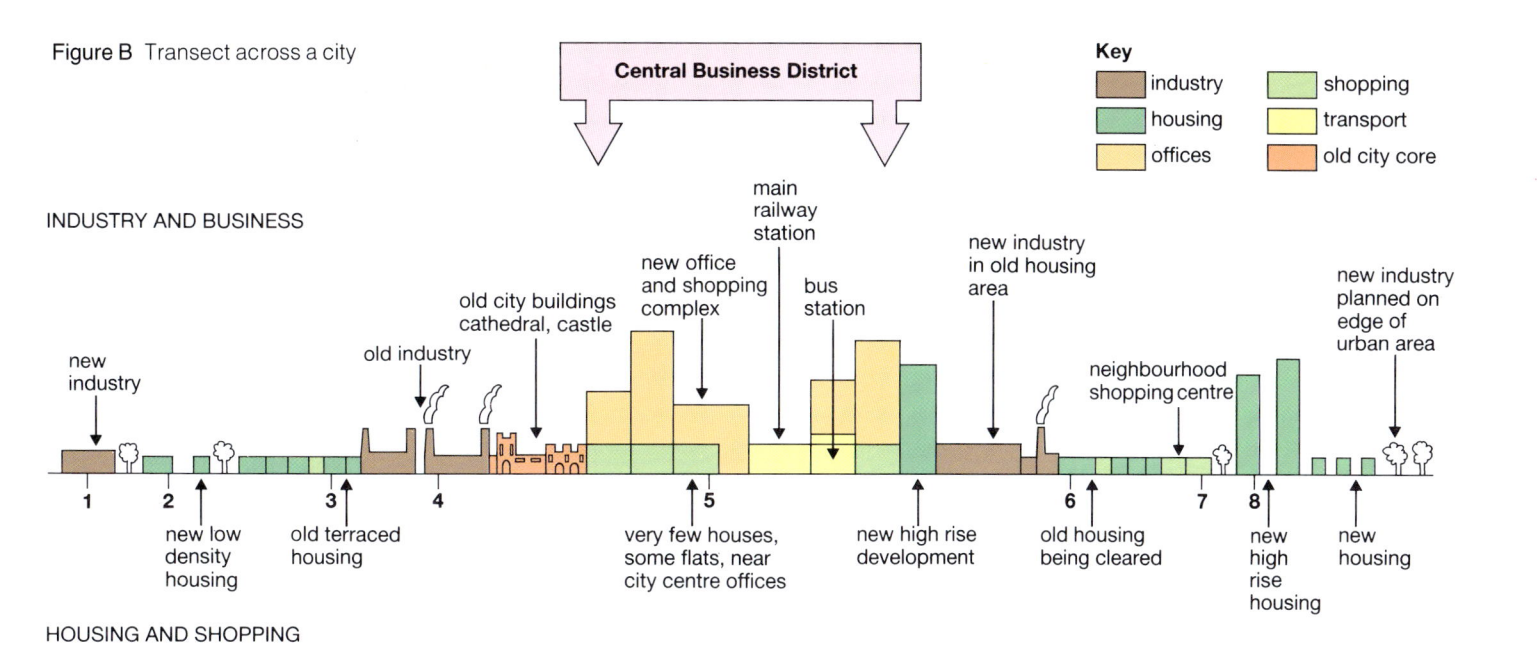

1 Link the eight photographs lettered **a** to **h** with the numbers **1** to **8** in Figure B. Check your choices with the answers on page 125.

2 Suggest answers for the following questions about photographs **a** to **h**.

a: What type of shops are you likely to find in this neighbourhood shopping centre?
b: Why is so much old industry wanting to relocate in the outer suburbs?
c: Why are these houses being demolished?
d: Why do you think people like this old style market in the CBD?
e: What are the problems with this type of housing development on the edge of the city?
f: Why are industrial companies building on the edge of the built-up area?
g: Where did the people living in these high rise housing schemes once live?
h: Why was the terraced housing built so close to the city centre?

2.7 Housing types: maps

For a detailed study of a town and fieldwork you need to use *large scale* maps or plans which show a lot of detail. The Ordnance Survey produce large scale maps. The ones on this page are small extracts from large sheets. The grid lines represent 100 metre squares.

The photograph looking along Hesketh Crescent (Figure B) shows detached and semi-detached houses with garages. Look carefully at Figure A and identify the exact houses.

The photograph of Winifred Street Post Office (Figure C) shows terraced houses. Look carefully at the map (Figure A) and identify the Post Office (PO), the telephone call box (TCB) and the letter box (LB).

Housing density refers to the number of houses in a given area. A large scale map shows housing density very clearly. One way of measuring density is to count the number of houses in a street length of 100 metres. The streets with terraced houses have a higher housing density than Hesketh Crescent. We can measure the density fairly accurately from the map.

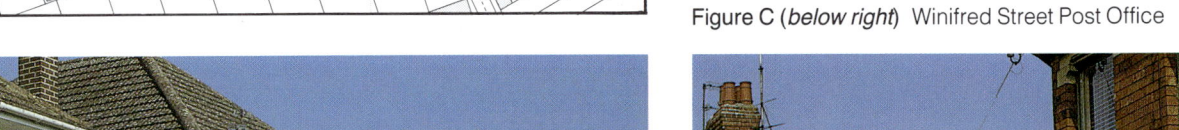

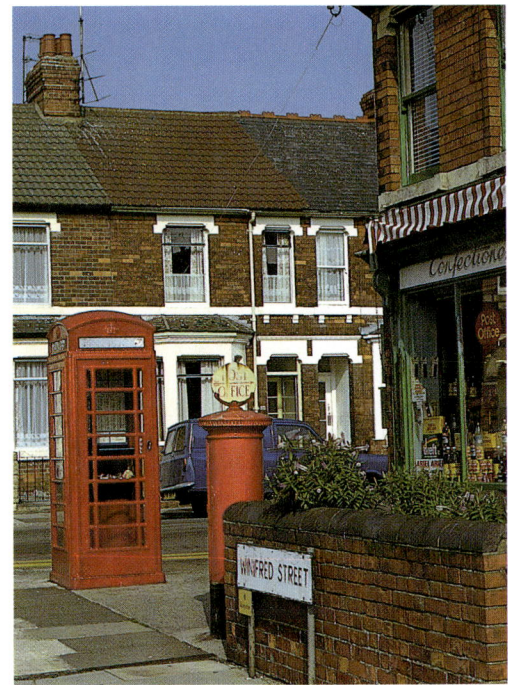

Figure A (*left*) Large scale map extract of a residential area. The arrows show the direction the camera was pointing to take photographs B and C

Figure B (*below left*) Hesketh Crescent

Figure C (*below right*) Winifred Street Post Office

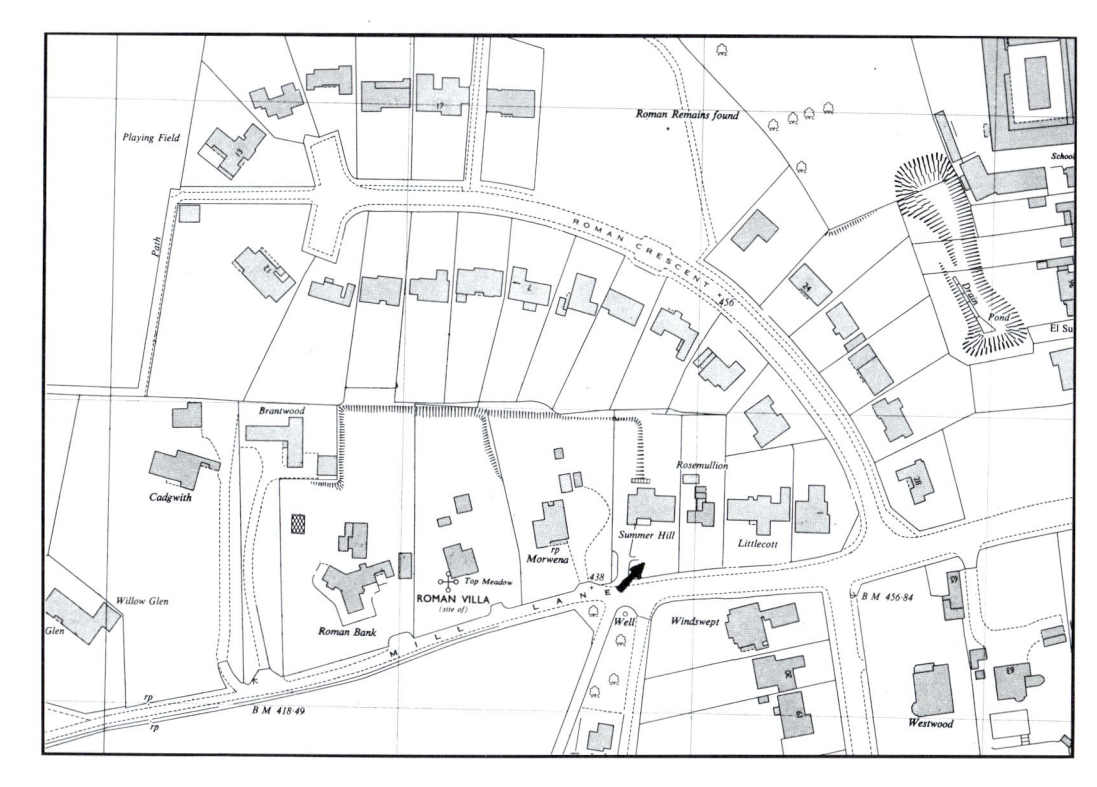

Figure D Large scale map extract of Roman Crescent in Swindon

Figure E Detached house in Mill Lane

QUESTIONS

1. Which St. Margaret's Road house numbers are shown in Figure C?
2. What house numbers in St. Margaret's Road have glasshouses in the gardens?
3. How high above sea level is the Post Office?
4. Approximately how long in metres are the gardens of the houses on the south side of St. Margaret's Road?
5. Where are the garages for the St. Margaret's Road houses?
6. Approximately how many houses are there in a 100 metres length
   a) on one side of St. Margaret's Road?
   b) on one side of Hesketh Crescent?
7. How would you compare the housing density in St. Margaret's Road with that in Hesketh Crescent?
8. Figure E is the photograph of a detached house in Mill Lane. Look at the map (Figure D) and find this house. Describe the house and its garden.
9. How does the housing density in Mill Lane compare with Hesketh Crescent?
10. Suggest what the houses in Roman Crescent are like. How do they compare with those in Mill Lane?
11. Why do you think this road has been named Roman Crescent?
12. **Further work** You can compare different housing types on large scale maps in your local area.
13. Try drawing out some different housing types on a made-up map. Include all types you have seen on these pages. Include also an area of high rise housing with separate garage blocks. Try to work out the approximate size of the high rise blocks.

2.8 Housing quality: fieldwork

Have you noticed how the quality of housing varies in a town or city? There are some streets where the houses are clean and quiet and others where there is litter and noise. Houses in some areas are well painted and have new roofs and windows. In other areas houses have a run-down appearance, the woodwork needs painting, there are broken roof tiles and old windows.

Is there a way of measuring housing quality? Is there a pattern to housing quality in an urban area? Students in a large Midlands town started their studies of housing quality by drawing up a housing quality list (see below, right). The quality of each item on their list could be recorded for a single house.

Figure A A line of transect from the centre of town to the edge of the built-up area. Houses were sampled along a main road which approximately followed the line X to Y

Figure C House sample 1

House quality checklist

paintwork	litter
roof	traffic noise
windows	people passing
front door	car parking
front garden	

Can you add any more items to their list? The students' plan was to give each item a number between 1 and 5, depending on the condition or state of repair of the house.

1 = excellent   2 = good   3 = average
4 = poor   5 = very poor

Each item was then discussed to see which ones were the best to measure.

The hypothesis

The students thought that housing quality would be better on the edge of the town and less good near the town centre. They wanted to test the following hypothesis; 'Housing quality improves away from the town centre'.

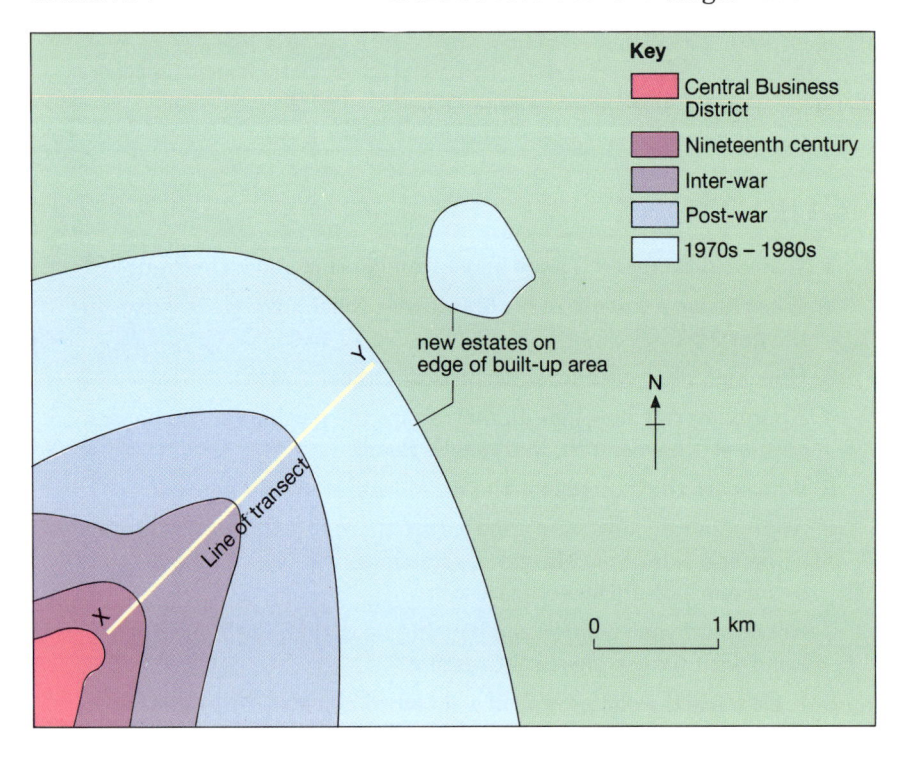

Figure B A table from a student's note-book

Sample	Paint	Windows	Roof	Litter	Noise
1	3	4	4	4	5
2	2	1	1	3	4
3	4	3	4	5	4
4	4	3	4	4	4
5	2	3	3	3	3
6	2	2	1	2	2

The method

A road leading out of the town centre was chosen, see Figure A. It was decided to sample every tenth house. The start was near to the centre of town and samples were from the right hand side of the road. One field note book contained the information shown in the table on page 36.

Figures C and E are pictures of house samples 1 and 6. The contrast between the two houses can be seen in the photographs. What do the photographs not show?

Graphs were constructed for each item of housing quality. The results of one student's work are shown on this page.

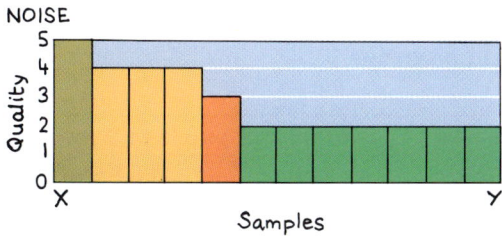

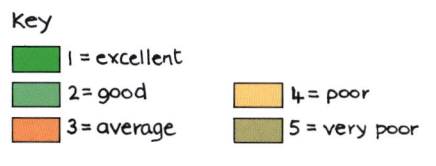

Figure E House sample 6

Figure D Housing quality along transect X to Y

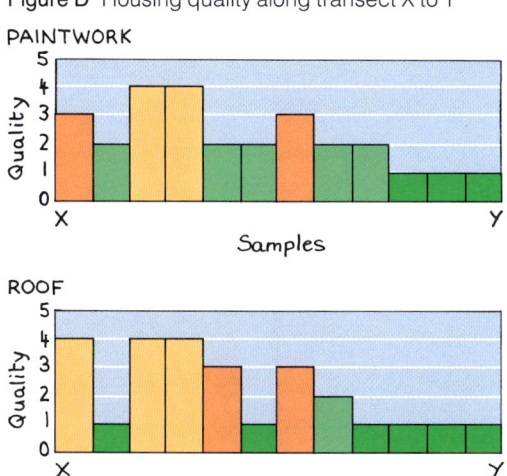

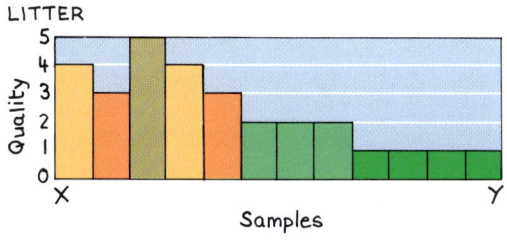

PAINTWORK

ROOF

LITTER

NOISE

Key
- 1 = excellent
- 2 = good
- 3 = average
- 4 = poor
- 5 = very poor

QUESTIONS

1. For each item on the housing quality list think of the difficulties of giving it a number 1 to 5.
2. Choose the *five* items which you think would give the best measure of housing quality.
3. Draw a graph for windows using the following figures.

Sample	Windows
1	4
2	1
3	3
4	3
5	3
6	2

Sample	Windows
7	2
8	2
9	1
10	1
11	1
12	1

4. a) Is there a pattern to housing quality along road transect X–Y?
   b) Did the students prove their hypothesis?
5. Suggest reasons for house sample 2 being an exception.
6. **Further work** a) Choose a house-lined road leading out of a town to sample.
   b) Write out your hypothesis.
   c) Decide on some items of housing quality that you wish to measure.
   d) Sample every fifth or tenth house.
   e) Write up your results in the same way as shown. State whether or not you proved your hypothesis.
7. Draw a summary graph for your survey which shows the overall housing quality for each sampled house. To do this add all your measurements together and find the average.
   For example . . .

Sample	Paint	Window	Roof	Litter	Noise	Average
3	4	3	4	5	4	3.6

2.9 Changing school patterns

The town in Figure A has six secondary schools. Schools G, H and I are comprehensives, each with 1200 pupils aged between 11 and 18. Schools J and K are also comprehensives, each has 800 pupils, ranging from 11 to 16 years old. School L is a Roman Catholic comprehensive with 800 pupils whose ages range from 11 to 18.

The pattern of schools in the town has developed since the 1960s. Each school has a *catchment area* consisting of one or two separate *neighbourhoods*. The school system has been a popular one with parents but now there is a problem. There are less children than there used to be; the schools are suffering from *falling rolls*.

The map shows you where the schools are in the town. It also gives details about the catchment areas. Figure B details the changes forecast for the schools.

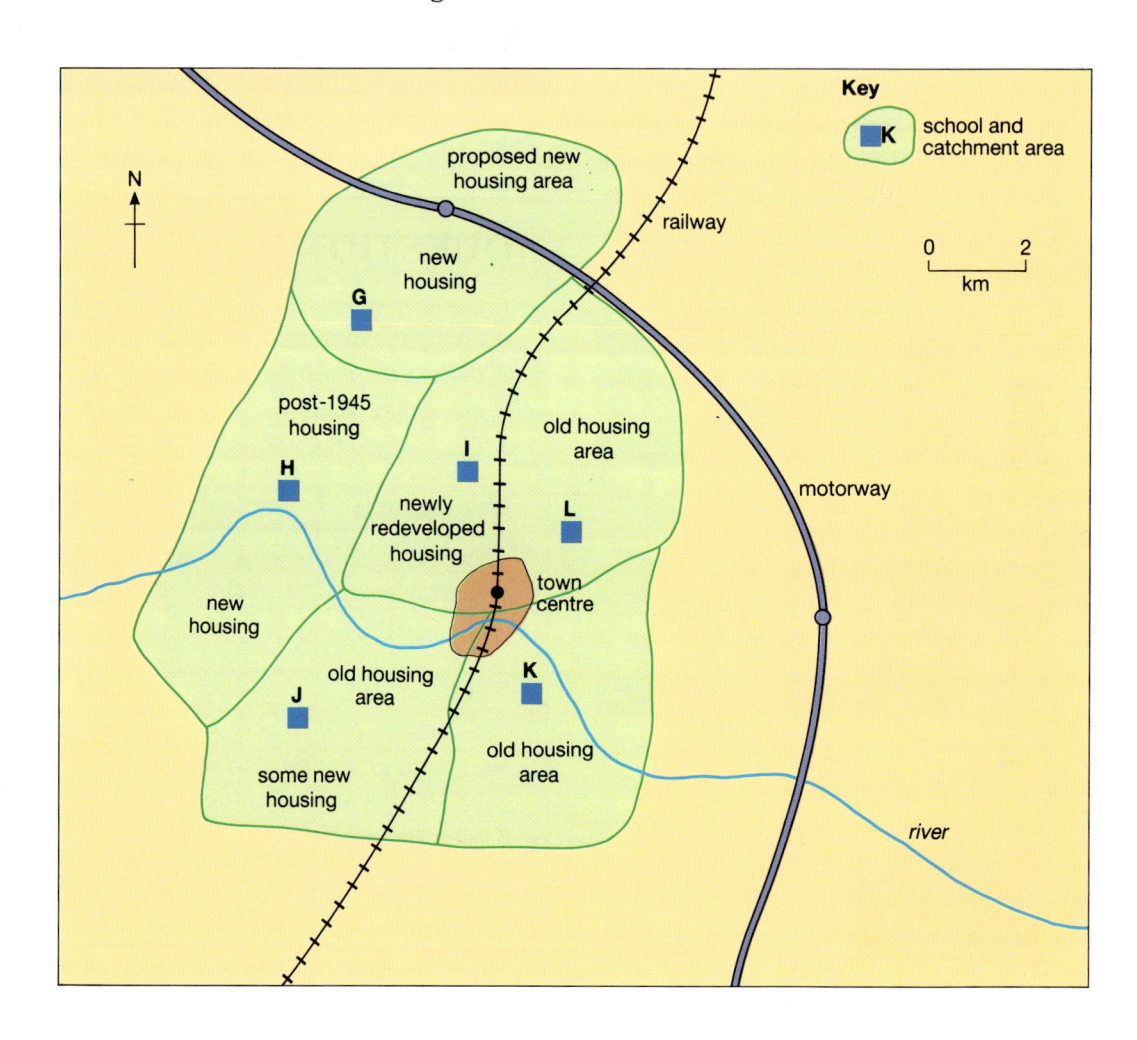

Figure A Schools and catchment areas

Changes in pupil numbers forecast for six schools

School	Age range	Number of pupils now		Number of pupils in 5 years	
		Total	6th Form	Total	6th Form
G	11–18	1200	150	1200	150
H	11–18	1200	150	800	100
I	11–18	1200	150	700	90
J	11–16	800	–	600	–
K	11–16	800	–	500	–
L	11–18	1000	120	800	100

The *Local Education Authority* (LEA) which provides and pays for all the schools says that a comprehensive school needs at least 1000 pupils in the 11–16 range and 150 pupils in the sixth form (16–18). It does not want schools to have less than:
a) 1150 pupils for an 11–18 school, or
b) 1000 pupils for an 11–16 school.

What the LEA wants

If the LEA gets its way, some of the schools will be closed immediately. Others will close within 5 years. Copy and complete the table below to show what will happen. The forecast table on page 38 and the text will help you fill in the gaps.

School closures

School	Now	In 5 years
G	?	?
H	?	?
I	Open	?
J	?	Closed
K	?	?
L	?	Closed

Figure B Pupils working in an 11–18 school

What parents want

The parents in each of the school catchment areas have met. No group of parents wants its school to close.

The LEA have come up with the suggestions shown on the right. The LEA are not moving from their stated minimum size for schools.

The parents and interested people meet again. They need your help. *What do you suggest?* Propose a new pattern of schools for the town.

Suggestion A
- All schools to be 11–16
- 11–18 schools to lose their sixth forms
- A new Sixth Form College to be set up

Suggestion B
- All schools to be 11–18 with sixth forms

QUESTIONS

1. What are your arguments for and against the two LEA suggestions? You should prepare one side of A4 paper setting out the LEA plans, your proposals and the advantages and disadvantages of each. [You could divide into groups to discuss the two suggestions and put your views to each other.]
2. Draw a map to show your new pattern of schools.
3. Write briefly about your proposals giving reasons for your decisions.

Unit 2 ASSESSMENT

Understanding spheres of influence

1. What do you understand by the sphere of influence of a shop? (2 marks)
2. How would you measure the sphere of influence of a post office? (4 marks)
3. Look at the 4 maps (Figure A) showing the spheres of influence of local radio stations in Surrey and Sussex.
   a) What is the approximate diameter of
   i) County Sound and   ii) Radio Sussex? (2 marks)
   b) Which radio station(s) can people pick up in
   i) Eastbourne and   ii) Brighton? (2 marks)
   c) You want to advertise a 'Festival of Sport' which is to be held in Guildford. You know people will be prepared to travel 30 kilometres for it. Which radio stations do you advertise with? (5 marks)

   Total: 15 marks

London, the capital

"London is the capital city and is the highest order centre in the British settlement hierarchy"

1. What do you understand by this quotation? (5 marks)
2. Study Figure B which shows some of the specialized areas in London. Which of these functions indicate that London is a capital city? (2 marks)
3. What other capital city functions would you find in and around London? (4 marks)
4. Which specialized areas would a regional capital like Newcastle-upon-Tyne or Cardiff have? (4 marks)
5. For a town or city that you have studied draw a map to show the approximate extent of specialized areas. Compare your results with the map of London and try to explain the differences. (25 marks)

   Total: 40 marks

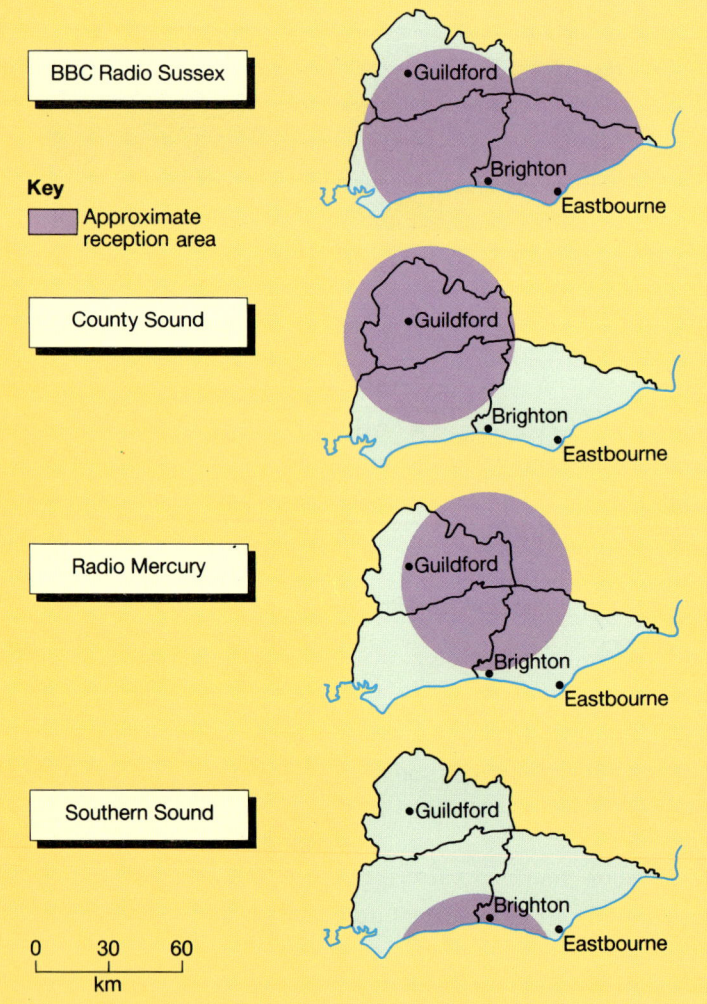

Figure A Local radio in Surrey and Sussex

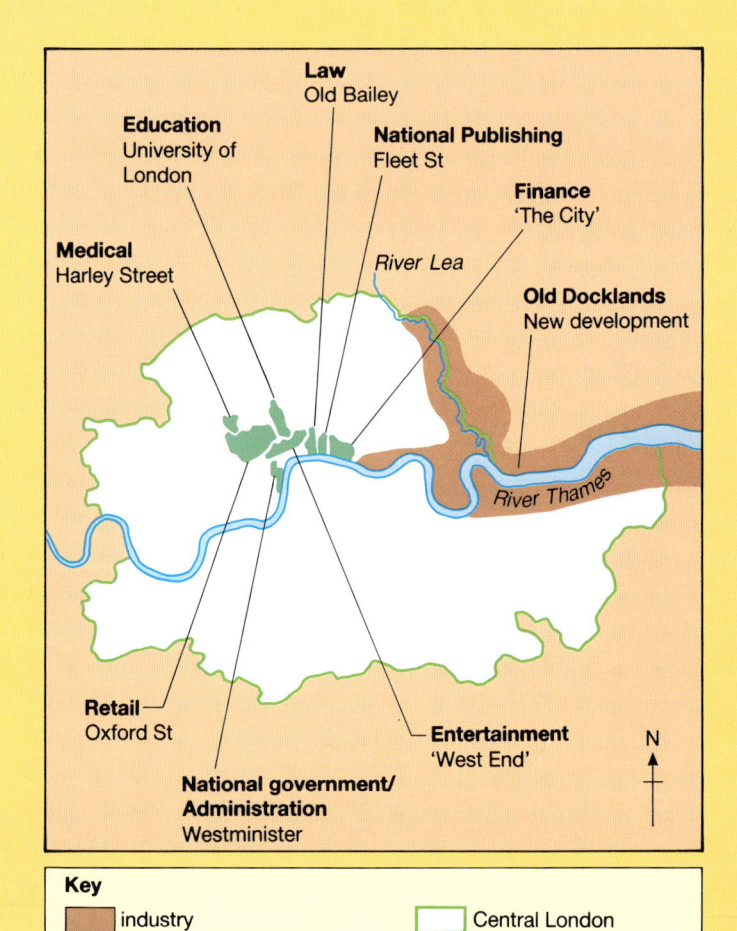

Figure B London's specialized functions

Fieldwork: housing

Plan a piece of fieldwork in your local area and carry it out. The aim of your fieldwork is to investigate one aspect of housing. You must choose your own hypothesis.

Urban example:
"All the terraced housing is near the centre of town."
  You could use one or two transects to test this hypothesis.

Rural example:
"The new houses in the village have smaller gardens than the old ones."
  Use the fieldwork methods explained on page 8. And refer to the Fieldwork Enquiry Route on page 18.

Plan	(10 marks)
Presentation	(10 marks)
Conclusion	(10 marks)
Total:	30 marks

Details for pupil profile sheets Unit 2

Knowledge and understanding

1. A settlement hierarchy
2. Functions of a capital city
3. Different functions have different patterns
4. Types of shops
5. Grading shopping centres
6. Growth of fast food chains
7. Superstores offer alternative shopping patterns
8. A city has distinct areas
9. Land values change in a city
10. Patterns of housing quality

Skills

1. Measuring distances on maps
2. Working out densities on a map
3. Reading a large scale map
4. Grouping and mapping information
5. Reading pie graphs
6. Using pedestrian flows
7. Using photographs
8. Linking photographs with maps
9. Using an urban transect
10. Using housing quality data
11. Making decisions (about types of schools)

Values

1. Understanding an old man's point of view about fast food
2. Understanding that people have differing views about shopping facilities
3. Realizing that you can make judgements about housing quality
4. Realizing that you can develop your own viewpoint after studying details (about schools)

3.1 Traffic in towns

Unit 3: Transport and Industry

The *traffic flow* graph (Figure A) shows three distinct peaks in traffic along a main road. This main road is just one of many serving a city centre.

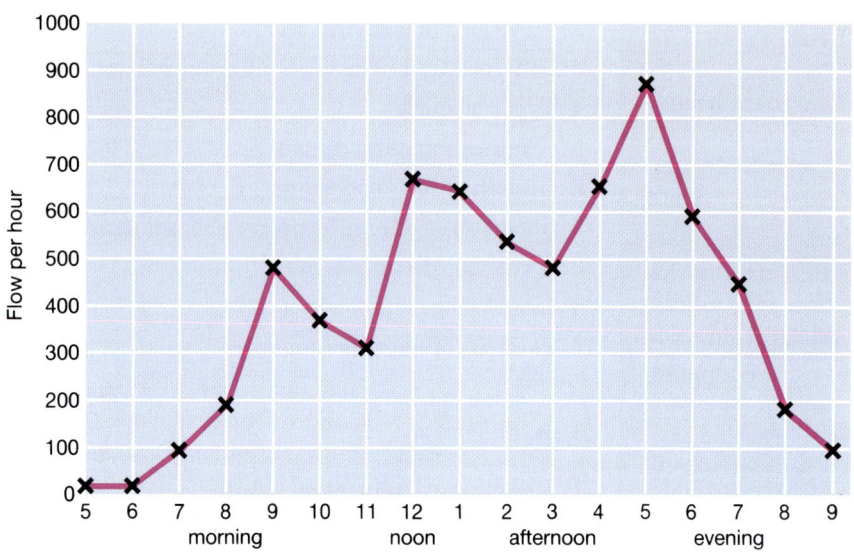

Figure A (*above*) Traffic flow along a main road

Desire lines

Traffic is made up of many individual journeys between different places. If individual journeys are plotted, then a *desire line* map can be drawn.

Figure B shows the results of a desire line survey. It is really the *demand* for car parks in a town centre. The figures show the number of people who would prefer to park in a particular part of town. The actual car parking capacity is also given.

Figure D shows where people from one housing street go for their work. You can see that several workers are travelling to the new factory. Planners use desire line maps to help them plan road improvements and new roads. In this case they may consider improving the road to the new factory.

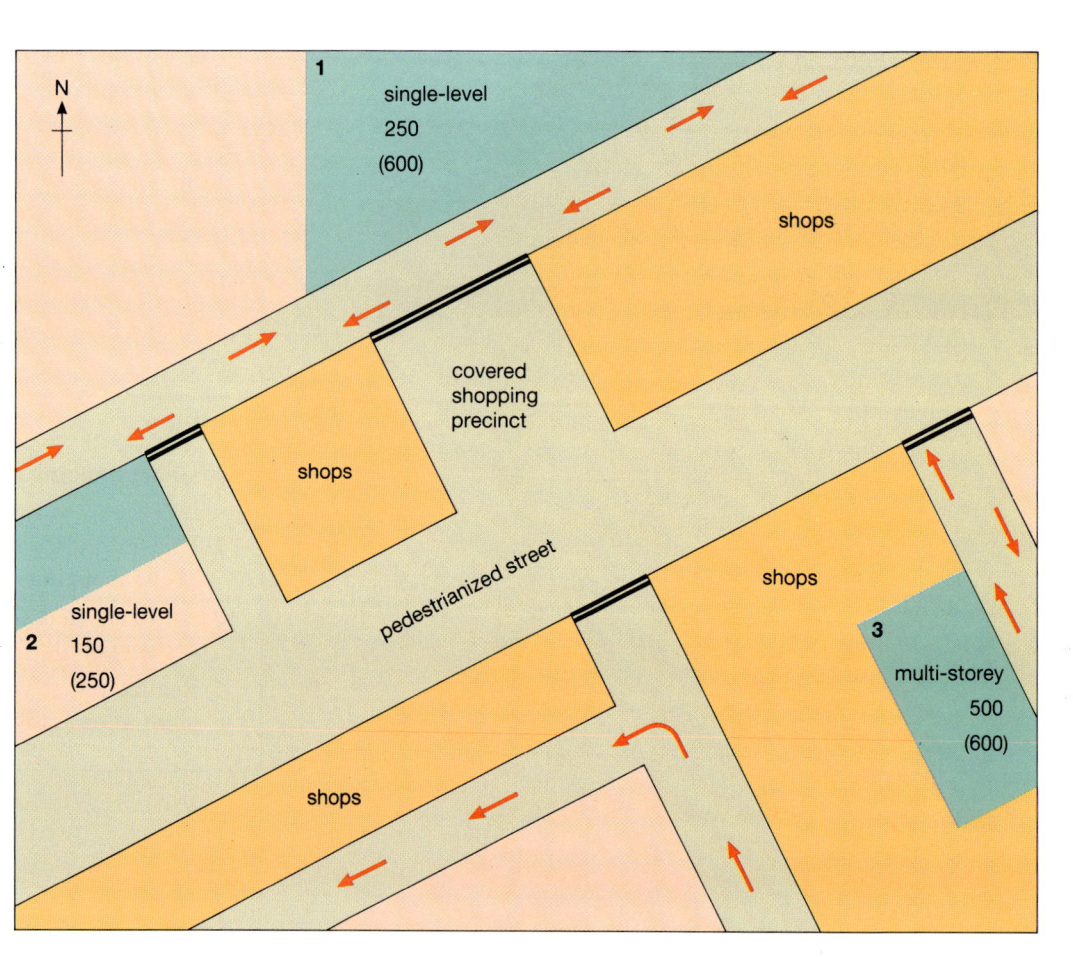

Key
- traffic direction
- blocked-off street
- car park
- 500 capacity
- (600) desired or preferred

Figure B The demand for car parking

42

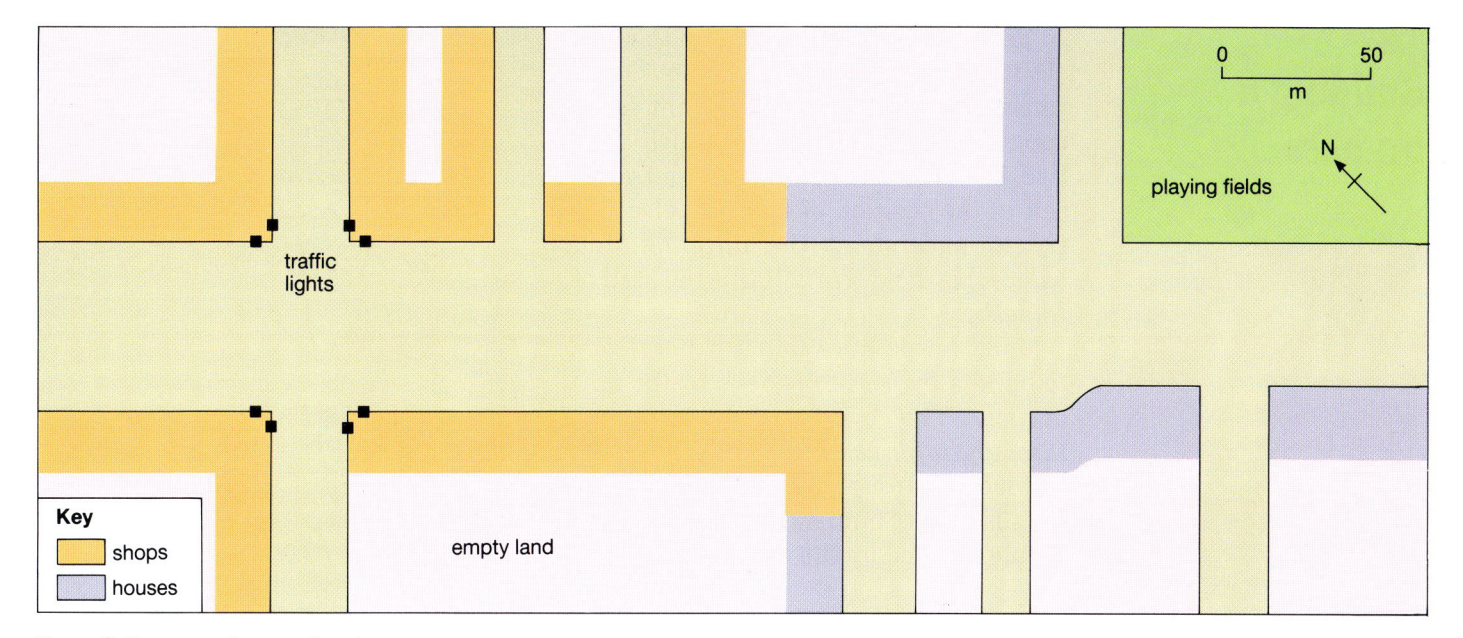

Figure C Base map for question 4

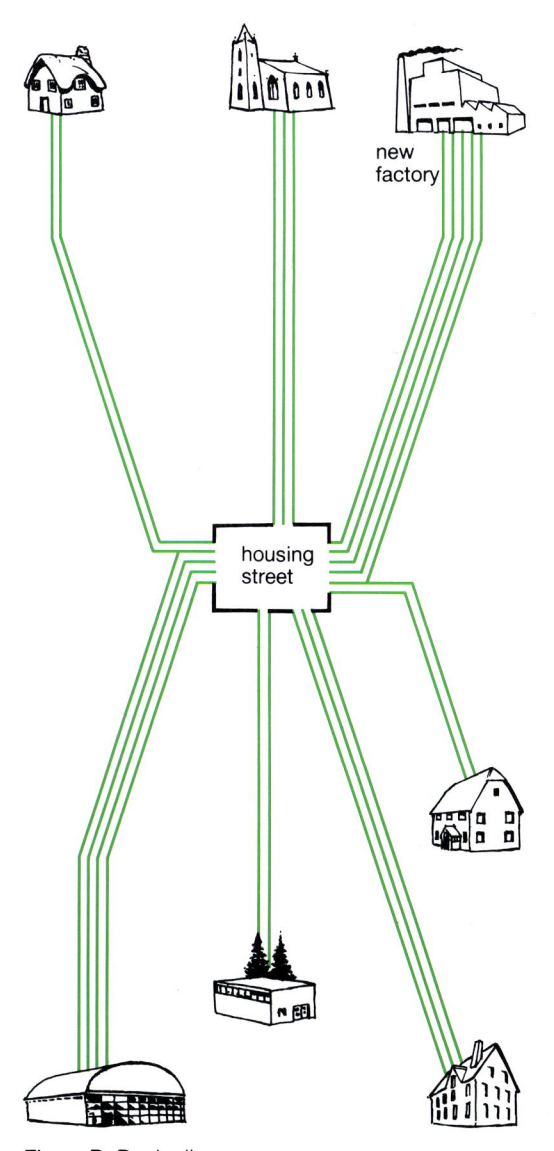

Figure D Desire lines

QUESTIONS

1. Which is the busiest time of the day on the main road?
2. Which way is most traffic travelling at a) 9.00am and b) 5.00pm?
3. On the day the traffic count was taken there was so much congestion at 9.00am that the flow was only 480 per hour.
   What situations can cause traffic hold ups (congestion)?
4. a) Make a copy of Figure D and on it show how you are going to control the traffic. You can use any of the following traffic control techniques. The numbers 1, 2, 3 refer to Question 5.

   double and single yellow lines
   mini-roundabout
   no right turns
   blocking off side streets
   pelican crossing
   banning heavy vehicles
   widening part of the road

   b) Explain your choice of traffic control techniques.
5. For a main road near you, think of the point where more traffic control is needed.
   a) State the location of your road.
   b) Describe the traffic problem – is it worse at a particular time?
   c) Explain how the traffic could be controlled?
6. The local council have a limited budget but realise they must spend more on car parking.
   What do you suggest they do? You should present the council with two alternative plans.
7. Apart from building new car parks can you suggest any other schemes for copying with shoppers cars?
8. If the council did not build new car parks what do you think the shoppers would do? How would this affect the shops in the towns centre?

3.2 Building a by-pass

In previous exercises you have thought about different people's viewpoints. Sometimes people have very different ideas about the environment in which they live. For this exercise you must put yourself in the position of someone else and try to understand the *attitudes* and *values* they hold. We call this the skill of *empathy*.

Many towns have found it necessary to build a *by-pass* to relieve traffic congestion. The by-pass takes all the *through-traffic* around the built-up area instead of through the middle of it. It sounds perfect but ... what about those people affected by the by-pass?

Figure A (*below*) Alternative by-pass routes

Figure B (*right, and facing*) Local opinions

> THE NEW ROAD AND THE BRIDGE WILL DESTROY THE WINTERING GROUNDS OF RARE WILD GEESE. THIS BREEDING GROUND IS UNIQUE ON THE EAST COAST.

CHAIR of the local branch of the Royal Society for the Protection of Birds.

> THIS IS NONSENSE. I HAVE SOME OF THE BEST FRUIT-GROWING LAND IN THE COUNTY AND THE BY-PASS WILL GO THROUGH THE MIDDLE OF MY ESTATE.

RETIRED ADMIRAL, land owner.

> THE VILLAGE HAS LOTS OF NEW HOUSES SOME OF WHICH ARE VERY EXCLUSIVE. THE NEW BY-PA[SS] WILL DEPRESS HOUSE PRICES AN[D] UPSET THE PEACEFULNESS OF THIS LOVELY VILLAGE.

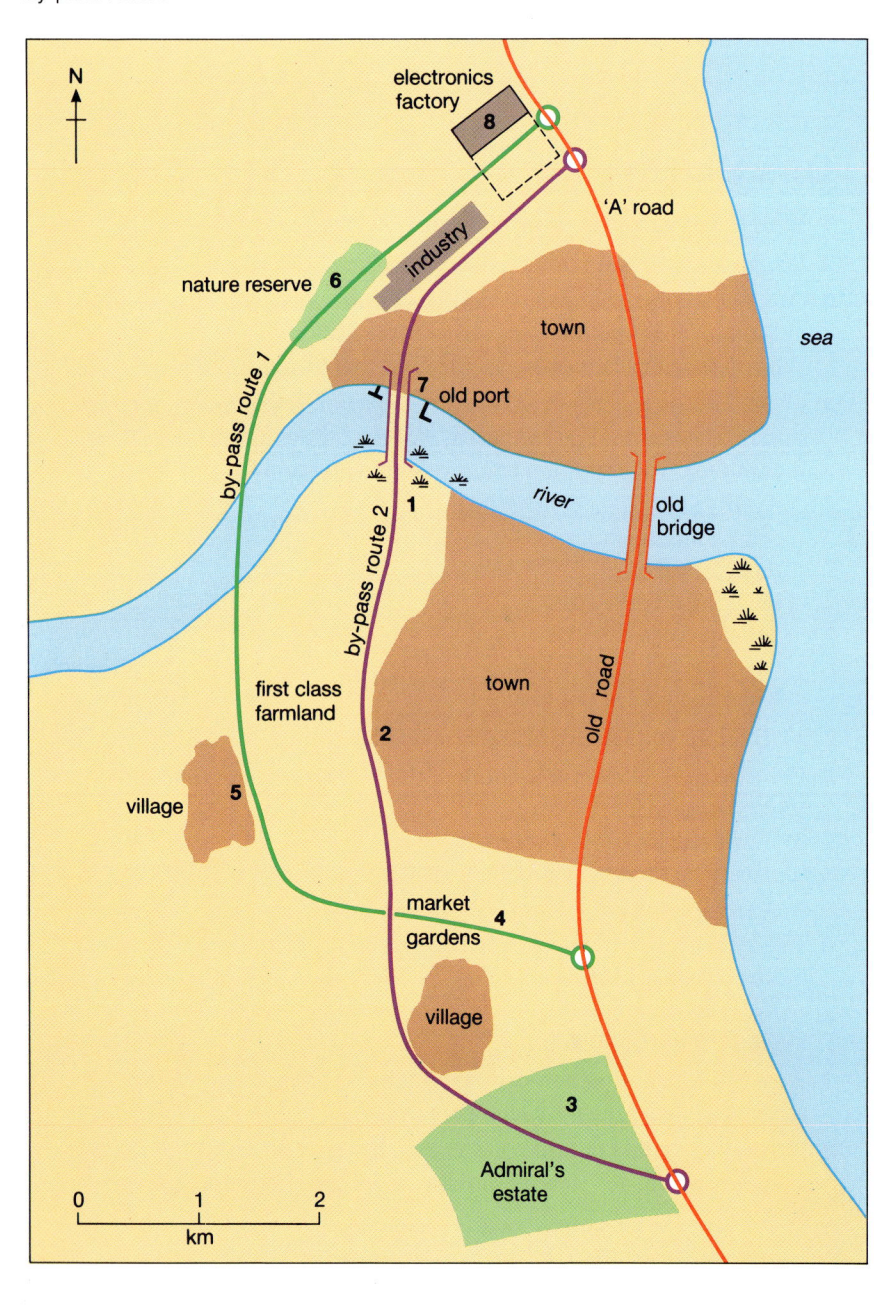

CHAIR of the Village Ratepayers' Association.

SECRETARY of the Residents' Association.

THE BY-PASS WILL BE TOO CLOSE TO THE PRESENT EDGE OF TOWN. RESIDENTS WILL BE UPSET BY ITS NOISE AND VIEWS WEST WILL BE SPOILT.

THIS IS A HIGHLY PROFITABLE FOOD GROWING AREA. THERE IS NO BETTER SOIL IN THE DISTRICT.

SPOKESPERSON for a group of market gardeners.

CHAIR of the Old Preservation Society.

WE HAVE WORKED FOR YEARS TO PRESERVE THIS ANCIENT PART OF THE TOWN. NOW THE NEW ROAD IS PLANNED TO GO OVER THE TOP OF IT!

WE HAVE JUST PURCHASED LAND TO EXTEND OUR MOST SUCCESSFUL FACTORY. NOW THE BY-PASS COULD BE ROUTED RIGHT THROUGH OUR EXTENSIONS!
JOBS BEFORE THE BY-PASS PLEASE.

THE LOCAL DIRECTOR of the Council of Nature Reserves.

THIS SITE HAS SOME OF THE COUNTRY'S RAREST BUTTERFLIES AND WILD FLOWERS. THE BY-PASS COULD COULD RUIN THIS EXCEPTIONAL RESERVE.

DIRECTOR of electronics factory.

QUESTIONS

1. Many towns have found it necessary to build a by-pass around the edge of town. What do you think the advantages of a by-pass are?
   (Hints: speed, time, congestion, pollution, noise)

2. Study the map of the coastal town. The county council have proposed two routes for the by-pass. Both plans cost about the same.
   a) Choose one of the people shown on this spread, or put all their names in a hat and pick one out.
   b) Read about the person and find what they are interested in on the map.
   c) Think about their attitudes towards the by-pass. Can you think of other reasons why they might oppose the by-pass?

3. Now listen to other people's views about the by-pass routes. Or you can read them yourself.

4. List the 8 viewpoints in rank order. Score them 8, 7, 6 … 1. You can see that you can now add up the scores for the two alternative routes. There are 4 viewpoints for each route.

5. Which by-pass should go ahead? Or can you suggest a better route for it. Remember, if you do you may come across other people who object to it.

6. Now you have decided on the by-pass route write the front page of a brochure. You must explain to the people of the town why the by-pass will be an advantage to them all.

3.3 Travelling by road

One hundred years ago people had never thought of a society dominated by the car. In the early twentieth century cars were for the rich and the roads linking settlements were narrow and winding. Today it is difficult to imagine a carless society. If your family does not have a car you will know many people who do have one. Certainly you will be aware at times of the problems of too many cars – traffic congestion, noise, danger and air pollution.

Reading road maps

To survive in our car-dominated society you must be able to read a road map. The Automobile Association (AA) Members Handbook contains maps like Figures A and B.

Urban motorways

Motorways have been built in cities throughout the rich world and increasingly in the poor world. Some motorways go through the centre of cities. To do so they have to be supported on stilts and use underpasses. Whatever the engineering difficulties, such motorways have costs and benefits. Figure C shows some of the costs of urban motorways. Can you think of any more. An *economic cost* refers to the financial cost and the *social cost* refers to the community losses or the 'cost' to the people.

Figure A AA map of the Norwich area

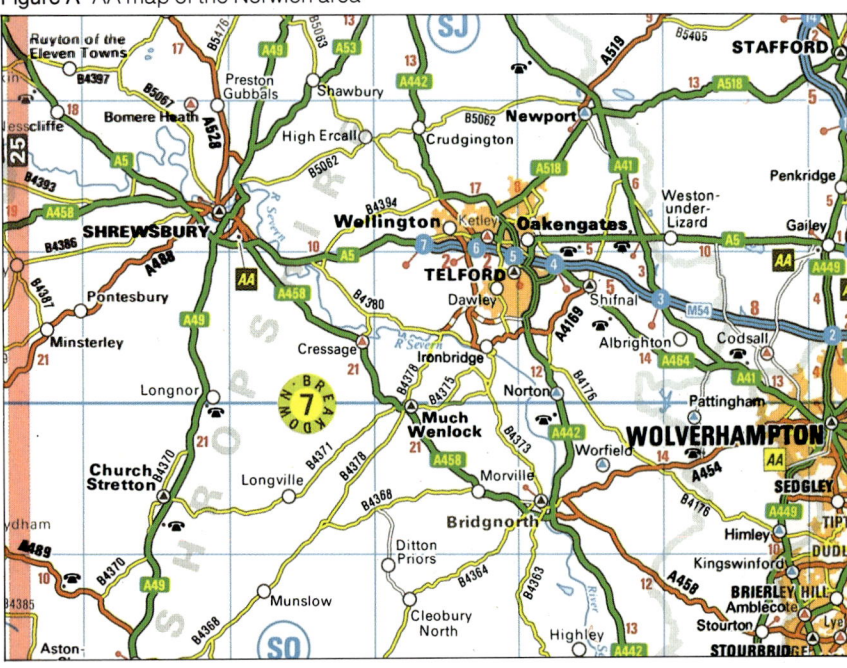

Figure B (*above and right*) The Telford motorway (M54)

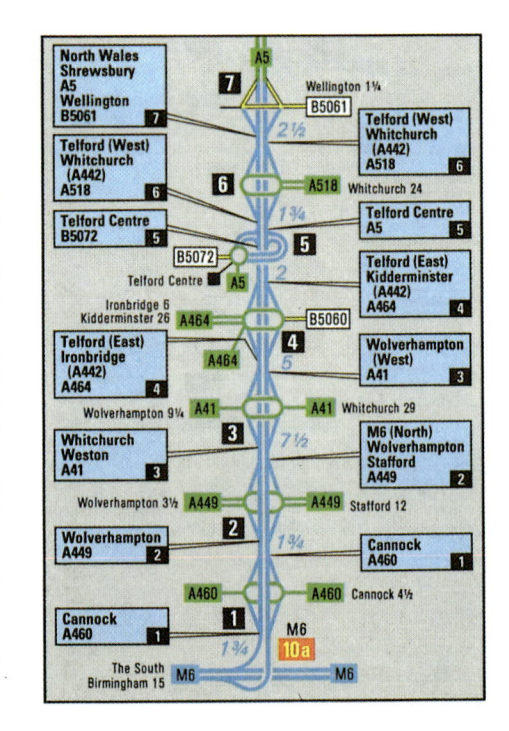

Figure D is an aerial photograph of the M25/M4 intersection near Heathrow Airport (see also Figure D on the next pages). At this point the M4 joins London's *Orbital Motorway*, the M25. This motorway is a ring road, it is 192 kilometres (120 miles) long and has 31 junctions. It was completed in 1986 after many years of construction. As with all motorways that serve urban areas, there is a mixture of costs and benefits. Some critics say it is too far out of London and is not really a ring road for London. They say it would have been better if it had been built much nearer the centre. The ring road that circuits Paris, the *Boulevard Pérepherique*, is much closer to the city centre. If the M25 had been built closer to London then more property and people would have been affected. As it is, a lot of good farmland and many pleasant areas of countryside have been disturbed.

Figure C The costs of a motorway

Figure D The M25 under construction

QUESTIONS

1. Use Figure A. You have to travel from Cromer in the north to Beccles, east of Lowestoft.
   a) How far is it in a straight line?
   b) How far is it by the main A roads (green)?
2. What do you notice about the road system in Norwich? Why do you think a *ring road* has been built around this city?
3. Which town on the map has a by-pass to the west of it?
4. Study Figure B. The map on the left is at a larger scale and shows a short section of motorway in the Midlands. On the right is another type of diagram showing the motorway. We call this a *topological diagram*.
   a) Why can the diagram not be called a map?
   b) What other topological diagrams do you know?
   c) Why are route diagrams often more useful than maps?
5. You have to travel from the centre of Wolverhampton to Minsterley which is West of Telford.
   a) Describe your journey.
   b) Draw a topological diagram to show your journey.
6. Study Figure C and make a list of some of the *economic benefits* and *social benefits* of urban motorways.
7. Why do you think it was necessary to build the M25?
8. Study Figure C and the photograph Figure D. In two columns list the costs and benefits of such a massive motorway intersection. This time you should divide the costs and benefits into *economic* and *environmental*.

3.4 Travelling between cities: London to Belfast

Look at the following facts which inform you about travelling between London and Belfast.

- **The short sea-crossing** between Cairnryan and Larne takes 2–2¼ hours. There is a similar sea-crossing between Stranraer and Larne.
- **The long sea-crossing** between Liverpool and Belfast takes 9 hours.
- **The Super Shuttle** service between London Heathrow and Belfast takes 1 hour 10 minutes.

Answer all the questions and decide which route you would choose. Think of all the different factors that would influence your choice of method of travel and the route you would take. For example, the cost of a single shuttle ticket is similar to the cost of a single ticket for car and driver on the sea-crossings. But with a car the petrol money must be added.

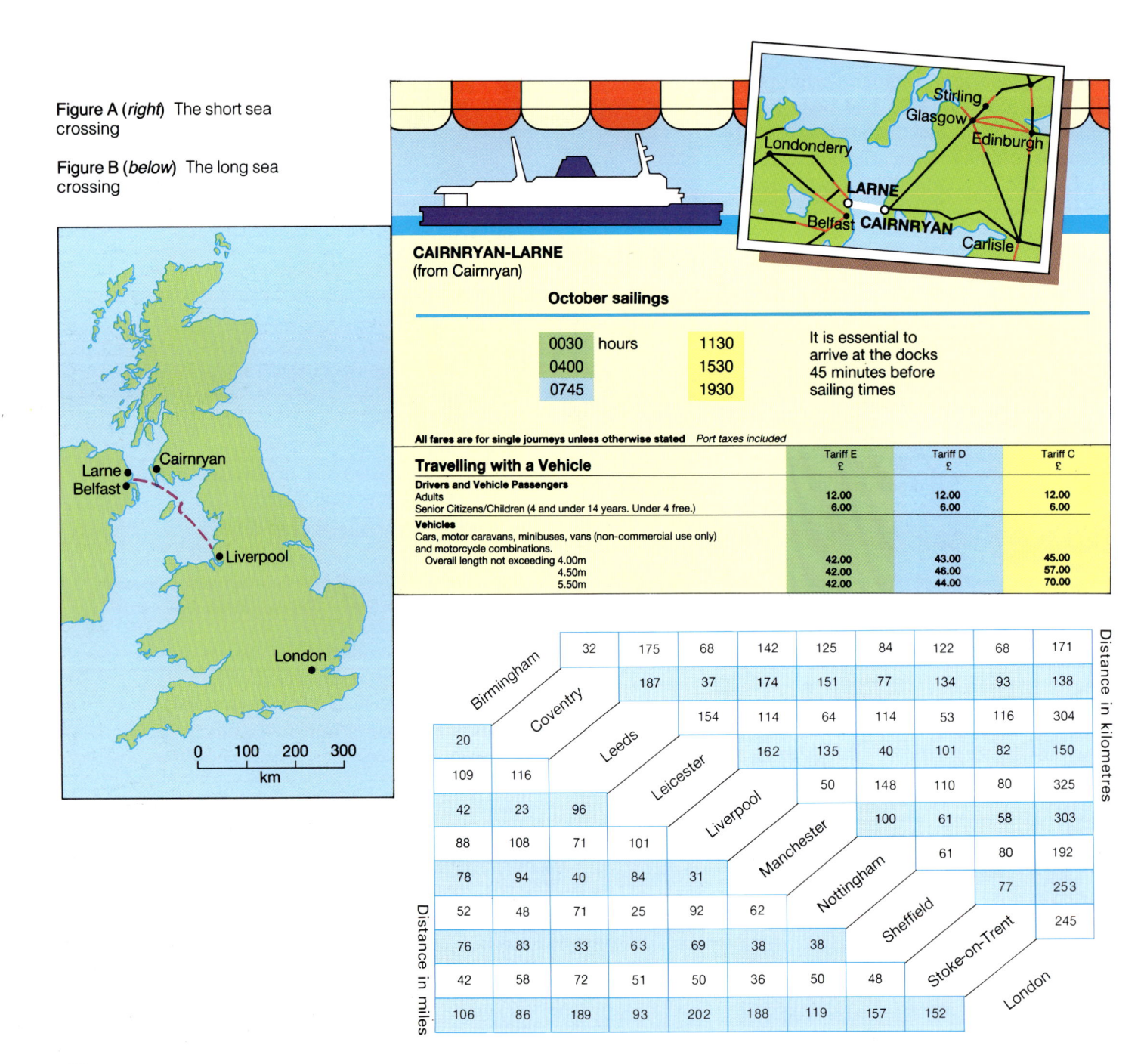

Figure A (*right*) The short sea crossing

Figure B (*below*) The long sea crossing

CAIRNRYAN–LARNE
(from Cairnryan)

October sailings

0030	hours	1130	It is essential to arrive at the docks 45 minutes before sailing times
0400		1530	
0745		1930	

All fares are for single journeys unless otherwise stated   Port taxes included

Travelling with a Vehicle	Tariff E £	Tariff D £	Tariff C £
Drivers and Vehicle Passengers			
Adults	12.00	12.00	12.00
Senior Citizens/Children (4 and under 14 years. Under 4 free.)	6.00	6.00	6.00
Vehicles			
Cars, motor caravans, minibuses, vans (non-commercial use only) and motorcycle combinations.			
Overall length not exceeding 4.00m	42.00	43.00	45.00
4.50m	42.00	46.00	57.00
5.50m	42.00	44.00	70.00

Distance in kilometres / Distance in miles

Birmingham	32	175	68	142	125	84	122	68	171
20	Coventry	187	37	174	151	77	134	93	138
		Leeds	154	114	64	114	53	116	304
109	116		Leicester	162	135	40	101	82	150
42	23	96		Liverpool	50	148	110	80	325
88	108	71	101		Manchester	100	61	58	303
78	94	40	84	31		Nottingham	61	80	192
52	48	71	25	92	62		Sheffield	77	253
76	83	33	63	69	38	38		Stoke-on-Trent	245
42	58	72	51	50	36	50	48		London
106	86	189	93	202	188	119	157	152	

BRITISH AIRWAYS

October
From LONDON HEATHROW to BELFAST
SUPER SHUTTLE SERVICE

Dep.	Arr.	Days	Flight No.	Class	Aircraft
0830	0940	123456	BA 4552	M	735/B11
1030	1140	Daily	BA 4572	M	757
1230	1340	Daily	BA 4592	M	757
1430	1540	Daily	BA 4612	M	735/757
1630	1740	Daily	BA 4632	M	735/757
1830	1940	Daily	BA 4652	M	757
2030	2140	12345 7	BA 4672	M	757

Explanation of abbreviations
735 – boeing 737-200
757 – Boeing 757
B11 – British Aerospace (BAC) One-Eleven
1–Monday 2–Tuesday 3–Wednesday 4–Thursday
5–Friday 6–Saturday 7–Sunday

Minimum check-in time is 10 minutes.
Flights depart from Terminal 1

SUPER SHUTTLE FARES (LONDON–BELFAST)

EARLY SAVER RETURN – £79. Tickets bought 2 weeks in advance
Travel between 1000 and 1530 hours

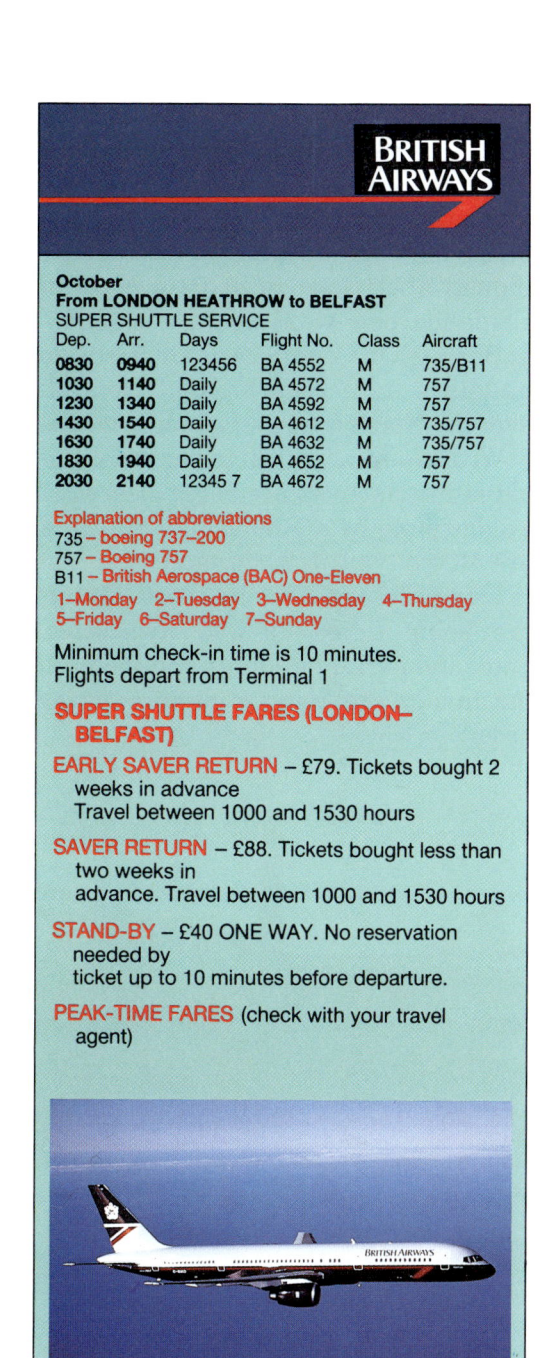

SAVER RETURN – £88. Tickets bought less than two weeks in
advance. Travel between 1000 and 1530 hours

STAND-BY – £40 ONE WAY. No reservation needed by
ticket up to 10 minutes before departure.

PEAK-TIME FARES (check with your travel agent)

Figure C The Super Shuttle

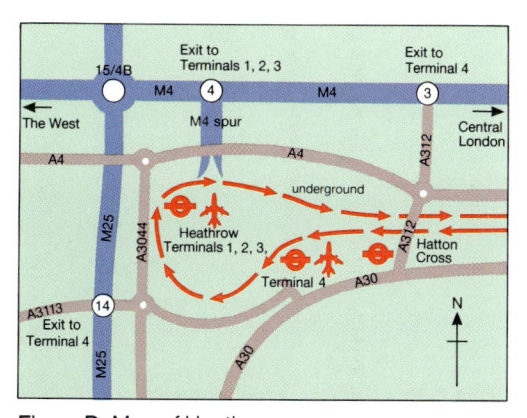

Figure D Map of Heathrow

QUESTIONS

The short sea-crossing

1 Find London and Belfast in an atlas. What is the straight line distance between them in a) miles and b) kilometres?

2 How far is the route from Cairnryan and Larne in a) miles and b) kilometres?

3 How much is a return journey from Cairnryan to Larne for a 4.50 metre long car and one passenger:
   a) on the 0400 hours sailing?
   b) on the 1530 hours sailing?

4 a) It is 600 kilometres by road from London to Cairnryan. If you were able to travel at an average speed of 80 kilometres per hour (including stops) how long would it take to drive this distance?
   b) If your car travelled 15 kilometres per litre of petrol and petrol costs 50p per litre, how much would this journey cost?

The long sea-crossing

5 Work out how far it is by sea in miles and kilometres from Liverpool to Belfast.

6 a) How far is it by road from London to Liverpool?
   b) How much would this journey cost you using the same figures as given in question 4 b)?

The Super Shuttle

7 How long is the flight from London to Belfast?

8 What do you notice about the check-in time for the Super Shuttle?

9 How much is a return ticket for one person:
   a) booking two weeks in advance and travelling between 1000 hours and 1530 hours?
   b) booking with less than two weeks notice and travelling between 1000 hours and 1530 hours?

10 Why do you think this service is called a 'shuttle'?

11 In three columns, list the advantages and disadvantages of the three routes to Belfast.

12 Which route do you think the following people would use? You are allowed to say "it depends" but if you do, say what it depends on!
   a) A Government official travelling to Belfast for a conference.
   b) A London family who do not like long sea journeys who are going on a touring holiday.
   c) A woman travelling from London to pick up her daughter who has just finished studying at University in Belfast.
   d) A London worker returning home for Christmas.

3.5 Industry in towns: preservation

Manufacturing industry based on coal made Britain one of the most powerful nations in the world in the nineteenth century. New towns grew up on the coalfields of central Scotland, northern England, the Midlands and South Wales. The majority of working people had jobs in manufacturing or mining. Today only about 25 per cent of Britain's working population is in manufacturing or *secondary* industry. The percentage employed in mining is now very small. In the latter half of the twentieth century many interest groups and local authorities have worked to preserve Britain's *industrial heritage*.

In 1968 the Ironbridge Gorge Museum Trust was established to *preserve* the remains of early industry. Today, at Blists Hill Open Air Museum at Ironbridge in Shropshire, there are rebuilt blast furnaces, an ironworks, a saw mill, a printing shop, and a colliery. All are preserved 'monuments' to the area's industrial heritage. In 1970 the North of England Open Air Museum was started at Beamish in County Durham. Here old buildings have been brought from all over the North East to the museum site.

Within our industrial towns and cities old industrial sites are being cleared at an alarming rate. Scenes like Figure A are all too typical. Fortunately the past is being preserved in the cities. Canals are being tidied up and revitalized. Some industrial buildings and pieces of machinery are being kept in working order.

Figure A Old steelworks in Sheffield

Figure B Derelict land in Sheffield

Figure C Disused steelworks alongside a little-used waterway

Sheffield

In the middle of Sheffield the *Kelham Island Industrial Museum* has been established in an old industrial area on the River Don. Visitors to this museum can follow a trail round the area which features many relics of the past. The photographs give you an idea of what this old industrial area is like. You probably know somewhere where there are industrial remains. Should they be preserved? But where do you draw the line? What should be kept and what should be demolished?

Housing conditions

The 1851 census shows up the poor living conditions of the area: 473 people lived next to a foundry and two pubs. They all shared just 18 water taps or pumps. The *Sheffield Independent* newspaper of 3 February 1872 said of the area:

> 'the courts and yards are close, narrow and full of offensive matter, which would be more valuable in another place . . . The rents paid in most of these wretched districts seem out of all proportion to the accommodation furnished'.

Figure D Entrance to the Green Lane Works

Figure E Part of the Kelham Island Industrial Museum

QUESTIONS

1. What do you understand by an open air museum?
2. Name two open air museums and describe the attractions on display.
3. Why do you think it is so important to preserve the industrial past?
4. Write down the evidence from Figures A and B that shows that Sheffield was an important steel centre.
5. Look at the derelict scene in Figure C. Why have people and industry left city centres?
6. Visitors to the Museum (Figure E) can read about the local area of Sheffield in the nineteenth century.
   Look at the details from the 1851 Census and the newspaper quote. Write in your own words what the housing conditions and living standards were like.
7. Figure D shows the entrance to the Green Lane Works which is seen being *renovated* and cleaned up. Do you think it is worthwhile keeping old buildings like this? Give your reasons.
8. a) How would you go about using this old industrial environment as a tourist attraction?
   b) How would you make it useful for school parties to visit?

3.6 The industrial estate: fieldwork

An industrial estate is an area set aside for factories, warehouses, repair shops, offices and other places of employment. It is a planned *industrial zone* usually located away from housing areas. You probably know an industrial estate near to where you live. These estates range in size from small areas containing a few industrial units to wide areas where large factories and warehouses have been built.

Many industrial estates are owned by local authorities. The authority builds factory units which can be rented or purchased. The idea of industrial estates started with the building of the Trafford Park Estate in Manchester in 1896. It was built to attract business to the newly built Manchester Ship Canal. Another early estate was the Slough Trading Estate. On both estates an *infrastructure* was provided. This means essential services were laid down, such as sewers, drainage, gas, electricity and water.

In 1936 the first Government trading estate was opened at Team Valley south of Newcastle-upon-Tyne. The building of industrial estates became a successful method of attracting new industry to Development Areas, New Towns and expanding towns.

Figure A The Compton Industrial Estate, Eastbourne. Students listed the following industrial units on the Estate:
Car sales
Tyre sales
SS Pumps (manufacturing)
Kingsway Publishing (distribution)
Decorators (sales)
Wine and spirit distributors
Glass merchants
Renault dealers
Leisure furniture manufacturers
Decorators (sales)
Eastbourne Borough Council (services)
Painting contractors
Anti-corrosion engineers
Builders
Shoe manufacturers
clean air installation
Furniture retailers
Engineering services
Furniture storage
Accident repairs
Electrical distributors

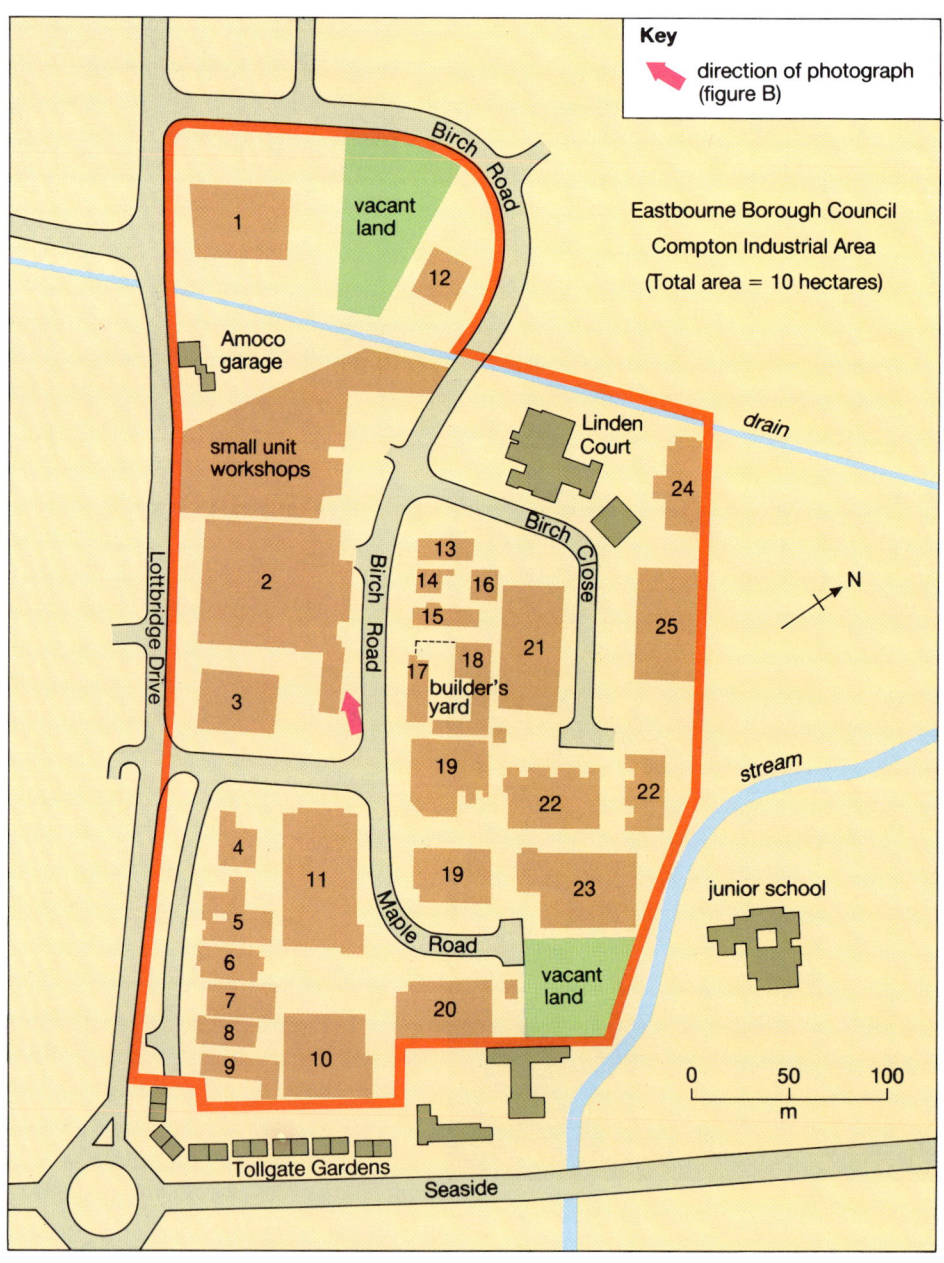

Figure B A stainless steel pump factory

Figure C Sample of questionnaire

A visit to the Compton Industrial Area, Eastbourne: fieldwork

Eastbourne, on the south coast of East Sussex, wants more industry. Like many local authorities it advertises for new industry. The town's industrial estates are said to be attractive to companies.

To find out what companies thought about the area, some students carried out an enquiry.

Organizing the enquiry

1 A map of the industrial area was obtained from the Borough Council. A simplified outline map was drawn for use on the visit.

2 Each industrial unit was identified and marked on the map.

3 Addresses of some sample companies were noted.

4 Letters were written to these companies enclosing a questionnaire. Part of the questionnaire is shown on the right, with the answers from the company shown in Figure B.

Figure D Part of the Compton Industrial Estate

```
Unit Number: 2
Company Name: SSP Pumps Limited
Address: Birch Road, Compton Industrial Estate,
         Eastbourne, East Sussex
```

Please answer the following questions in the spaces provided:

a) What exactly do you do at your unit/factory?
   We make stainless steel pumps.

b) How long have you been on this estate?
   We moved here in 1970.

c) Why did you move to this estate?
   The company needed a bigger site because it was expanding its production.

d) Are you pleased with the facilities on the estate?
   The estate is very good. But as you know this is very low-lying land and the site has been flooded a few times.

e) Are there any other facilities which you would like the estate to provide?
   Better drainage.

f) How many people do you employ?
   We employ 185 people at present, but this figure changes slightly from time to time.

QUESTIONS

1 What is an industrial estate?
2 Name one of the earliest industrial estates.
3 Why have industrial estates been so successful in attracting industry?
4 You are a director of a small company making double glazing units for homes. The company wants to move to a factory away from its cramped town centre site. Make a list of what you would look for when attempting to find a new location.
5 Study the map and key.
   a) How many entrances are there to the industrial estate?
   b) Which is the largest industrial building?
   c) What does this firm do?
6 How many factories (units making things) are there on the estate?
7 How many units are linked to the motor trade?
8 Find Tollgate Gardens on the map. What do you think the problems are of living next to an industrial estate?
9 Study the photograph Figure D. Find the unit on the map.
   a) Which way was the camera pointing?
   b) Name the company on the right of photograph.
   c) What type of company is it?
   d) Describe the landscaping.
   e) Why does an industrial estate like this have landscaping?

Unit 3 ASSESSMENT

Grouping information and drawing a graph

An industrial estate

Study the map on the previous page of the Compton industrial area in Eastbourne. On a fieldstudy visit, students identified most of the industrial units that were occupied. The industrial units can be grouped into the following groups or types.

- **A** Manufacturing (factories)
- **B** Warehouses (buildings for storage)
- **C** Wholesalers and retailers (sales and distribution)
- **D** Services (repairs, builders, paint spraying)

Draw a bar graph to show the types of the 21 industrial units given in the caption to the map. (8 marks)

Figure A A view of the Compton Industrial Estate

An investigation

Quality of the environment

Study Figures A and B. Figure A shows part of the Compton industrial area in Eastbourne. Figure B is an area of older industry near Eastbourne railway station.

i) The general aim of the investigation is to compare the quality of environment in the two areas.

ii) The hypothesis to be tested is "older industrial areas have a less attractive environment than newer industrial areas".

a) List the *four* features of the industrial environment to which the students' description refer. (4 marks)

b) For each industrial area give each of the features of the environment a quality grade 1 to 5. State what your grades mean. (8 marks)

c) Compare the environmental quality of the two industrial environments by means of a graph. (8 marks)

d) Add up your grade totals for each area. has the hypothesis been proved?

e) Why do you think towns like Eastbourne are keen to build industrial areas which have pleasant environments? (6 marks)

Total: 30 marks

Figure B Industry near the Eastbourne railway terminus

People's viewpoints

Planning an industrial museum
The local council has decided to open an industrial museum on some waste land near the city centre. Read the following people's comments about the proposal.

> THIS WILL GIVE YOUNG PEOPLE JOBS.

> THIS WILL ATTRACT THOUSANDS OF VISITORS.

> THIS DEVELOPMENT WILL BRING UNWANTED TOURISTS TO OUR AREA.

> THIS WASTELAND IS A LONG ESTABLISHED HABITAT FOR WILDLIFE: IT WILL BE DESTROYED.

Figure C (*top left*) the Mayor, (*top right*) member of the Trades Council, (*bottom left*) chair of the Resident's Association, (*bottom right*) member of the Wildlife Association

a) What jobs will the museum provide? (2 marks)
b) How do you think the visitors could upset local residents? (2 marks)
c) Why is the Wildlife Society so against the plan? (2 marks)
d) Write possible comments about the planned museum for:
　i) The manager of a local public house that provides pub lunches
　ii) The chair of the 'Campaign for Better Housing'
　iii) A founder member of the 'Society for the Preservation of Steam Engines' (6 marks)
f) Write four reasons why *you* think the industrial museum scheme should go ahead *or* should not go ahead. (6 marks)
Total: 20 marks

Details for pupil profile sheets Unit 3

Knowledge and understanding

1. Traffic flow and control
2. Desire lines and demand
3. The use of by-passes
4. Economic and social costs (motorways)
5. Industrial heritage
6. Industrial estates

Skills

1. Deciding on car parking
2. Ranking different viewpoints
3. Explaining a decision
4. Using road maps
5. Planning journeys – reading timetables
6. Using a large scale industrial estate plan
7. Drawing a bar graph

Values

1. Planning decisions should take account of people's needs
2. Empathizing with different interest groups
3. Balancing economic and social costs
4. Planning journeys for people with different priorities
5. Awareness of the need to preserve old industry
6. Realizing that development (old industry) is viewed differently by various interest groups
7. Investigating the quality of the environment

4.1 Inside an urban area: land use

Unit 4: Urban Organization

On the map, Figure A, six major types of land use have been mapped. You could probably think of a few other land uses. There is also industrial land, derelict land and land being built on. You could also map shops and services separately.

Figure A (*right*) Types of land use in an urban area

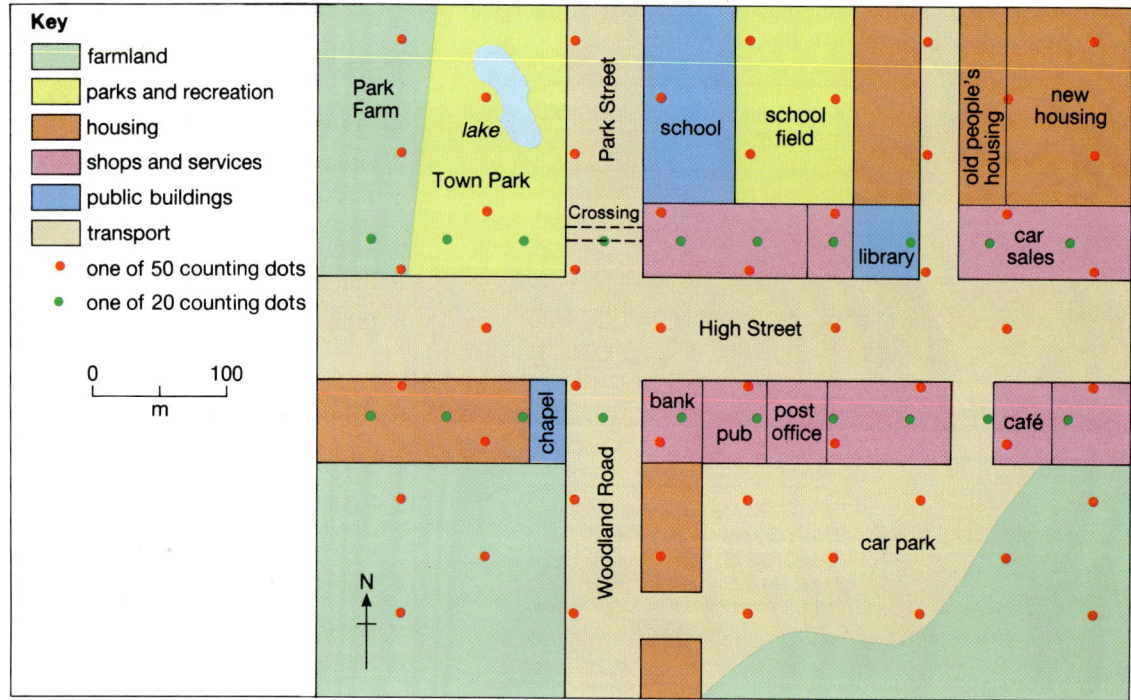

Key
- farmland
- parks and recreation
- housing
- shops and services
- public buildings
- transport
- • one of 50 counting dots
- • one of 20 counting dots

0 — 100 m

Park Farm, lake, Town Park, Park Street, school, school field, old people's housing, new housing, Crossing, library, car sales, High Street, chapel, bank, pub, post office, café, Woodland Road, car park

Figure B (*below*) Land use in the High Street shown in Figure A

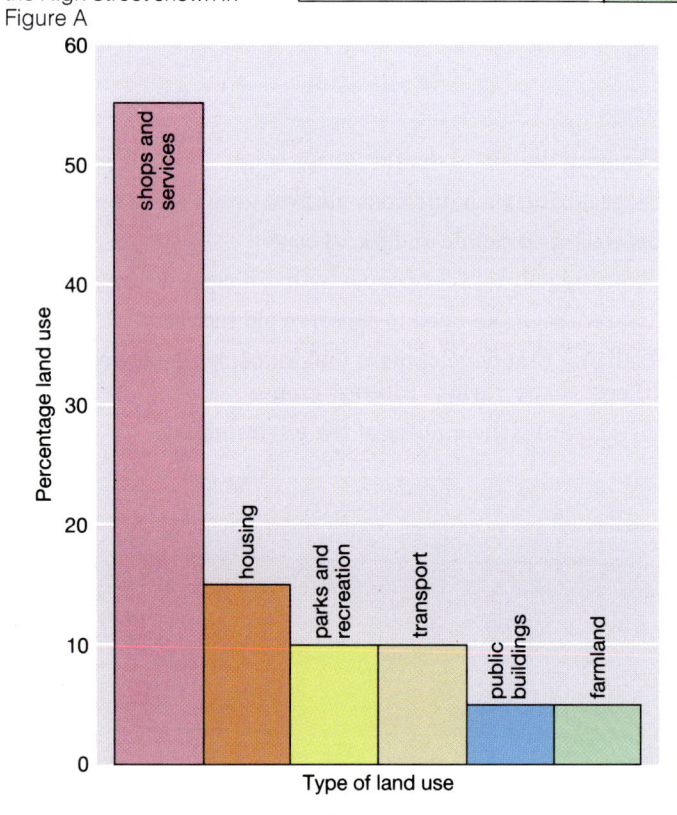

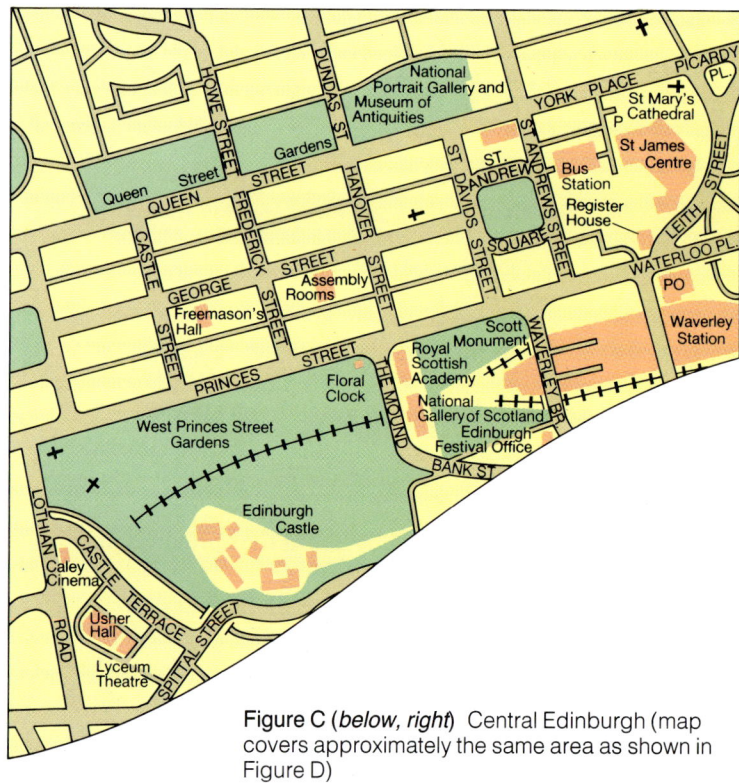

Bar chart — Percentage land use vs Type of land use:
- shops and services: 55
- housing: 15
- parks and recreation: 10
- transport: 10
- public buildings: 5
- farmland: 5

Figure C (*below, right*) Central Edinburgh (map covers approximately the same area as shown in Figure D)

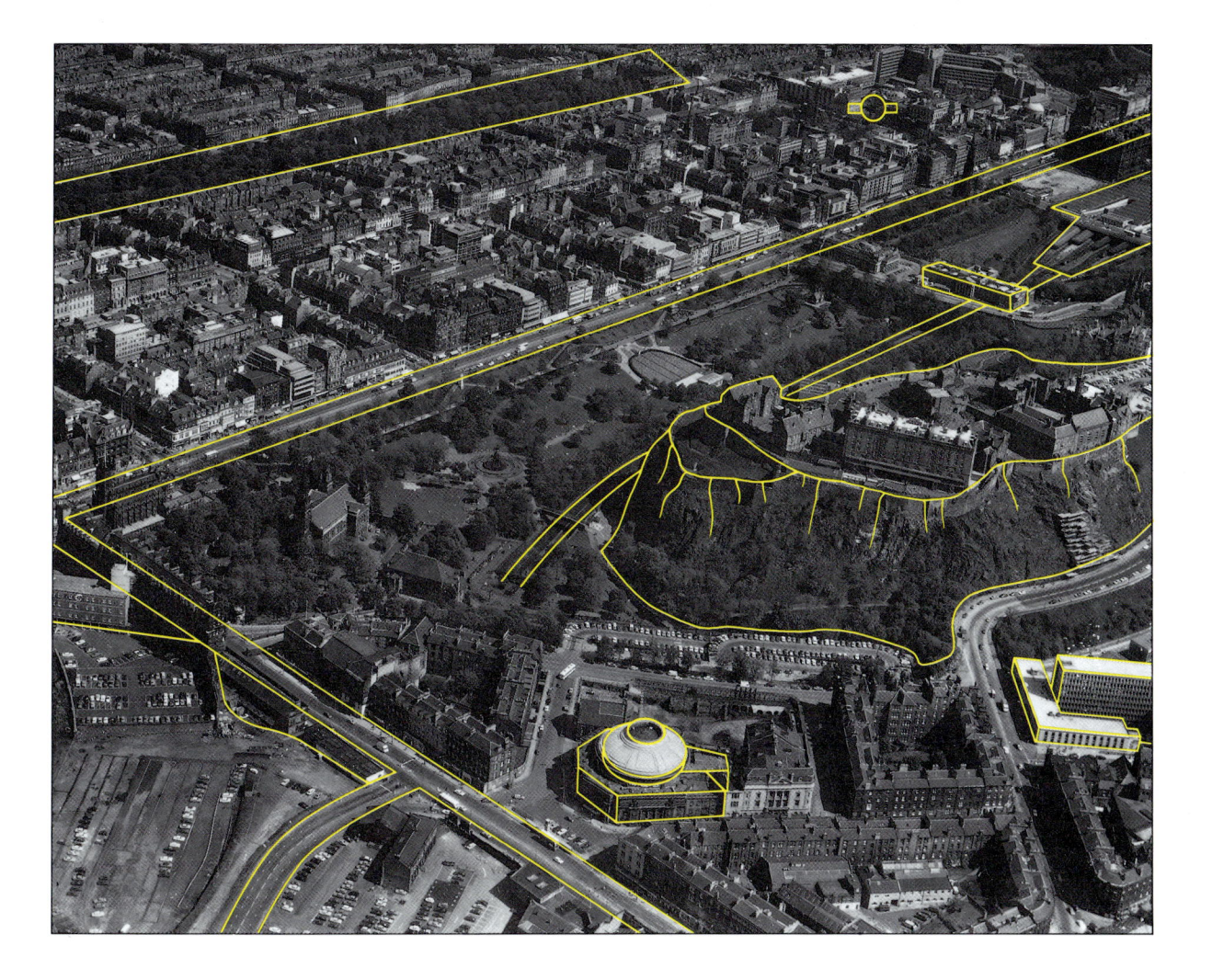

Figure D View over Edinburgh
a) the Castle and grounds
b) Waverly railway station
c) the railway line
d) an old railway station now being used as a car park
e) areas of parks and gardens
f) Princes Street – shopping
g) Lothian Road
h) the Usher Hall – concerts
i) the bus station
j) offices in Spittal Street
k) National Gallery of Scotland

Figure B shows the percentage of each category of land use along High Street. The calculations were made by plotting 20 equally spaced dots on the map. These are then counted for each land use and multiplied by 5. This method of gathering information is called *sampling*. Sampling can be used for collecting statistics of any type.

QUESTIONS

1. Study Figure A. Calculate the percentage of each land use for the whole map. There are 50 red counting dots so you will need to double each total for the percentage.
2. Draw a bar graph to show the percentages.
3. **Land use in Edinburgh** a) Trace the coloured outline on the aerial photograph of Edinburgh.
    b) Add a key and labels to show the land use and features listed under the photograph.
4. What buildings shown on the map (Figure C) indicate that Edinburgh is the national capital of Scotland?
5. Apart from shopping what other city functions would you expect to find in Princes Street/George Street area?
6. **Further work: fieldwork** Map land use along a main road in an urban area. Only use 6 to 9 land use categories. Present your map in colour with a clear key.
7. Measure out a number of sampling dots and use them to calculate the land use percentages.
8. Draw a graph to show your results.

4.2 Inside an urban area: racism and vandalism

The places shown in this spread are in major British cities. Each place is somebody's home area. Home is where people find comfort, friendship and security. The group of young people talking to the policeman in Cardiff (Figure A) look secure in their community. But like many people belonging to *ethnic minorities* they live with the problems of *racism*. Racism is the term used for the combination of racial prejudice and the exercise of power. In Britain, the white people have control of the major institutions, the banks, the factories, shops and schools. It is a powerful white society in which there is prejudice against ethnic minority people.

In inner city boroughs, the ethnic minority population may make up 50 per cent of the community, but this section of the community suffers *disadvantage*. Unemployment rates are higher amongst *Afro-Caribbean* and *Asian* groups. The 1981 census revealed an unemployment rate of 15.6 per cent for white men aged between 16 and 29, but 25 per cent for Afro-Caribbean and Asian men. They find it more difficult to obtain good housing and further education. In some city areas there are racial attacks and ethnic minority people may live in a state of fear.

In the Moss Side area of Manchester (Figure B), some of the *immigrants* who came to the city in the 1950s and 1960s live in high rise housing built in the 1970s. Today their children and grandchildren also live in the area. The older black people have lived in Moss side for over 30 years. The racial prejudice they experienced in the 1950s might have been more obvious, but the hidden racism has not changed. One resident commented "I went for a job as an office secretary. They were very nice to me but I knew I wouldn't get the job as the other girls were white".

Figure A A Sikh policeman with some Cardiff teenagers

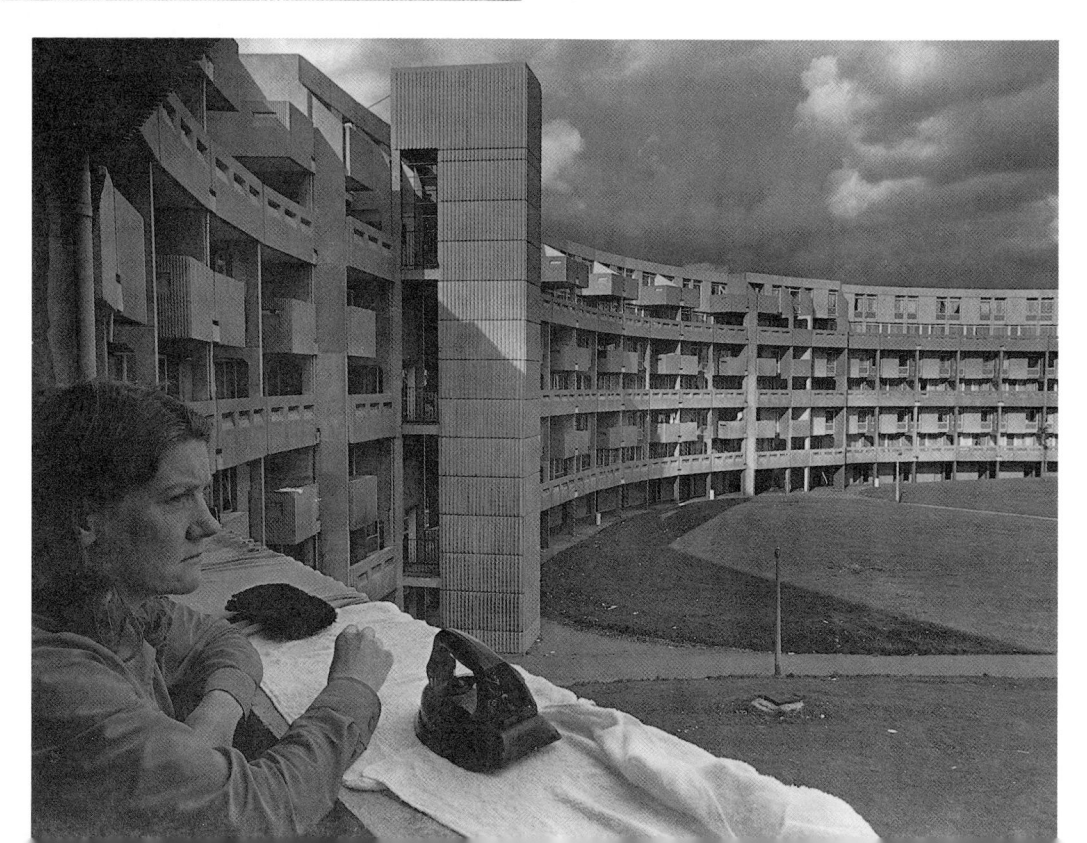

Figure B High-rise housing in Moss Side, Manchester

In Kirkby, near Liverpool, vandals have forced people to leave the housing area shown in Figure C. *Vandalism* refers to deliberate damage of buildings, telephone boxes, lamp posts, etc. You can see that some homes are still occupied. This is not an old environment, but the local community has simply broken down. In such areas of vandalism there are also crimes of violence and muggings. The people live in fear and insecurity. They may be the old, the sick, the ethnic minorities. Whoever they are, home is not as good as it could be.

Figure C The results of vandalism on a housing estate in Kirby, Liverpool

Figure D A high rise block of flats in Manchester

QUESTIONS

1. What do you understand by racism?
2. In what way do the ethnic minority people in urban areas **suffer from racism**?
3. In a recent survey people living in a city said they would prefer to live in a house with a garden.
   What problems do you think can occur for people living in the high rise blocks in Figures B and D?
4. Study the type of housing in Figure C.
   Describe the type of housing here.
5. Imagine you are an old person still living in the housing block shown in Figure C. Write about your fears of living in this housing area.
6. Think of your own housing environment.
   In two columns write five points about each of your likes and dislikes about where you live. Try to put the points in rank order.
7. **Further work** Think carefully about racism and vandalism in your home area. Write down some of the evidence for each of these problems. If you wish you can interview some of the residents about the two problems. Can you suggest any solutions for some of the problems you have identified?

4.3 Social areas in a town: 1

By using census information, detailed analysis of an urban area can be made. This study will concentrate on Swindon. All the information has been taken from the Small Area Statistics 1981 Census.

First find Swindon on an atlas map. Swindon grew rapidly in the nineteenth century as an industrial town. There has also been much recent growth.

Figure A shows the nineteen census divisions for the Swindon area. The whole area is known as Thamesdown. The small divisions are called *wards*.

Age structure

The census collects information on people's ages. We can use the statistics in the columns headed 'Percentage population' in the table on the right to test the following hypothesis:

'The older inner area of Swindon has more people who are over 60 years old than the newer outer areas'.

Now compare Central, a ward in the older central part of Swindon, with Toothill, one in the outer area. Answer questions 1–3.

Figure A Car owners in the Thamesdown area, Wiltshire

Key
Percentage households without cars
- more than 48
- 33–48
- 21–33
- less than 21
- ■ Swindon town centre

Statistics based on census information from the Thamesdown area

Ward	Percentage population		Percentage of household	
	Retired (female 60 +, male 65 +)	Under 16	With no car	With two cars
1. Blunsdon	17.3	21.3	18.5	27.1
2. Central	21.2	17.6	53.6	5.3
3. Chiseldon	16.8	22.2	23.1	20.7
4. Covingham	4.1	24.1	10.4	19.8
5. Dorcan	5.3	31.9	19.8	14.7
6. Eastcott	21.0	18.5	48.7	7.4
7. Gorse Hill	19.4	22.9	49.0	6.8
8. Highworth	11.2	26.1	20.0	20.9
9. Lawns	20.9	18.4	24.0	21.0
10. Moredon	12.3	26.0	31.0	13.6
11. Park	10.4	26.6	52.1	6.4
12. Ridgeway	19.7	20.1	18.3	29.8
13. St. Margaret	12.1	23.1	17.3	17.4
14. St. Philip	15.6	23.5	32.2	12.4
15. Toothill	4.9	28.5	19.8	13.8
16. Walcot	17.1	21.1	44.7	9.3
17. Western	19.8	20.7	41.9	9.0
18. Whitworth	12.8	23.5	52.1	6.9
19. Wroughton	14.8	23.4	25.1	16.3

Figure B (*right*) A scattergraph is helpful to find groupings for car-owner statistics

Car ownership

The census collects statistics on the number of cars per household. Which type of wards are likely to have a high percentage of households with no cars? It is likely to be the wards in the older areas where people have less income and where there are more pensioners. Are there other reasons why households in the older central parts might not have a car?

Figure A is a *choropleth* map showing households in Thamesdown not owning a car. The colour shading has been chosen to show up the contrast in ownership. You can easily pick out the wards in the centre of Swindon with a high percentage of households with no car.

To find the best groupings for the figures use a *scatter graph* like the one in Figure B. It was used to find the groupings for the map of households with no car.

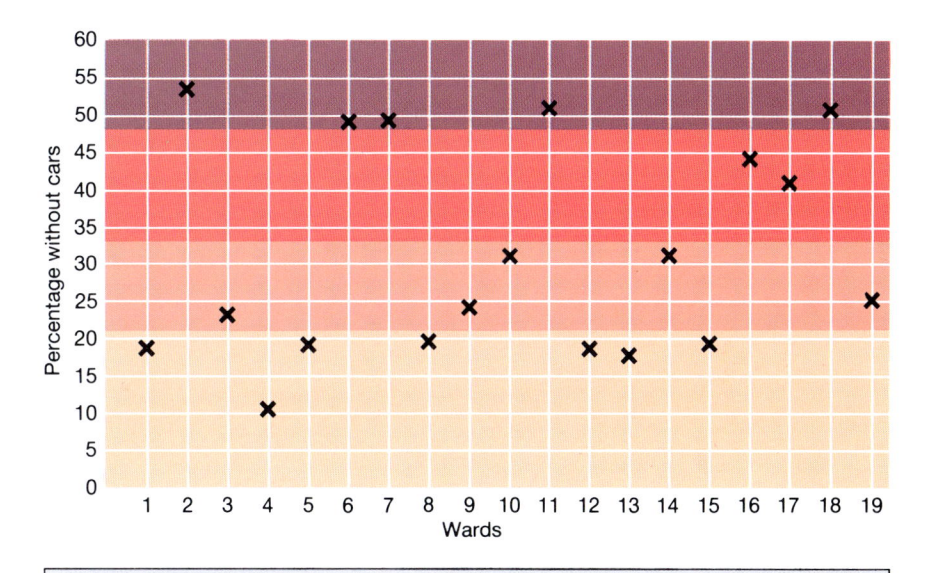

QUESTIONS

1. Is the hypothesis proved when Central and Toothill are compared?
2. Now compare the statistics for Eastcott and Dorcan. Do these prove the hypothesis?
3. Test the following hypothesis: '*The new housing districts such as Toothill have more children than the central areas of town.*' This time choose the same wards and use the statistics in the column 'Percentage under 16 years'.
4. Construct a map to show the percentage of households with two cars. Use an outline map similar to Figure A. Use colour shadings or black and white.

4.4 Social areas in a town: 2

Room density

The statistics collected in the census for room density can show where houses are crowded or where few people live in a house.

Census statistics for households in Thamesdown

Ward	Percentage of households with 0.5 or fewer persons per room	Rank order	Percentage under 16 years Rank order
1. Blunsdon	53	?	13
2. Central	63	4	19
3. Chiseldon	59.5	5	12
4. Covingham	42	?	6
5. Dorcan	38	?	1
6. Eastcott	65	3	17
7. Gorse Hill	55.3	?	11
8. Highworth	54.5	?	4
9. Lawns	66.9	2	18
10. Moredon	50	?	5
11. Park	37	?	3
12. Ridgeway	67.2	1	16
13. St. Margaret	50	?	10
14. St. Philip	52.6	?	7
15. Toothill	51	?	2
16. Walcot	52.8	?	14
17. Western	59.4	6	15
18. Whitworth	49	?	8
19. Wroughton	52.7	?	9

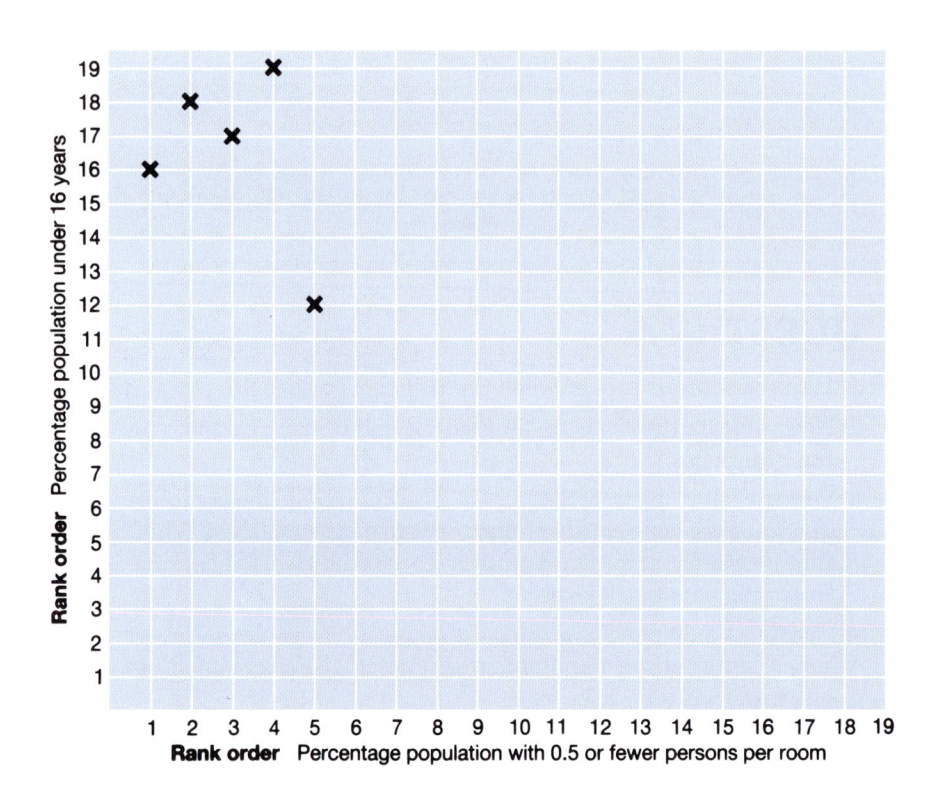

Types of employment and social class

The census also collects information on the types of work people do. The types of employment data is used to place people in social classes. Six social classes are used by the Registrar General:

A Upper professional/managerial/administrative
B Lower professional/managerial/executive
C1 Supervisory/clerical (white collar)
C2 Skilled workers
D Semi-skilled workers
E Unskilled manual workers

Figure A Rank order of room density figures plotted against rank order of percentage population under 16 years for Swindon wards 1–19 (see question 2)

Figure B Central Swindon from the air

Social classes in Swindon

Ward	Social Class (%)	
	A	E
Blunsdon	3.3	2.3
Central	0.8	8.8
Chiseldon	1.7	3.4
Covingham	2.4	3.0
Dorcan	2.2	4.5
Eastcott	2.0	3.9
Gorse Hill	0.6	6.9
Highworth	4.6	2.4
Lawns	3.8	0.8
Moredon	1.6	4.1
Park	0.5	7.2
Ridgeway	3.3	2.8
St. Margaret	1.5	3.4
St. Philip	1.1	2.9
Toothill	2.0	2.5
Walcot	2.0	6.1
Western	0.6	5.4
Whitworth	0.3	17.5
Wroughton	2.1	11.0

QUESTIONS

1 a) Study the statistics in the table on page 62. Then complete the rank order.
b) In which four wards are there the highest percentages of households with 0.5 persons or fewer per room? (These are those with the highest rank order.)
c) Can you suggest why these four wards might have a high percentage with low room densities?
d) Covingham and Dorcan are new housing areas with a high percentage of young children. Do they have a low percentage with low room densities?

2 Figure A is to be used to compare percentage of households with 0.5 or fewer persons per room and percentage of population under 16 years. Make a copy of the graph.
a) Plot the ranks from 6 to 19 on the horizontal axis.
b) Write about the pattern shown on your completed graph. Are the two sets of figures linked?

3 Answer the following from your knowledge of the Thamesdown area. Then check your answers using the statistics in the table on the left.
a) Name four wards where you would expect to find the highest percentage of people in Social Class A.
b) Name four wards where you think the percentage of people in Social Class E is high.

4.5 Urban growth: models

If you visit any large city in the developed world you will find similar patterns of growth. Figure A is not a real city; it is a *model*. This model simplifies the real city but it includes the main features of its growth. It shows the city has grown in rings. The oldest buildings are at the centre or core. The newest areas are on the outskirts or in the outer suburbs. Even small towns and villages outside the city have grown in a circular way.

Figure D is a more complex model of a developed world city. Similar *land use* or *activity areas* can be found in many cities. The original city grew outwards from the old core. Circular growth was not dominant because the city grew in *sectors* along the railway and the river, and more recently along the motorways on the edge of the city.

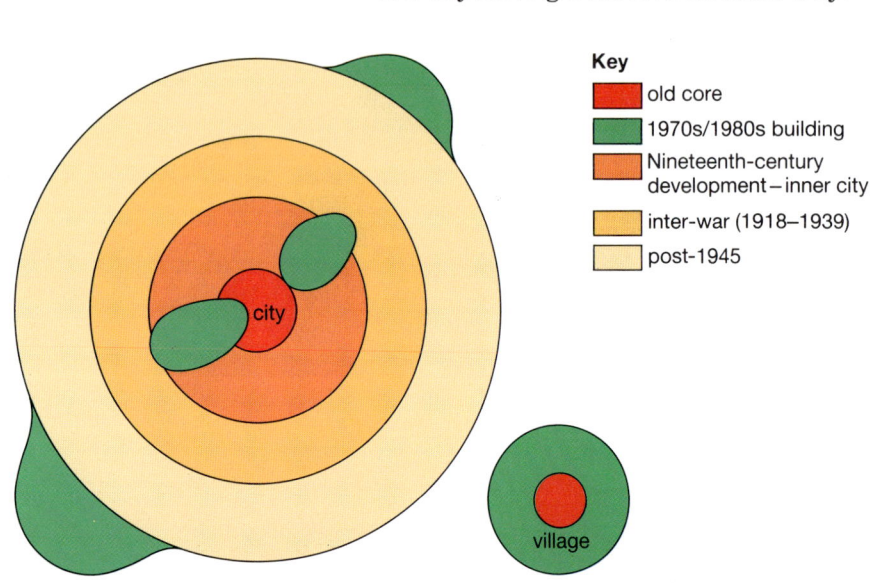

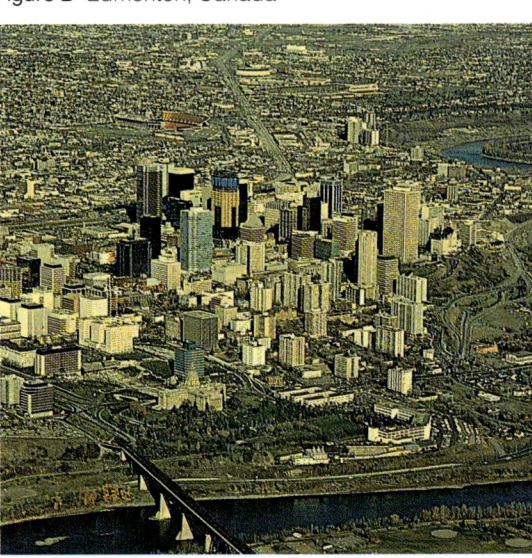

Figure B Edmonton, Canada

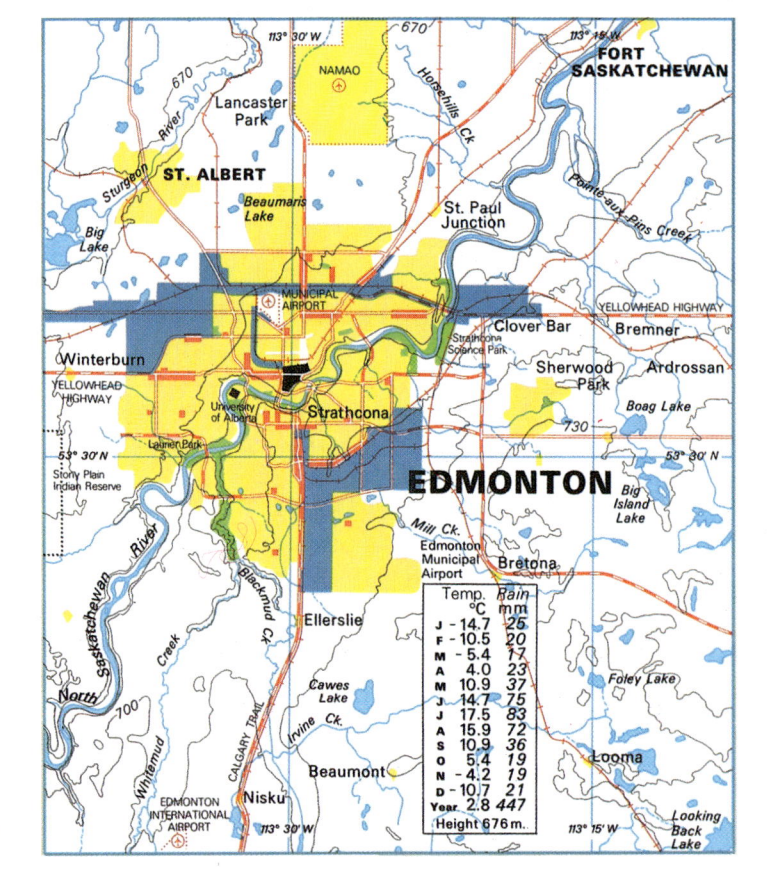

Key
- old core
- 1970s/1980s building
- Nineteenth-century development – inner city
- inter-war (1918–1939)
- post-1945

Figure A (*above*) Circular development in a city, by age

Figure C (*right*) Activity areas in and around Edmonton

Key
- Central business
- Lesser commercial centre
- Industrial districts
- Built up area, mainly residential
- Major parks and open areas
- Major military installations

Highways
- Limited access and rapid transit
- Other main highways
- Railways
- Airport

Scale : 1 : 4 000 000

0 — 10 km

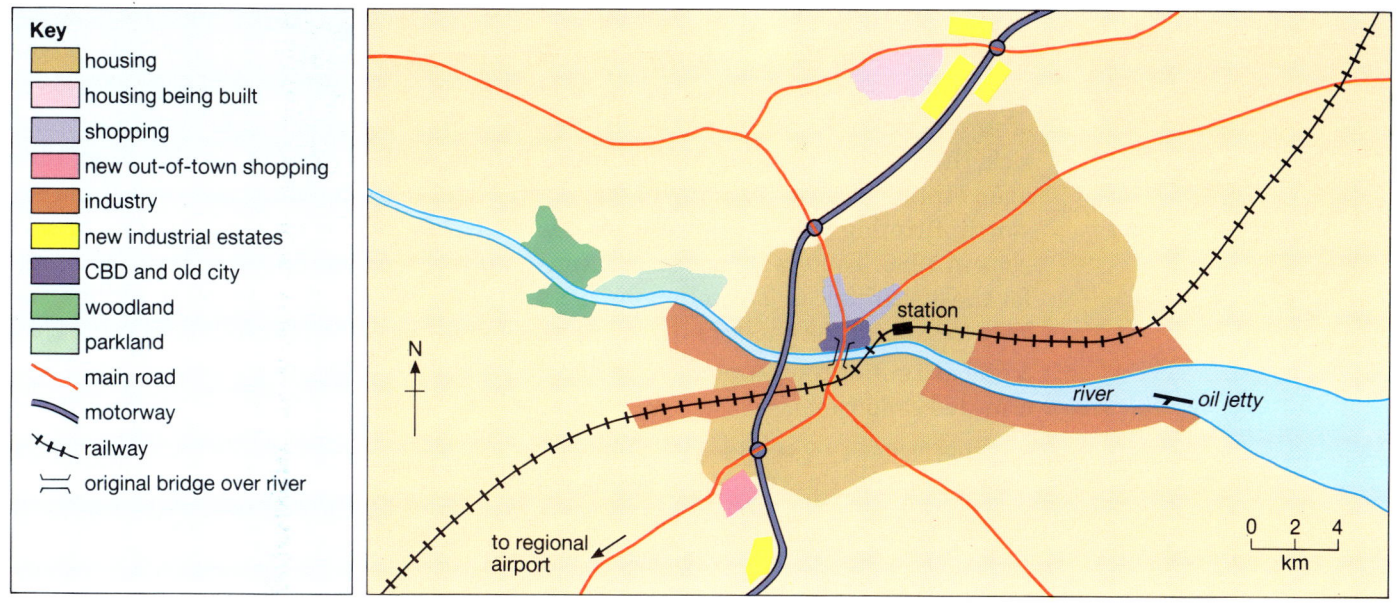

Figure D Activity areas in a developed-world city

Figure E Sector development in a city

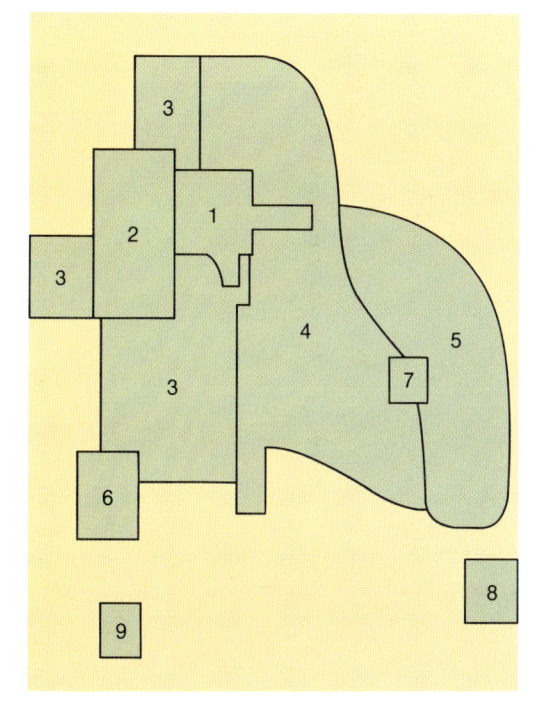

Key

District
1 central business district
2 wholesale light manufacturing
3 low class residential
4 medium-class residential
5 high-class residential
6 heavy manufacturing
7 outlying business district
8 residential suburbs
9 industrial suburbs

QUESTIONS

1 Study the model of the city, Figure A.
   a) What is the age of the inner city?
   b) Where are the two types of location for the 1970s/1980s building?
   c) Why do you think there is little 1970s/1980s building in the inter-War zone?
   d) When did the old village outside the city begin to expand?

2 Study Figure C. Edmonton is a city in the Canadian prairies.
   a) Describe the shape of the industrial areas.
   b) What has been the main influence on the location of the industrial area to the north of the city?
   c) What has influenced the location and shape of the smaller commercial centres?
   d) Where is most of the parkland and open space?

3 Study Figure D.
   a) What was the reason for the siting of the old city?
   b) What were the two reasons for the location of the older industrial areas in the city?
   c) What is the reason for the location of the new industrial estates?

4 Study the urban model, Figure D. Describe the layout of the model urban area.

5 a) In what ways is Edmonton similar to the city model Figure E?
   b) In what ways does Edmonton not fit in with the model?

6 Identify some of the growth zones in your own town or city. Has the settlement grown in a circular way?

7 For your own town or city identify an example of each of the nine shaded zones in Figure E. For each example state what has influenced the zone's location.

4.6 Inner city problems

In most old cities in Britain, Europe and North America there is an *inner city* area. Here there is a greater proportion of *people in need* – the unemployed, the sick, the old, the low paid, the disadvantaged ethnic minority groups. In Handsworth, Birmingham, there were serious riots in 1986. There were several reasons for the disturbances. The following facts help to explain the background to them:

- 16 per cent of the people live in overcrowded conditions
- 36 per cent are unemployed
- 50 per cent of the 19–24 age group are out of work
- 70 per cent of the population are seriously deprived
- there was tension between the police and the ethnic minority groups
- there was a high rate of drug abuse and petty crime

In England's inner cities there are almost 156 square miles of *derelict land*. This is as much as the total area of central London! Unfortunately people have to live close to derelict land, there is a lack of good quality woodland and parkland. *Housing* in inner city areas is often old and in poor state of repair. *Housing densities* are often higher than in other parts of the city. In some cities the problem of *homelessness* is acute. In London there are 20 000 people sleeping on the streets or in inadequate shelter. Many homeless people are young.

It is no surprise that people have been leaving the inner cities. Those who have been able to afford to do so have moved out. Those who remain suffer *poverty*. The 1986 Church of England Report, 'Faith in the City', said "poverty is about how people are treated and how people regard themselves ... Yet the lack of an adequate income is at its heart".

Figure A Urban areas of Hulme—Moss Side, Manchester

Redevelopment in Manchester

As the residential and industrial areas of Manchester fell into disrepair, redevelopment schemes were started. The maps and photographs tell a story of change.

Figure B New housing, Bedwell Close

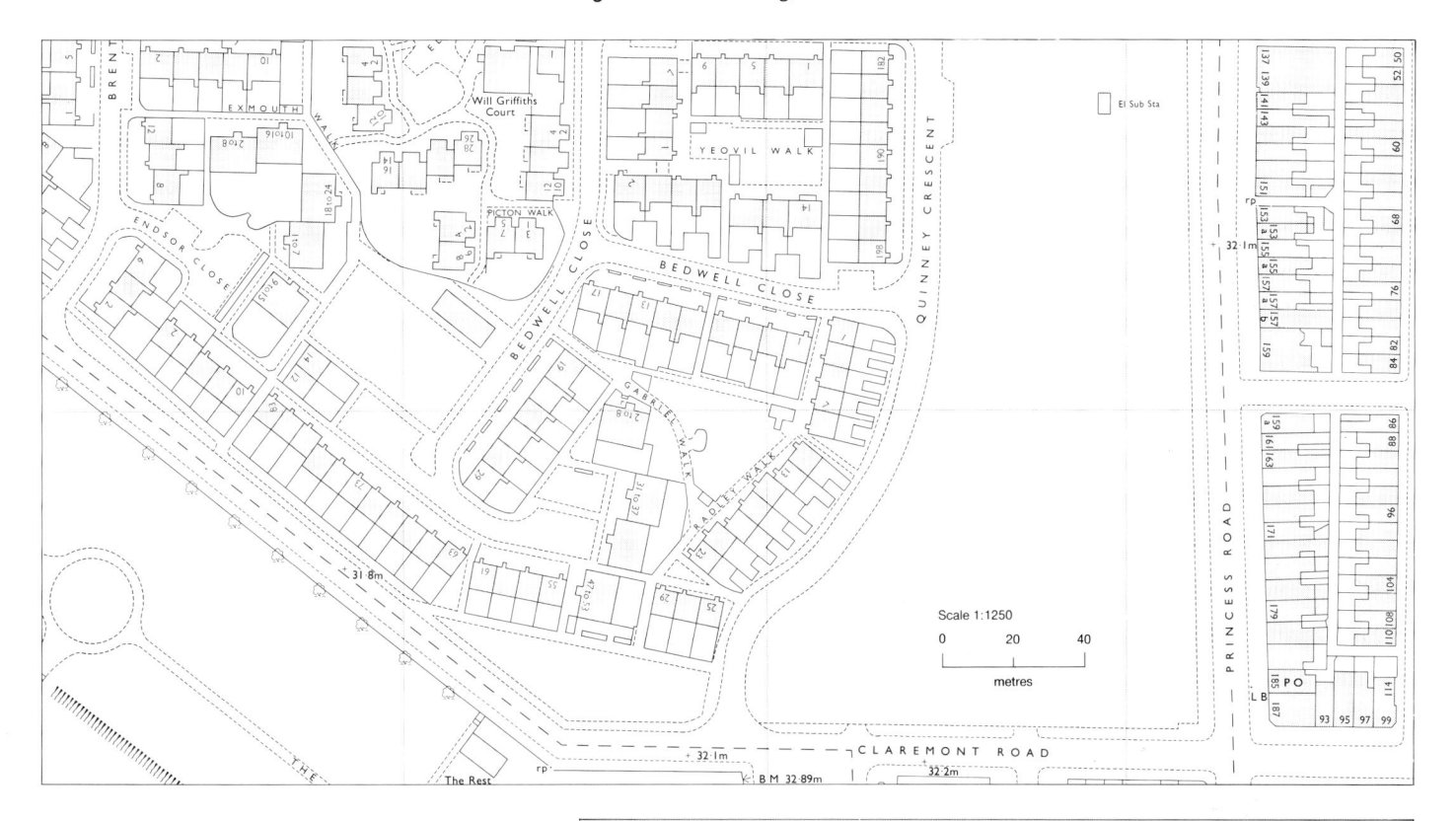

Figure C The Moss Side area

Figure D (*below*) Housing awaiting demolition before redevelopment

QUESTIONS

1 Find Bedwell Close on Figure C. Locate this area on the photograph opposite (Figure A).
   a) Describe the types of streets and housing before redevelopment.
   b) Describe the present street pattern and new housing.
   c) What evidence is there that the area in the east of the map is about to be redeveloped?
   d) Why has redevelopment been necessary in this part of Manchester?

2 Study Figure A. The photograph was taken in the middle of redevelopment in 1973.
   For each of the areas numbered 1 to 9, describe in detail the urban environment. For each area, note the changes that have occurred or are soon to occur.

3 Imagine you are living in a high rise housing block in Manchester. Write to a friend who has just moved into a small new house with a garden. In your letter explain the problems of living in your block and say why you would like to move to a new house.

4.7 Inner city renewal

Apart from housing redevelopment there have been many schemes that try to solve inner city problems. In London, Glasgow, and Paris and in some American cities, areas have been cleared and rebuilt. The London Docklands Development Corporation (LDDC) has started to revitalize London's Docks. In Glasgow, the Glasgow Eastern Area Renewal scheme (GEAR) is revitalizing an old industrial and residential part of the city. In Paris there are many redevelopment areas. La Défense is a new urban centre in Paris providing homes for 20 000 people and work for 100 000.

Liverpool and Stoke have both held *garden festivals*. In 1986 the Stoke National Garden Festival was one of Europe's top five attractions. Two million people visited the festival which was sited on reclaimed land in the city. During the year 1000 permanent jobs were provided at the site. In 1988 the National Garden Festival used derelict land along the River Clyde in Glasgow.

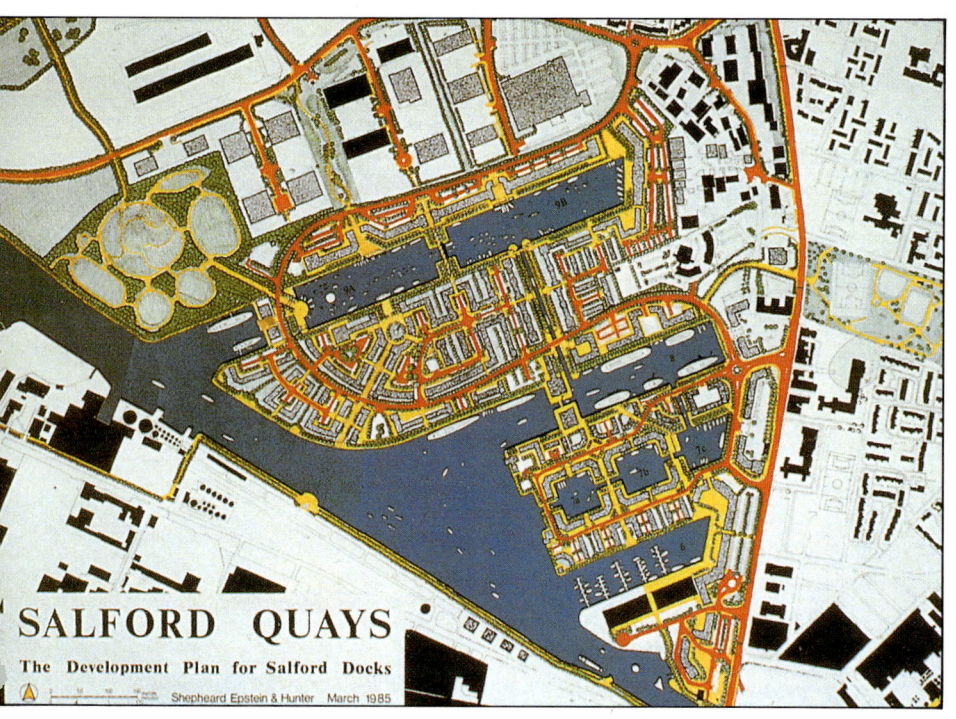

Salford Quays – Greater Manchester

Salford Docks were built at the end of the Manchester Ship canal and were opened in 1894. They gradually fell into decline and by the early 1980s shipping had finished. In the 1985 Development Plan for the Docks, the Salford City Council said:

> 'the trade and the jobs have gone; the land and the water remain and, if let to rot, would have a devastating effect on surrounding areas for years to come. That cannot be allowed to happen'.

A new four-star hotel is now on the quayside at Salford's Number 6 dock. Docks 6, 7, 8 and 9 are the centre of a new waterside development. There are 600 homes, many new factories and warehouses. A new leisure complex includes an eight screen cinema, and a boat and yachting marina.

Such a large scale *regeneration* project cannot be funded by the local city council. The Salford Quays scheme has attracted funds from the EC. It also receives financial aid direct from the Government.

The Figures A and B show the original *development plan* and the site. The plans have changed in detail since 1985 but today the area is lively and busy. It has not been allowed to rot!

Figure A Original development plan for Salford Quays

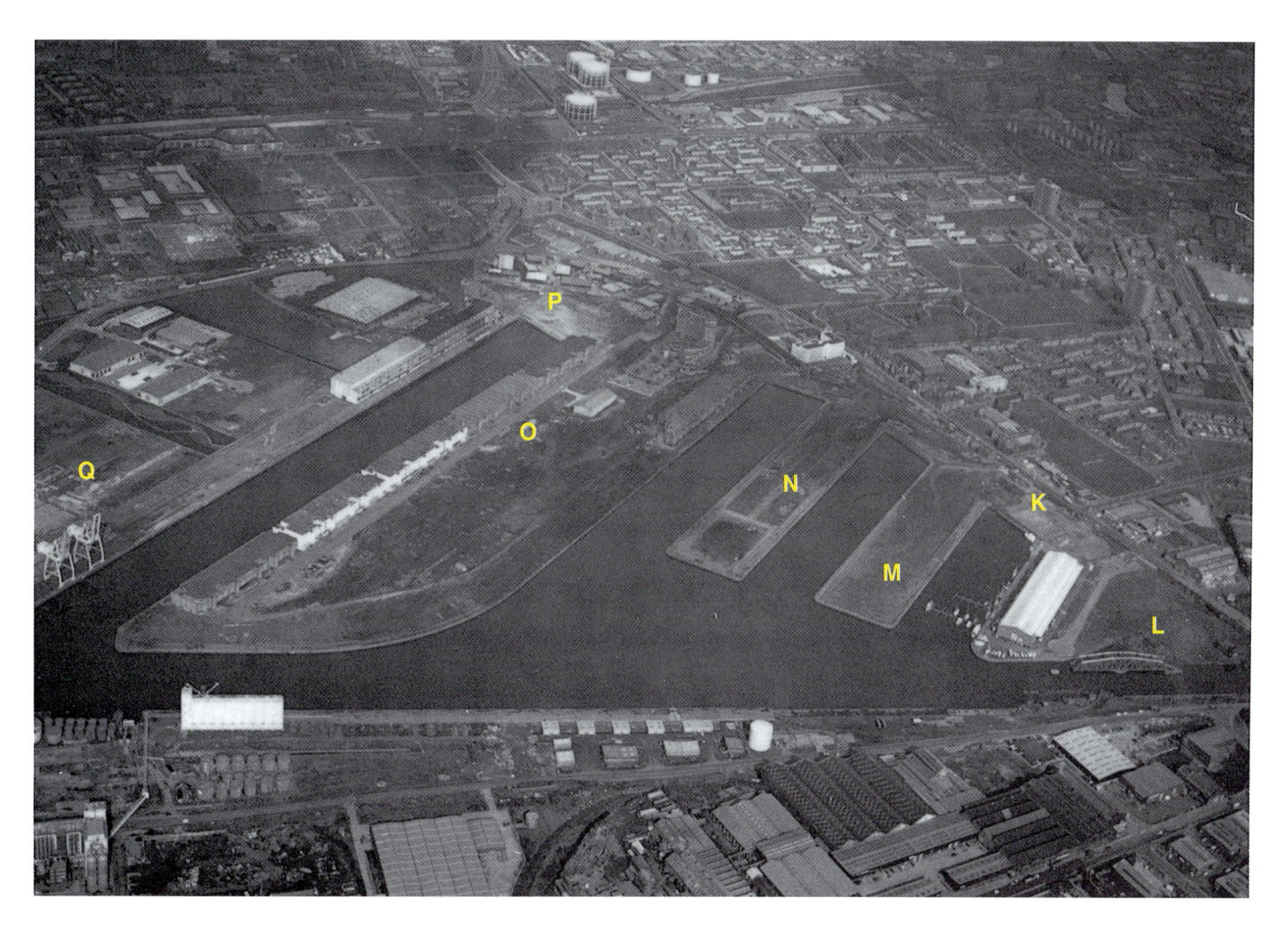

Figure B Area under development:
K new hotel
L cinema complex
M housing estate
N business park
O housing estate
P leisure/commercial centre
Q recreational area
R Manchester Ship Canal
S Trafford Park Industrial Estate

QUESTIONS

1. Using Figures A and B, draw your own map to show the developments labelled K to S on Figure B.
   Note: i) the red routes on Figure A are roads, ii) the shapes of the hotel (K) and the cinema (L) are different from the original plan.
2. Why has it been necessary to 'revitalize' dockland areas in cities like London and Salford?
3. Make a list of the types of redevelopment taking place in Salford. Use the text and Figures A and B.
4. What will the Salford Quays scheme provide for the people of the area? Which do you think is the most important part of the whole development? And why?

69

4.8 New towns

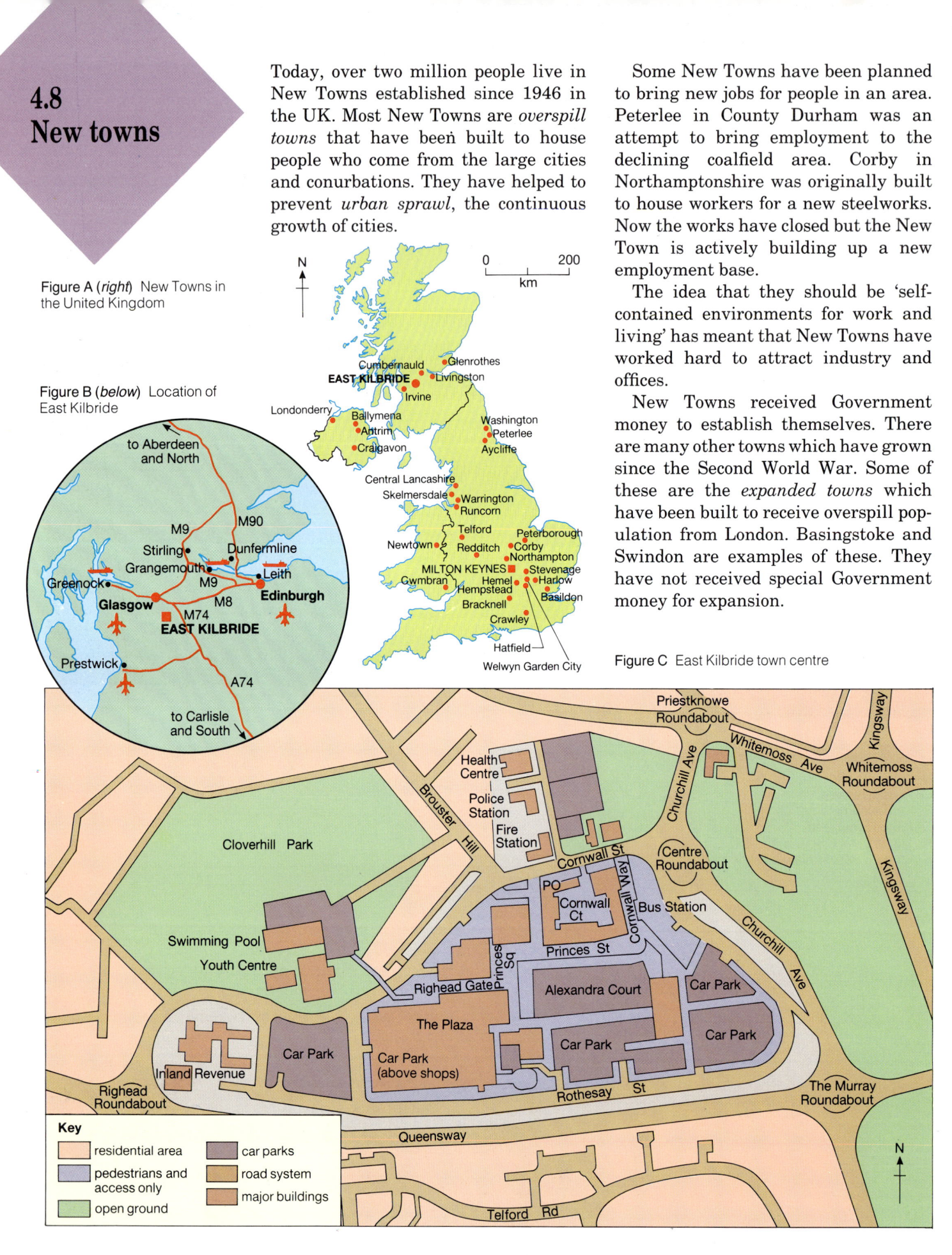

Today, over two million people live in New Towns established since 1946 in the UK. Most New Towns are *overspill towns* that have been built to house people who come from the large cities and conurbations. They have helped to prevent *urban sprawl*, the continuous growth of cities.

Some New Towns have been planned to bring new jobs for people in an area. Peterlee in County Durham was an attempt to bring employment to the declining coalfield area. Corby in Northamptonshire was originally built to house workers for a new steelworks. Now the works have closed but the New Town is actively building up a new employment base.

The idea that they should be 'self-contained environments for work and living' has meant that New Towns have worked hard to attract industry and offices.

New Towns received Government money to establish themselves. There are many other towns which have grown since the Second World War. Some of these are the *expanded towns* which have been built to receive overspill population from London. Basingstoke and Swindon are examples of these. They have not received special Government money for expansion.

Figure A (*right*) New Towns in the United Kingdom

Figure B (*below*) Location of East Kilbride

Figure C East Kilbride town centre

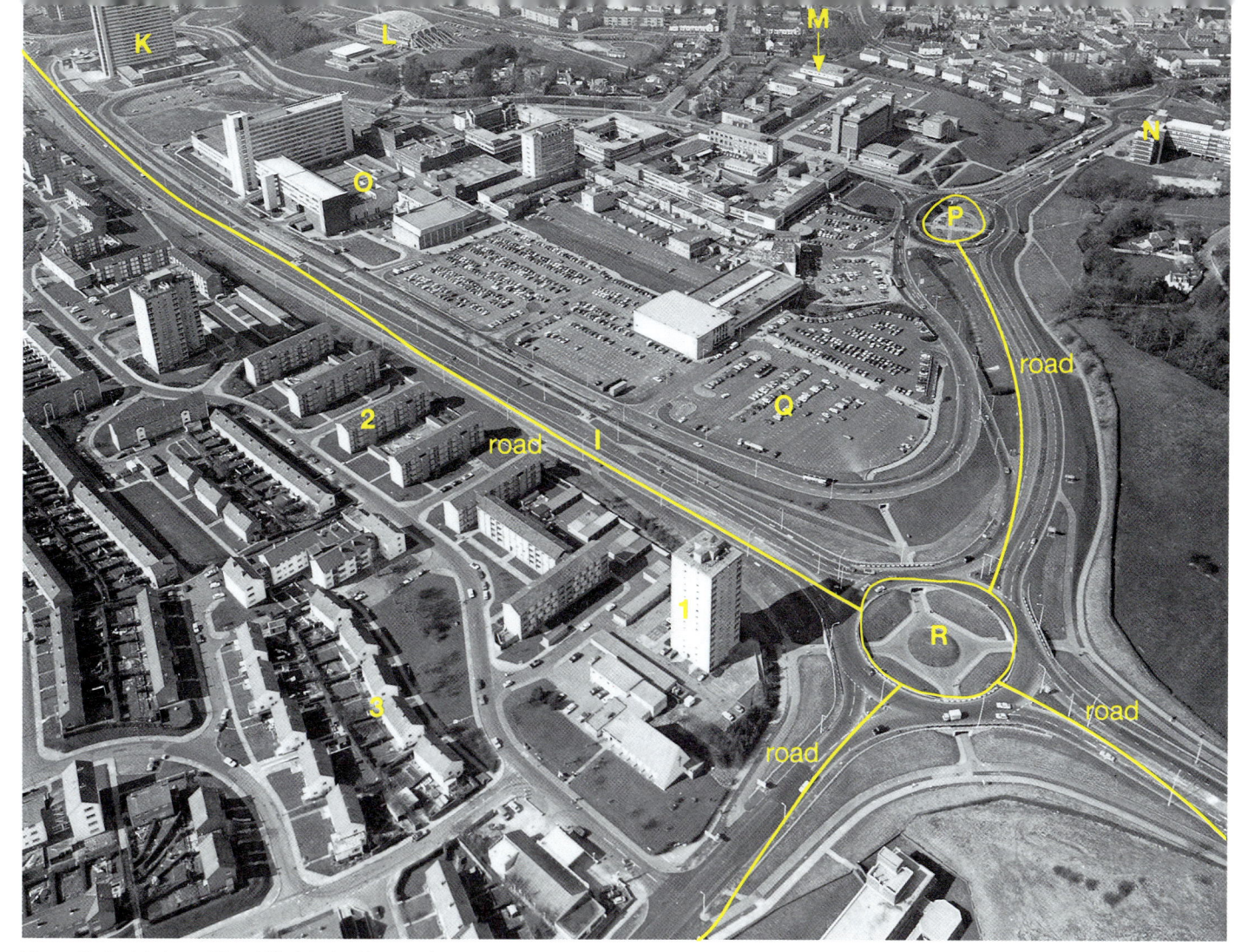

Figure D Aerial view of East Kilbride, looking north

East Kilbride – Scotland

East Kilbride is one of five New Towns in Scotland and was established as an overspill town for Glasgow. It is situated 14 kilometres south of Glasgow. Since 1946 the population has grown from 2400 to over 70 000. This New Town has been successful in attracting manufacturing companies. The percentage employed in manufacturing is 40 per cent which is much higher than the national average. There is an engineering and electronic bias to the manufacturing. Firms include Rolls Royce (aero engineering), Rockwell International (valves for the oil industry), Medical Production (heart pacemakers).

QUESTIONS

1 What is a New Town?
2 Explain why New Towns were built.
3 Which is the nearest New Town to where you live?
4 How does a New Town differ from an Expanded Town?
5 What do you understand by 'self-contained environments for work and living'?
6 Study Figure B.
   a) Where is East Kilbride?
   b) How far from Glasgow is East Kilbride?
   c) Which road connects East Kilbride with England?
   d) Why do you think East Kilbride was built here?
7 What type of employment has East Kilbride attracted?
8 Study Figure C which shows the East Kilbride town centre. Using the map, identify and name the places labelled K to S on the photograph.
9 Describe the three different types of housing numbered 1 to 3 in the foreground of the photograph.
10 What evidence is there that road transport is important and efficient in East Kilbride?

4.9 Planning the urban area

Using the information on this page, make your own plan for part of an urban area. Use a blank piece of A4 paper. Place the town centre in the bottom left corner of the paper, you are not planning the whole town. To give you ideas for your plan look at Figure A, and also at the town centre map and photograph of East Kilbride on the previous page. Remember to use shading (colour or black and white) and a good key, but do not spend too much time drawing detail.

Figure A Llantarnam Park industrial estate, Cwmbran New Town

ADVANCE FACTORY UNITS FROM ONLY

Develop your business in one of Cwmbran's latest Advance Factory Units

- 750–20,000 sq. ft. Units
- High Quality Units
- Superb Labour Force
- 5 mins from M4
- Loans and Grants can be arranged
- Rent Free Periods

A SQ. FT.

Cwmbran
Britain's best located Assisted Area.
Cwmbran Development Corporation Gwent House, Cwmbran, NP44 1XZ
Tel: Cwmbran (06333) 67777

Figure B Part of a brochure promoting East Kilbride

EAST KILBRIDE
YOUR MARKET BASE FOR EUROPE

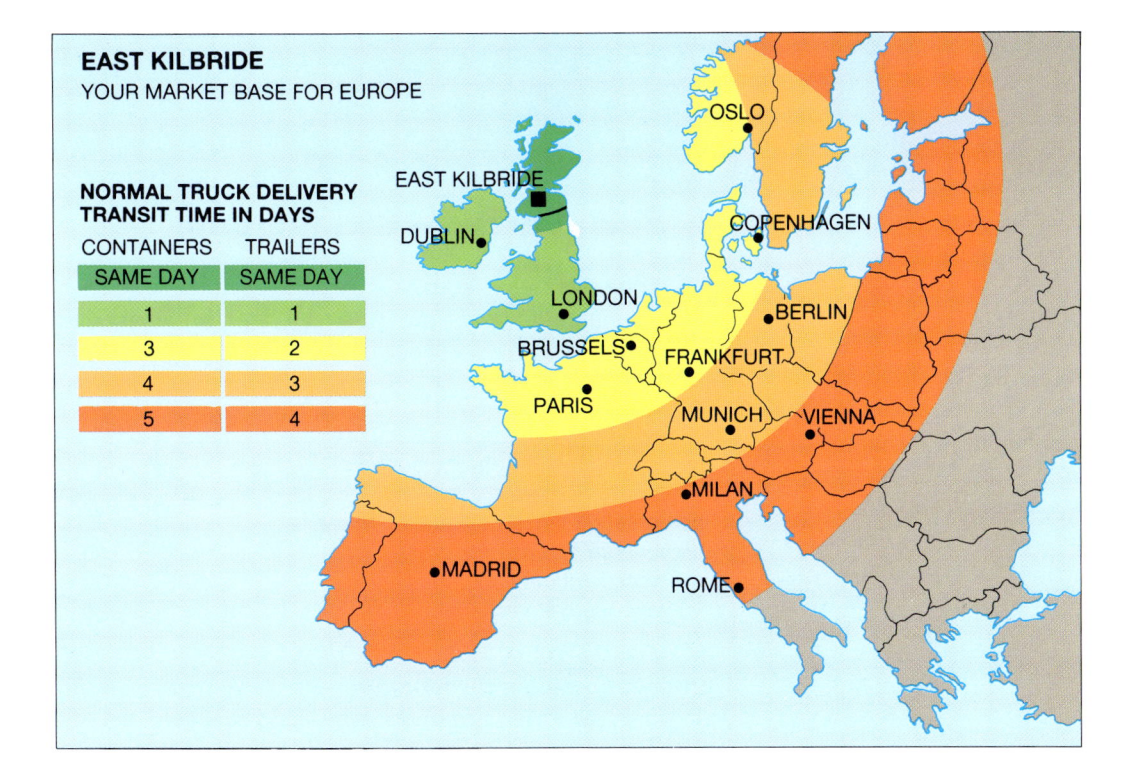

NORMAL TRUCK DELIVERY TRANSIT TIME IN DAYS

CONTAINERS	TRAILERS
SAME DAY	SAME DAY
1	1
3	2
4	3
5	4

Figure C Advertising poster

Omega: East Kilbride
The Omega development is a prestige high quality facility set in its own landscaped grounds totalling around 5 acres.

QUESTIONS

1 Draw your own plan. This is what your new urban area needs:
   a) A *town centre* with *shops, offices, car parks*
   b) A *public service area* with *police, fire, ambulance*
   c) A *leisure area* with *sports centre* and *swimming pool*
   d) Two separate *housing areas* called *neighbourhood units*.
      Each neighbourhood has a *neighbourhood shopping centre and two primary schools*. One of the neighbourhoods has a *comprehensive school*
   e) An *industrial estate*
   f) *Dual-carriageway roads* with *roundabouts* linking the different areas of the town
   g) *A large hospital in its own grounds*
   h) Around the edge of the town is a *green belt*. This is an area of land preserved for farming and recreation; new building is not allowed

2 You can locate your town anywhere in the United Kingdom. Give it a name.
   a) Draw a *regional map* to show where your town is. You need to show the nearest city or cities, the motorway and the 'A' class road links. See Figure B on the previous spread to help you.
   b) In one of the corners of your map you need a small *inset map* to show where the town is within the United Kingdom.

3 Design a poster to advertise the New Town you have helped to plan. You are trying to encourage companies to move to the town. You particularly want to advertise the town's pleasant environment. You can use some of the ideas from Figure C.

4 Write about the advantages of the town, mentioning its transport links with other parts of the United Kingdom and Europe.

Unit 4 ASSESSMENT

1. City planning

Study the development plan (Figure A) for an area of Solihull, 11 kilometres south of Birmingham.
a) What is an industrial park? (2 marks)
b) List *five* types of land use surrounding the industrial park. (5 marks)
c) Describe how the industrial park has been separated from the nearby residential areas. (3 marks)
d) Describe the pattern of road transport serving the new industrial park. (4 marks)
e) Why are industrialists attracted to this type of city environment? (6 marks)
Total 20 marks

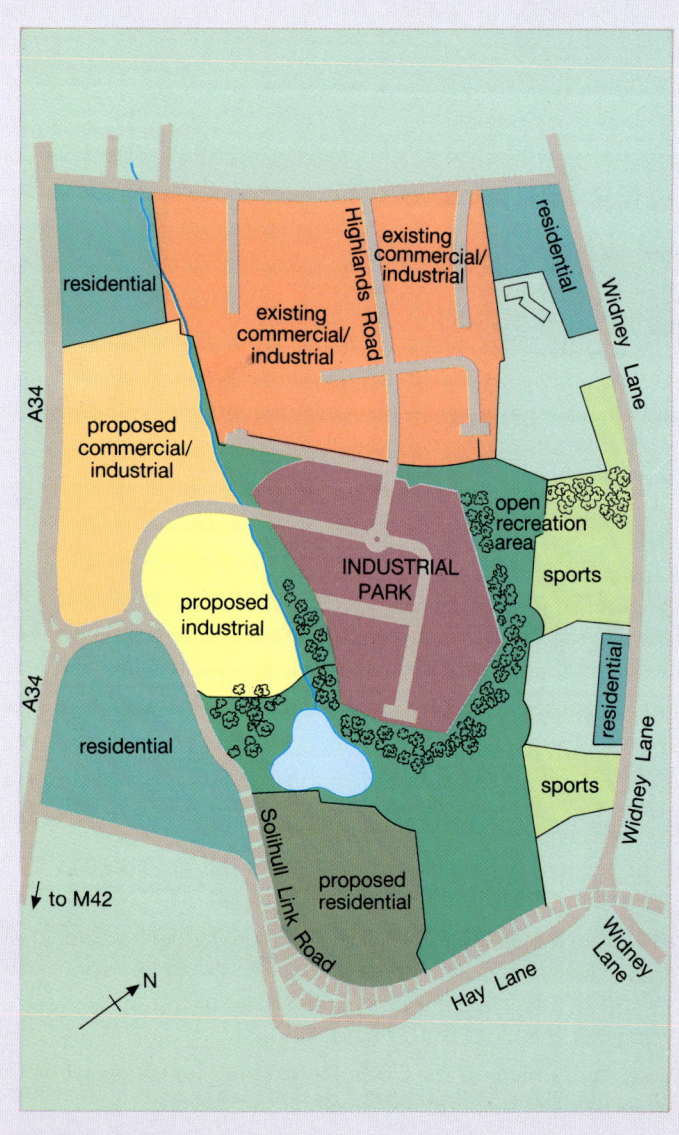

Figure A Development plan for an industrial park

2. Social areas – Birmingham

Study the two sets of statistics. Area K includes the area of the development plan Figure A. Area L is an inner city area in Birmingham.

Criteria	K	L
percentage of households lacking or sharing a bath	0	5
percentage of households with no car	22	72
percentage of born outside the UK	3	35
percentage of men unemployed	6	30
10 year population change	+ 3	−30

Attempt to explain the following:
a) The great difference in car ownership between Area K and Area L (2 marks)
b) Why do 5 per cent of households in Area L lack or share the use of a bath? (2 marks)
c) Why does a higher percentage of ethnic minority people live in Area L than Area K? (2 marks)
d) Why is such a large percentage of men unemployed in Area L? (2 marks)
e) Why has Area K gained population while area L has lost population over a 10 year period? (4 marks)
f) Suggest what the differences would be between Area L and M for:
   i) housing density (2 marks)
   ii) the amount of good quality parkland? (2 marks)
g) Plot the following statistics for wards in a large British city on a copy of the graph shown on the right Figure C. Two wards have been plotted for you. (4 marks)

Ward	Percentage of households with no car	Rank order
A	75	1
B	20	
C	35	
D	55	
E	70	2
F	39	
G	56	
H	42	
I	28	

h) Which two wards are old inner city wards? (2 marks)
i) Which two wards are on the edge of the city? (2 marks)
j) Explain the pattern of car ownership in a typical British town or city (6 marks)
Total 30 marks

3. Residential development

Figure B is a photograph of new housing in Byker, an inner city area of Newcastle-upon-Tyne.

a) Referring to examples describe the problems of inner city areas. (10 marks)

b) Draw your ideal development plan for an old nineteenth century inner city housing area. The redevelopment should contain new areas of industry as well as housing. A range of amenities is also required including a new primary school, shops, and public playing fields. (15 marks)

Total 25 marks

Figure B New housing in Byker, Newcastle-upon-Tyne

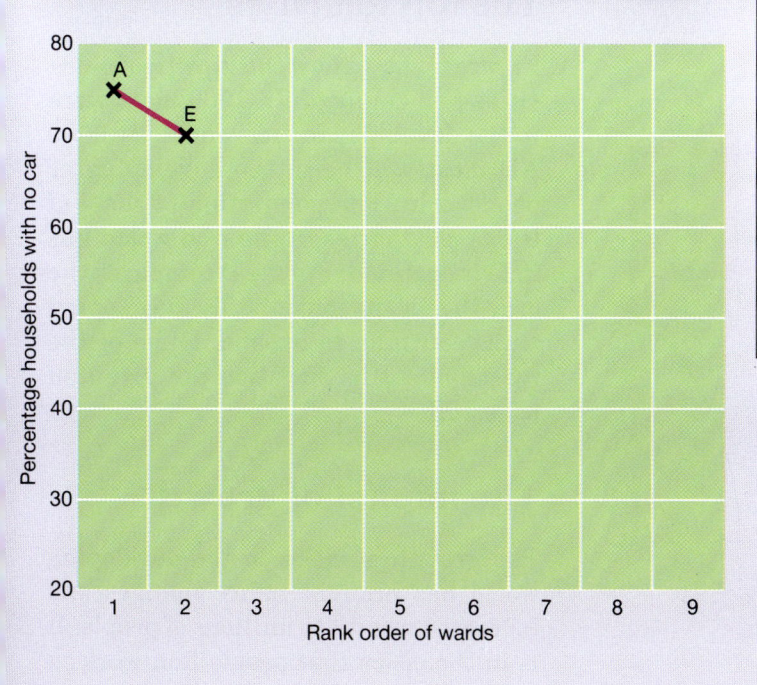

Figure C Rank order of households without cars

Details for pupil profile sheets Unit 4

Knowledge and understanding

1. Land use
2. Racism – ethnic minority people
3. Social areas in a town
4. Census statistics
5. Urban models
6. Inner city problems – derelict land, housing
7. Dockland regeneration
8. New Towns, neighbourhood units, green belts

Skills

1. Calculating percentages from samples
2. Land use mapping
3. Linking photographs and maps
4. Testing a hypothesis using social statistics
5. Constructing a choropleth map
6. Using a scatter graph
7. Reading a development plan
8. Planning your own urban area

Values

1. Understanding racism
2. Looking for racism and vandalism
3. Empathizing with inner city problems
4. Awareness of the role of redevelopment in cities
5. Appreciating that redevelopment may lead to new problems
6. Designing a poster to advertise a pleasant environment

5.1 Urban growth in the developing world

Unit 5: The developing world

Throughout the whole world the percentage of people living in cities is increasing. Figure A shows the increase in the world's population living in urban areas. The change from rural to urban living is called *urbanization*.

Figure B shows urbanization by continent. Two of the three developing world continents have an urbanized population similar to the developed world. But Africa's lower percentage is increasing quickly. By the year 2000, South America may be as urbanized as Europe.

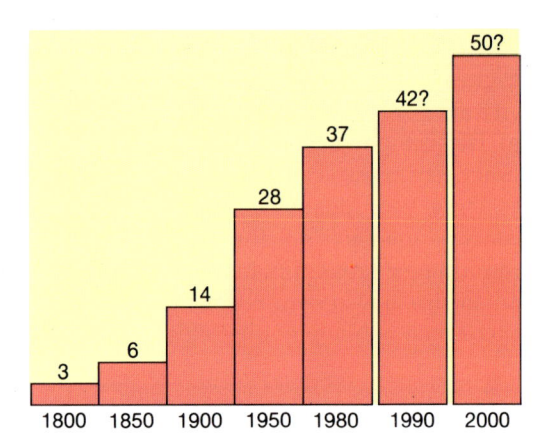

Figure A Growth of world population living in urban centres (percentage figures)

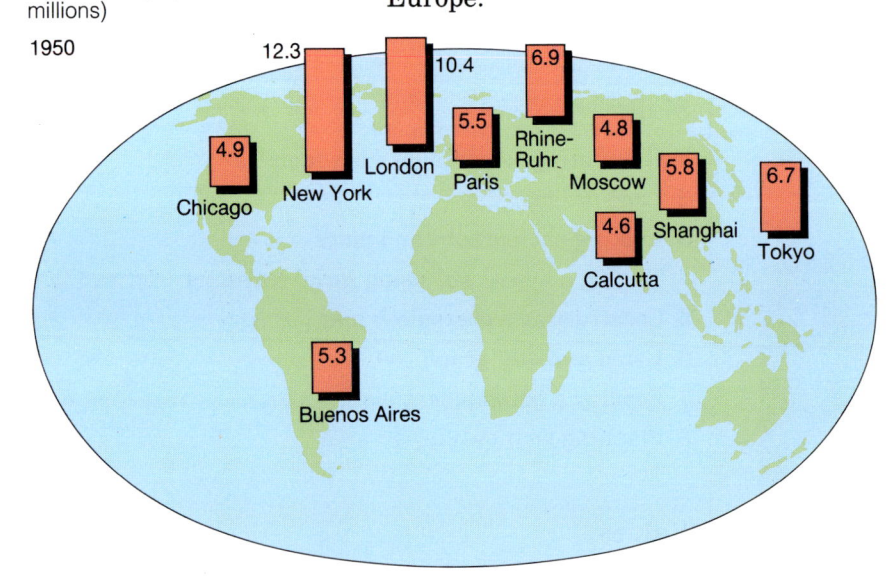

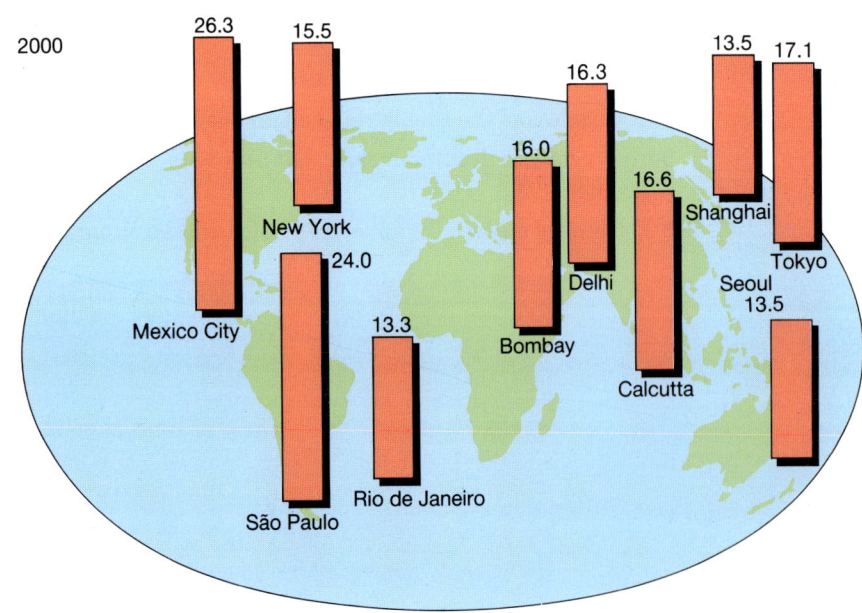

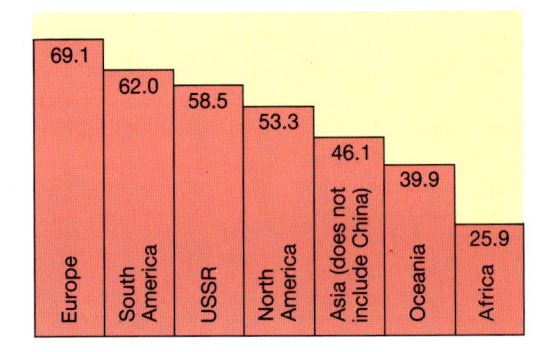

Values: 1800: 3; 1850: 6; 1900: 14; 1950: 28; 1980: 37; 1990: 42?; 2000: 50?

Figure B Percentage of world population living in urban centres

- Europe: 69.1
- South America: 62.0
- USSR: 58.5
- North America: 53.3
- Asia (does not include China): 46.1
- Oceania: 39.9
- Africa: 25.9

Figure C The changing top ten world cities (population in millions)

1950:
- Chicago 4.9
- New York 12.3
- London 10.4
- Paris 5.5
- Rhine-Ruhr 6.9
- Moscow 4.8
- Calcutta 4.6
- Shanghai 5.8
- Tokyo 6.7
- Buenos Aires 5.3

2000:
- Mexico City 26.3
- New York 15.5
- São Paulo 24.0
- Rio de Janeiro 13.3
- Bombay 16.0
- Delhi 16.3
- Calcutta 16.6
- Shanghai 13.5
- Seoul 13.5
- Tokyo 17.1

The top ten cities

Figure C shows how the growth of giant cities has changed. In 1950 most were in the developed or rich world. By 2000 AD most will be in the developing or poor world. The population of some of the largest cities in the rich world has in fact declined. Figure D compares the growth of some major cities. Developing cities continue to expand. Some of the reasons for this situation are given on page 108.

The impact of growth

The growth of cities in the developing world has brought many changes and increased wealth to millions of people. It is in the cities that people find work in shops, services, offices, factories and within the transport system. People have been able to participate in modern twentieth century life in the urban areas. By moving to cities in the developing world millions of people have experienced the way of life most people in the rich world take for granted. Urban people have a better chance of seeing a doctor, and of going to college. They have a better chance of having piped water, electricity and access to a telephone.

Problems

Some poor world cities are having problems because too many people have moved to them too quickly. It is not always possible to provide roads, drains, water and electricity if there are too many people.

In Guayaquil, Ecuador's largest port and industrial city, 60 per cent of the city's people live in *squatter settlements* on mud. At high tide, the settlements are flooded. Eventually the city authorities will raise the level of the settlements and the flood problem will not exist. But by then thousands more people will have moved to Guayaquil. They will live in new 'stilt' houses above the mud and water.

It is common for people living in the rich world to hear about the problems of the poor world cities. Not all cities have so many environmental problems as Guayaquil. The people living in the stilt houses do not see the problem as we do. They go about their daily lives like others. If you were to go there, you would see people sitting talking, cooking and going to and from work. Maybe the makeshift homes look poor but they do provide some shelter and privacy. The people are struggling against poverty and ill-health but they live and work in the *hope* of a better life in the future.

The homeless

If people have no fixed home and live on the streets they are *homeless*. People living in squatter settlements outside developing world cities may be moved by the authorities. For some time they will be forced to sleep where they can. In the big cities of the rich world people also lose their homes – some may be unable to pay rent and are *evicted*. Some are young people who have left their homes.

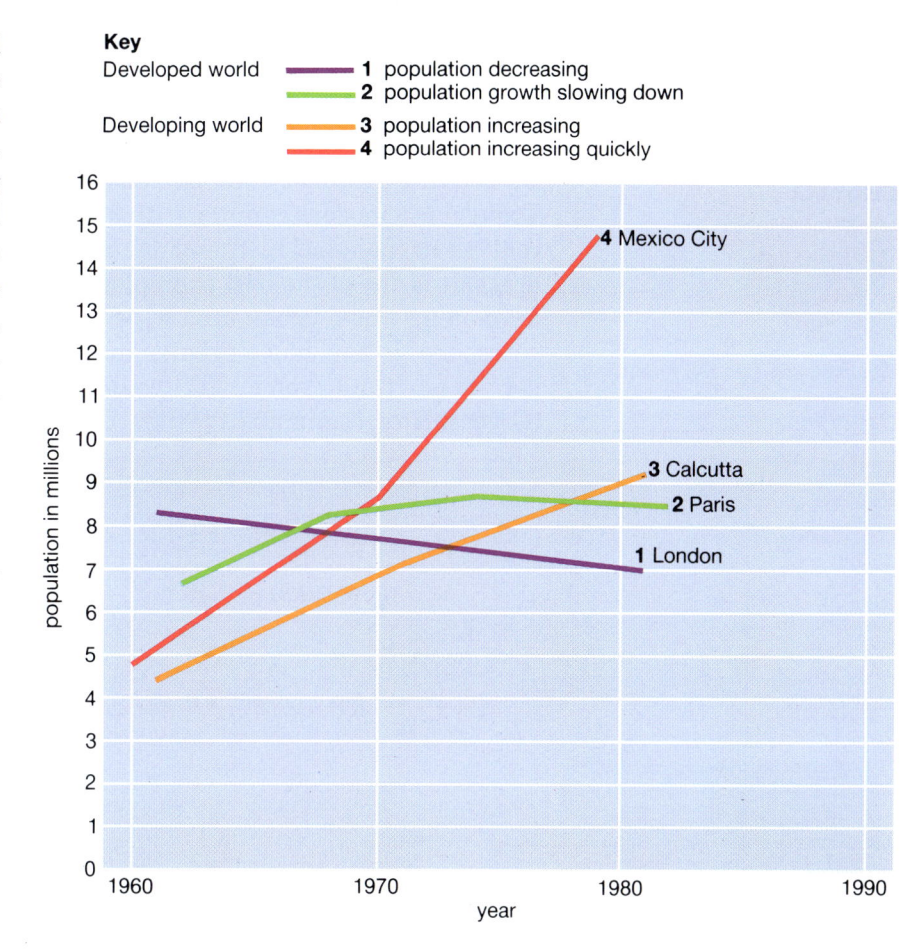

Key

Developed world
— 1 population decreasing
— 2 population growth slowing down

Developing world
— 3 population increasing
— 4 population increasing quickly

Figure D Population change in four major cities

QUESTIONS

1. What is the percentage of the world's population living in cities?
2. Which continent is:
   a) the most urbanized b) the least urbanized?
3. Which of the top ten cities were in the developing world in 1950?
4. Which of the top ten cities will be in the rich world in 2000 AD?
5. Which other developing world city could you add besides Mexico City to Figure D?
6. In two columns make lists of the advantages and disadvantages of living in a developing world city.
7. 1987 was the International Year of Shelter for the Homeless.
   a) Write a newspaper article about homeless people in the poor world. How did they become homeless?
   b) Write another newspaper article about homeless people in London or another large rich world city. How did they become homeless?

5.2 Hong Kong: coping with growth

In 1842 Britain began its colonial rule of Hong Kong. By the end of the present century Hong Kong will be officially Chinese again. At the beginning of British rule the colony was 'barren rock'. Today it is a modern country with 92 per cent of its population living in urban areas. It is one of the best examples of a developing world urban area which has succeeded. It now has a greater income per head than some EC countries (Greece, Eire, Spain and Portugal).

Since 1970 Hong Kong has developed very quickly. Its manufactured goods have a world-wide market. They were once cheap toys and textiles but today they are high quality fashion clothes and electronics. Hong Kong is a major world port and a world conference and exhibition centre. It is the fourth largest financial centre in the world after New York, London and Tokyo.

The building numbered 1 on the photograph, Figure B, is the Hong Kong and Shanghai Bank. It is one of the latest 'skyscrapers' in the Hong Kong skyline. The building is said to be the most expensive in the world – 50 storeys for £600 million!

Perhaps Figures B and C do not look like a developing world city. But if you visit another bank being built you will see a different scene. Chinese labourers, helped by their wives, hand-dig the foundations. There are 5.5 million people in Hong Kong and the majority work in crowded factories and live in crowded housing areas. The population density in the whole of Hong Kong is 5200 people per square kilometre; the highest in the world for a single country. The lack of

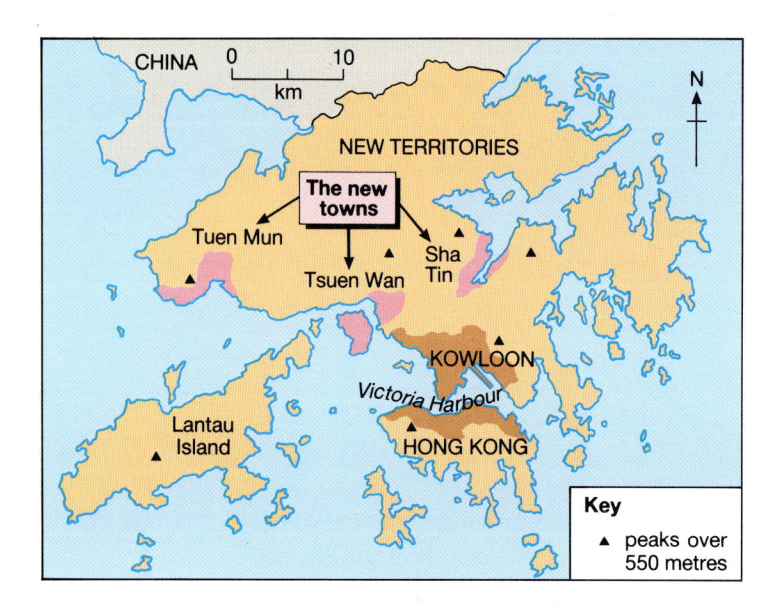

Figure A Location of Hong Kong

Figure B Hong Kong's commercial centre, looking towards Kowloon

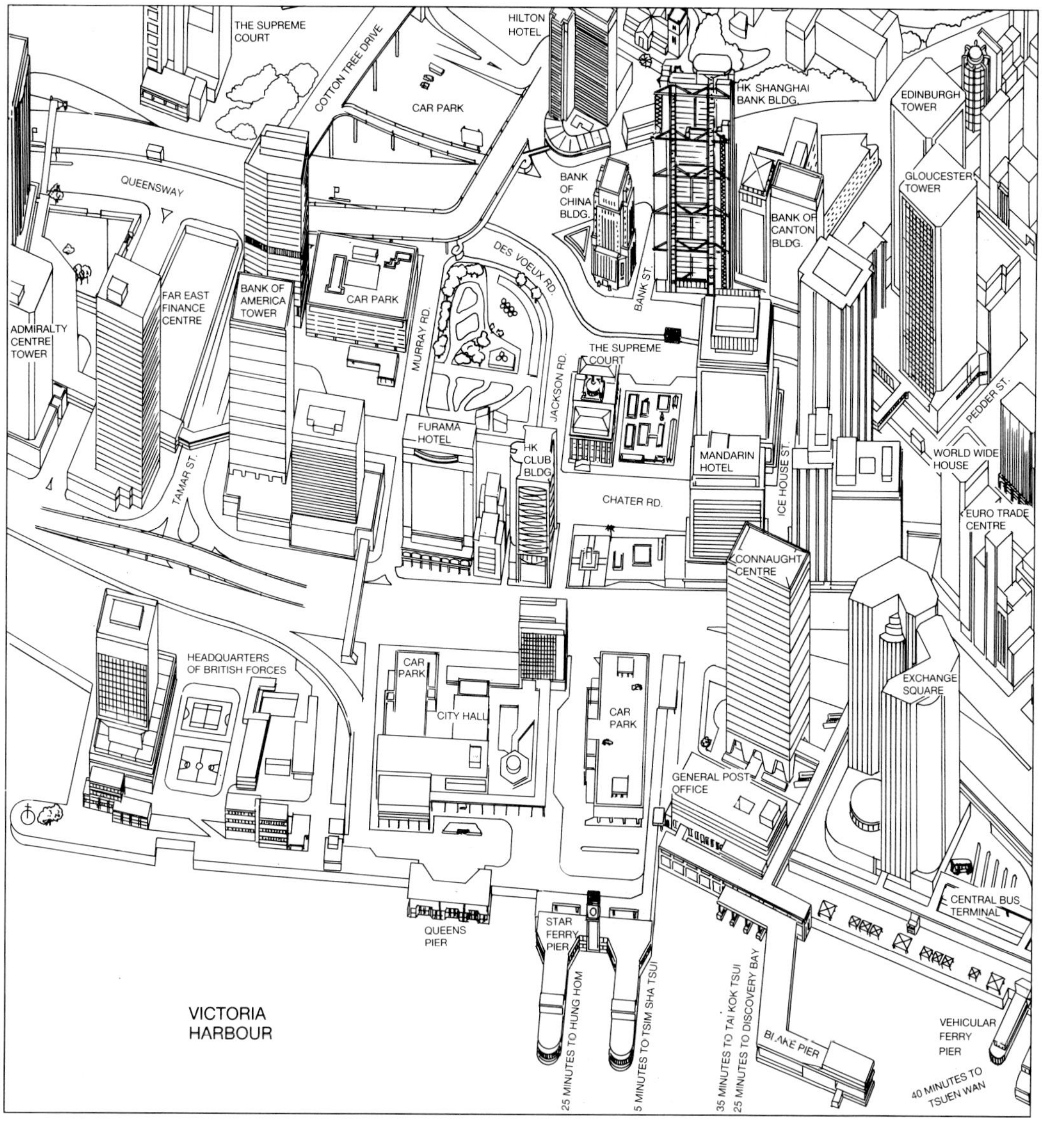

Figure C An unusual map of the Central District of Hong Kong

space is so extreme in Hong Kong that in the Sha Tin new town (Figure A), 30 storey tower blocks house 8 000 people each.

Hong Kong's new towns are being built on the small amount of available flat land. Hills have been levelled and land reclaimed from the sea. There is an overcrowding problem in Hong Kong similar to other developing world cities. What is the future for Hong Kong's growth? Most of the land is too rugged for housing development as we know it today. Some land must be kept for farming and recreation. Some of the steep slopes must be left forested to prevent soil erosion.

QUESTIONS

1. Study the maps and photograph.
   a) Which way was the camera pointing in Figure B?
   b) Which part of Hong Kong is across the water?
   c) What is the name of this harbour area?
   d) Write two sentences about the building numbered **1** on the photograph.
   e) Name the buildings numbered **2, 3, 4** and **5**.
   f) What is the name of the high rise building numbered **6**?
   g) Describe the function of the area shown in the photograph.
2. Describe the overcrowding problems of Hong Kong.
3. What has been done to solve the overcrowding problems?
4. What are your solutions to Hong Kong's future growth? How can such a small place cope with even more people?
5. In what ways is Hong Kong not typical of a developing world country?

5.3 Living in a self-help city

In cities in South America, Africa and Asia, people are working hard to improve their standard of living. Many have recently arrived from the countryside to start a new life. Think of the situation facing these two city newcomers. Pedro and Maria have left their Brazilian village and moved to the city of Rio de Janeiro. They are young, recently married and they want to share in the excitement of city life. Their home village can offer no employment except in the sugar cane industry. This is poorly paid seasonal work and its future is uncertain. They have arrived in Rio full of hope.

Where do they live?

- They could live on the streets – many do.
  - But it is not safe or hygienic and Maria and Pedro want a better start than this.
- They could stay with friends and relatives who have been in the city some years.
  - But their homes are small and can not house anyone else.
- They could rent a room in one of the *shanty towns* or *favelas* that have grown up around the city.
  - But they could be exploited and find it difficult to pay the rent.
- They could rent an apartment in a public housing scheme.
  - But there is a long waiting list of people who have been living in the city for years. Also the rents are just too high.
- They could build their own home.
  - But it is illegal to do this and it is difficult to find a good site.

To begin with, Pedro and Maria stay with Pedro's Uncle and his family in a favela home. It proves to be a good start. The uncle explains to them how they too can build their own home. He knows where there is some spare land along a railway track. Strictly it will be an illegal home and Pedro and Maria will be *squatters*. Materials are no problem as there is a factory nearby which throws out wood, metal and polythene.

Figure A Rio de Janeiro, Brazil

Figure B Pedro and Maria's first home

Where do they work?

Both Pedro and Maria need to earn money to pay for food and other essentials. There are many jobs in the *informal sector* of the city's economy (see page 82). Pedro finds a job selling postcards and souvenirs to Rio's tourists. His uncle knows someone who supplies the goods very cheaply. It is a job with no insurance or work licence and to make money Pedro has to work long hours. There is also a long journey to the tourist beaches from the favela; it costs Pedro a lot of his hard earned income.

Maria finds work in a small clothing factory which is really an upstairs room where young girls make children's shirts. The wages are no real reward for the hours Maria has to work.

In the evenings and at weekends Pedro, Maria and Pedro's uncle work on building the new home. They meet new friends and plan their new city life. They see the hundreds of consumer goods in the shops on their way to work. One day they will be able to afford some of them.

Do they start a family?

Some of Maria's friends have children and they want to know when Maria will have a family. Pedro and Maria know about contraception and Maria is using the pill. They are both determined to put off having children until they have more money. Neither want as many children as their parents had. Pedro is one of six brothers and two sisters (another sister died when still a baby).

Life in the 'self-help' favela is hard for Pedro and Maria. They work hard and improve their home. Later they will look for better work and then hopefully start a family. They will need a lot of good health, energy and their fair share of good fortune! The diagrams in Figure D show the cycle of improvement that people like Pedro and Maria are part of.

Figure C Pedro's first job

CYCLES OF IMPROVEMENT

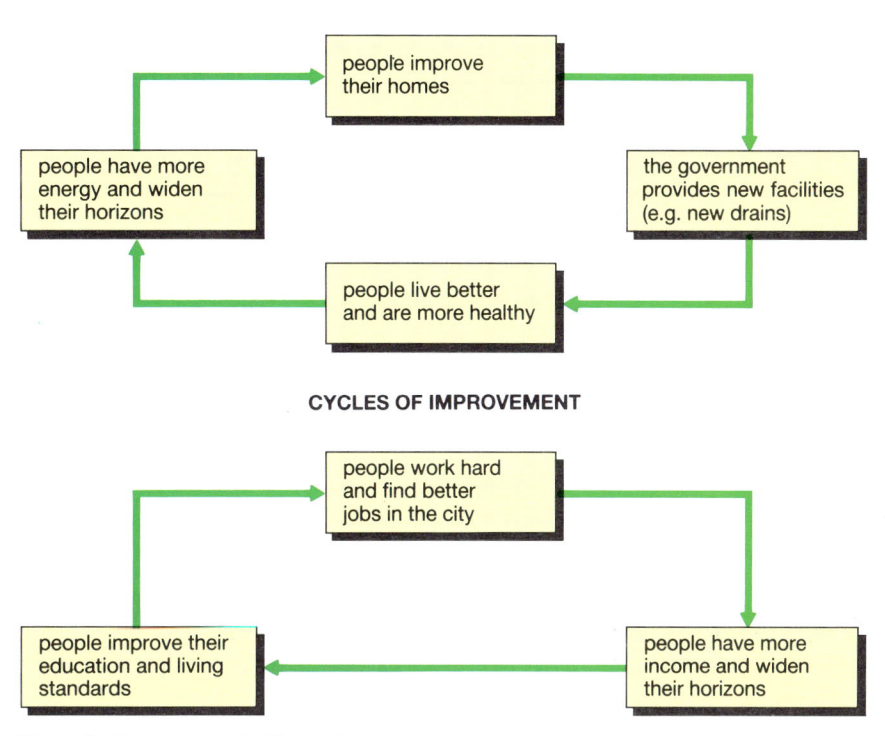

Figure D Two ways at looking at how people improve their way of life

QUESTIONS

1 Why do you think Pedro and Maria wanted to move to Rio de Janeiro?
2 Where did they stay on arrival in the city?
3 In what ways did Pedro's uncle help the couple to start their new life?
4 What are the problems with Pedro's and Maria's jobs?
5 Why are Pedro and Maria squatters?
6 How did they build their first home?
7 Choose one of the sketches and redraw it to show how Pedro and Maria have become part of the improvement cycle.
8 Think of Pedro and Maria in ten years time. Most things have gone well for them. Write about a) where they live, b) where they work and c) their family.

5.4 Living in a poverty trap

The story of Pedro and Maria on pages 80/81 is full of hope and optimism. It can be repeated throughout cities in the developing world. But the improvement in Pedro and Maria's living standards is not guaranteed. A quick change of fortune can take people out of the cycle of improvement.

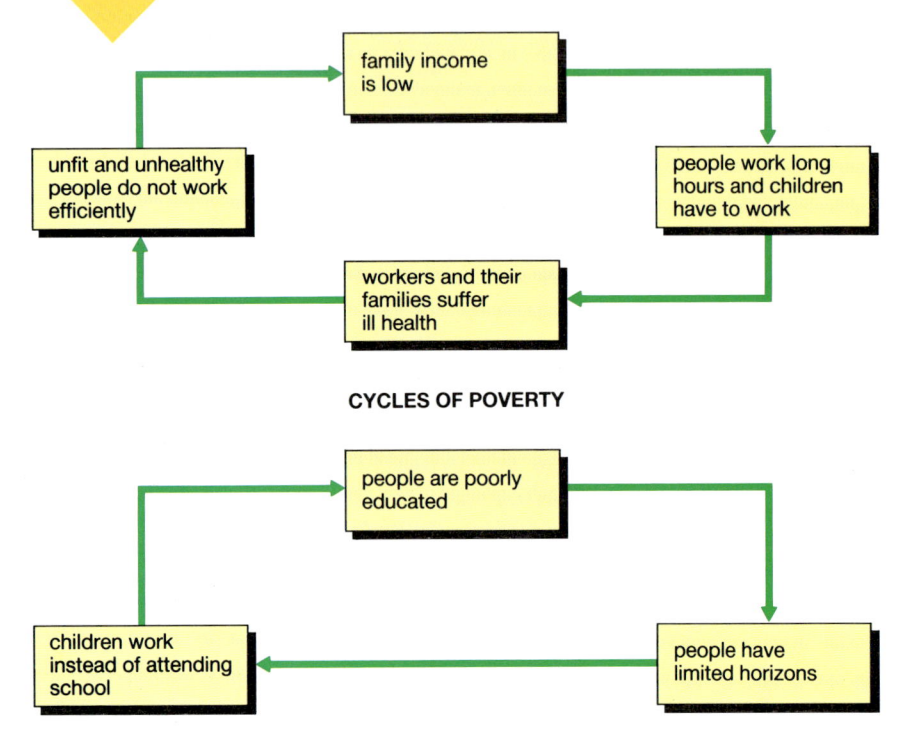

Often in the developing world, employment is hard to find. When it is found it is often underpaid and people have to work very long hours. A high percentage of people have jobs which are irregular and there is not enough work for them; they are *underemployed*. Not enough work means not enough income and perhaps not enough food. Instead of living in a cycle of improvement people are caught in a *cycle of poverty* or a *poverty trap* (Figure A). Millions of newcomers to cities in South America, Africa, and Asia cannot break out of the poverty trap.

> 'In Lagos, Nigeria's capital, thousands of people cannot improve their condition. 85 per cent of the school children have hook-worm or roundworm. Infantile deaths are common, many of the babies dying of dysentry. About 80 per cent of the houses near Lagos Lagoon have no public refuse disposal . . .'

Clearly many people living near Lagos Lagoon are unfit and unhealthy and can not work efficiently. Figure A shows you that it is difficult to break out of this situation.

CYCLES OF POVERTY

Figure A Two ways of looking at how people are trapped by poverty

Figure B Despite low pay, long hours, and crowded conditions these people have probably broken out of the poverty trap

Figure C Services in the informal sector

A way out – improving the informal sector

The problem of too many people chasing too few jobs is not an easy one to solve. One way forward is for governments to give more help to the *informal sector* of the economy. In many cities over 50 per cent of people work in the informal sector – Figure C. This type of employment is small scale, uses hand labour or old equipment and local resources. It is not recognized by the authorities in terms of the law.

The informal sector needs more aid and encouragement. The following could be provided:
- small amounts of starting capital
- simple premises for work
- easier work licences
- education for accounting
- encouragement to rich people and tourists to use the informal sector

A richer informal sector would mean that people would have more money and could break out of the cycle of poverty.

The other way out

People living in poverty do find other ways out of the poverty trap. The sex industry flourishes in some developing world cities. Prostitution is a way out of poverty for some young women. Drug selling can bring in the income to support a large family. People turn to crime and street violence, and muggings are unfortunately another way of obtaining money.

Services in the informal sector

shoe cleaning · mending clothes · washing clothes · selling crops · selling souvenirs · cooking food · providing cheap transport · selling drinks · repairing cars

QUESTIONS

1. Explain the term underemployment.
2. What do you understand by a cycle of poverty or poverty trap?
3. Why are the people living near Lagos Lagoon caught in a poverty trap?
4. Why might the woman in Figure C never be able to break out of the poverty trap?
5. Choose an example of a service which is part of the informal sector in a developing world city.
   a) Describe the characteristics of this type of employment.
   b) How could the government help to make this service more successful?
6. Why will a more successful informal sector help people living in a developing world city?

5.5 Urban growth in Brazil

In the 1850s Paris and London became the first cities in the world with one million inhabitants. Today there are over 180 of these *million cities*. Most of the recent additions have been in the developing world. All of Brazil's top ten cities have populations of over one million; the top two are over five million.

Brazil's big cities have grown very quickly in the last forty years. The graphs (Figures A and B) show the quickening growth of four Brazilian cities. The slope of the graph indicates the rate of growth.

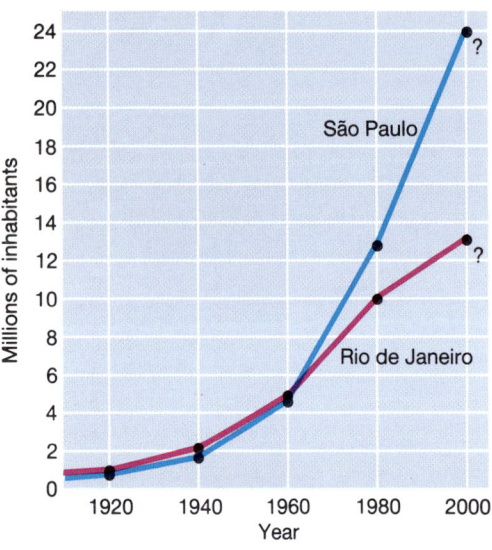

Rio de Janeiro

From 1763 to 1960 Rio de Janeiro was the capital of Brazil. It was not a *primate city* which dominated the country like many South American capitals. It shared its position as the economic and political centre of Brazil with São Paulo. In 1960 Brasilia became the new capital. It was planned to take some of the growth away from Rio. It was situated in the middle of the country to help open up the interior.

Figure A (*right*) The growth of São Paulo and Rio de Janeiro

Figure B (*far right*) Population growth in Recife and Belo Horizonte (see question 2)

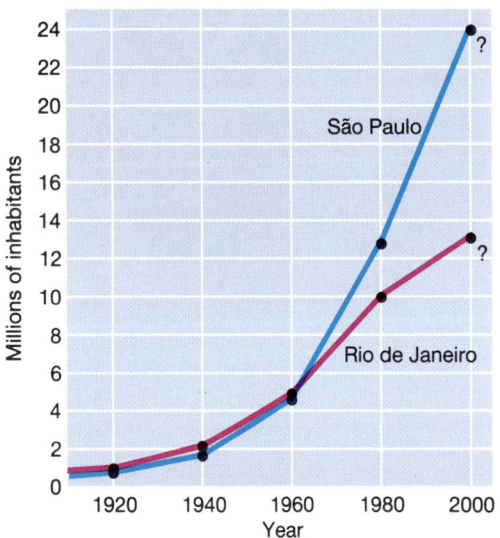

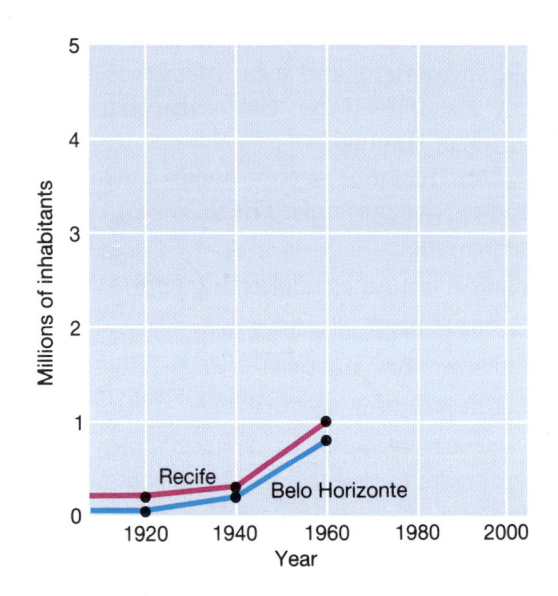

Figure C Downtown Rio

Rio's functions	
financial:	stock market
	banking
industrial:	printing and publishing
	clothing
	food processing
	Alfa Romeo car plant
	oil refining
	shipbuilding
tourism:	the February 'carnival'
	museums
	sports
	sea and beaches
transport:	largest airport in Brazil
	new Metro system
	important seaport

Figure D (*above, right*) The 200 000 capacity Maracana Stadium

Figure E (*below*) Cars parked on the pavement in Rio

Rio's problems
restricted site
overcrowding
more than 25 per cent live in favelas – unhealthy, lacking drainage and piped water
city has sprawled
traffic congestion, parking problems
great contrast between the rich and the poor

QUESTIONS

1 Study the line graphs in Figure A.
   a) Which city is at present growing faster?
   b) When did São Paulo become bigger than Rio de Janeiro?
   c) What is the approximate present population of i) São Paulo and ii) Rio de Janeiro? (Read the present year as best you can along the horizontal axis.)

2 Draw out the line graph Figure B.
   a) Title the graphs – 'Population growth of Recife and Belo Horizonte'.
   b) Complete the line graphs using the following information.

Recife	1980	2.1 million
	2000	4.0 million (estimate)
Belo Horizonte	1980	2.5 million
	2000	5.6 million (estimate)

   c) Read off your graph approximately when Belo Horizonte overtook Recife.
   d) How do you know from the graph that Belo Horizonte is growing faster than Recife?
   e) Both cities are approximately doubling in size every 20 years. If these rates continue what will the population of i) Recife and ii) Belo Horizonte be in 2020?

3 Study Figure C.
   a) Describe the type of city development.
   b) What type of activities will be found in this area of the city?

4 Study Figure D.
   a) What sports are catered for in this area?
   b) Imagine you live in a favela and scarcely earn enough money to feed your family. What would you feel about the splendour of this sports complex?

5 Study Figure E.
   a) What transport problems does this picture show?
   b) Describe the type of housing shown in this photograph.

5.6 Villages in Tanzania: ujamaa

Tanzania is a large country in East Africa. It is four times larger than Britain. Tanzania is now a country of villages – 87 per cent of Tanzania's 21 million people live in the countryside. The percentage of people living in urban areas is low, as it is in many African countries.

In the past, settlements in Tanzania's countryside consisted only of scattered hamlets of a few homes each. It was impossible to provide even basic services for each isolated hamlet. The *pattern* of settlement had to be changed.

Figure A The making of two ujamaa villages

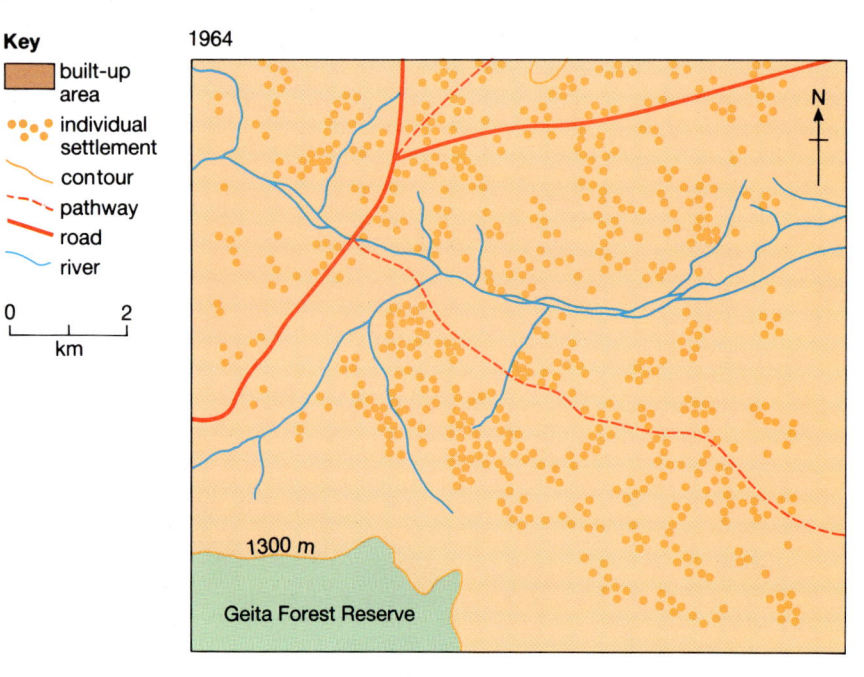

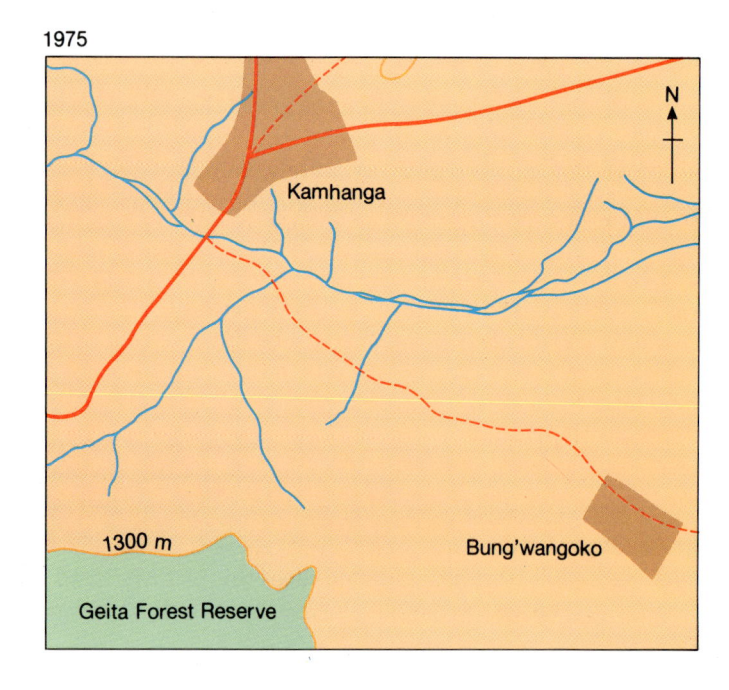

Figure A shows how this was done in one area. Hundreds of individual settlements have been reorganized into just two very large villages. The reorganization policy is called *ujamaa* a Swahili word meaning 'family life'. Each family in the ujamaa village grows its own food around their house. Much of the land is owned and farmed by the villagers on a *collective* basis. This means that all the farmers work together to produce more food than they could produce on their own. This system is similar to the collective farms of Israel and the USSR. Tanzania has had a socialist government since its independence in 1961.

What advantages do the ujamaa villages have?

1 It is easier to provide roads, electricity, and water.

2 It is easier to build schools, clinics and shops to serve a larger number of people.

3 It is easier to afford machinery and improve farming methods.

From small beginnings ujamaa spread quickly in the 1970s. In 1967 there were only 48 ujamaa villages. By 1986 there were 8 200 and over 80 per cent of Tanzania's population lived in them.

Figure B The products of successful farming

Success of ujamaa

- **Education** The schools are for adults as well as children. The adult literacy rate is now the highest in Africa.
- **Health** Health centres and dispensaries have been built in the villages. Most of the medical staff are Tanzanians.

Evidence of improvement

Criteria	1961	1986
school attendance	22%	nearly all
adult literacy	25%	80%
infant mortality	190 per 1000 births	98 per 1000 births
life expectancy	37 years	50 years

Failure of ujamaa

- Food production has not increased as hoped
- Production of cash crops for export has declined
- Many collective farming schemes have collapsed
- Many people were forced to move from their homes to the ujamaa villages

QUESTIONS

1. Why did the Tanzanians start ujamaa villages?
2. Why is it easier to develop villages than isolated hamlets?
3. Imagine it is your job to plan a new ujamaa village in a rural area of Tanzania. The people live in over 100 scattered farms and hamlets. Design a poster (using several sketches) to help convince the people that ujamaa is a good idea for them.
4. You have to decide what aid to give to a new ujamaa village. Which four of the following would you provide? Put them in rank order.

    a health centre
    a school for 5–11 year olds
    a reliable vehicle
    a metalled road to market
    an electricity supply
    a travelling library
    a repair workshop
    a piped water supply

5. Study the following statistics.

Urban population of some developing countries

Country	Percentage population living in towns and cities
Tanzania	13
Kenya	13
Mexico	67
Brazil	68
Venezuela	76
Nigeria	13
Ghana	36
Egypt	44
Ecuador	45
Peru	65

a) Which countries are in Africa and which are in South America?
b) Work out the average (mean) percentage for each continent.
c) Summarize your results in one sentence. Can you suggest reasons for the difference? (It is not because of ujamaa policies in Africa – this is only a policy in Tanzania.)

Unit 5 ASSESSMENT

A city model

It is possible to generalize about world cities and draw a model to show their development. There are similarities with and differences from the developed world models (p. 64).

1. Study the city model:
   a) What is the function of the CBD? (1 mark)
   b) Suggest why slums have developed near the centre of the city. (2 marks)
   c) Find the 'periferia':
   i) What type of amenities would you be likely to find in this area?
   ii) How will this area differ from housing in a similar zone in a developed world city? (2 + 2 marks)
   d) What are favelas? Write about their characteristics.

2. Name three differences in the zones of this model compared with a developed world city model. (3 marks)

3. In what way is this model similar to a developed world model? (4 marks)

Total 14 marks

Figure A Model of a developing-world city

- CBD – shops, offices, traffic problems
- perifera, poor quality, permanent housing with some basic alternatives
- high-class suburban housing
- zone of slums and poor quality housing – better-off people have moved out
- modern factories along main transport lines
- expensive high-rise apartments with modern amenities
- low-cost government housing
- self-help areas, squatter settlements, favelas

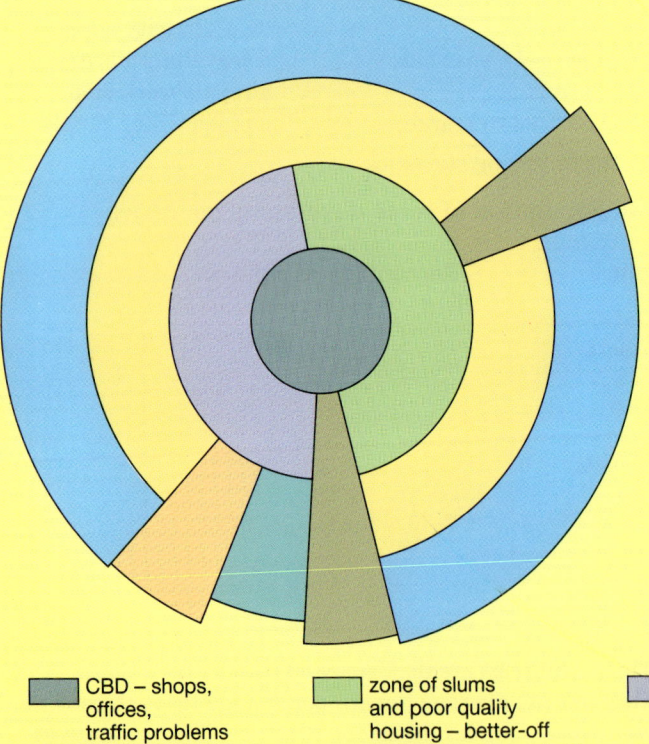

Brasilia

Brazil's new capital city, Brasilia, was officially 'opened' in 1960. Today, over one million people live in the new city. The building of Brasilia has taken a lot of pressure off the old capital Rio de Janeiro. Rio was growing so fast that its housing and transport facilities were not coping. Brasilia has also taken away urban growth from the other centres in the south east of the country. It has given growth and hope to the formerly remote inland regions of Brazil.

In a pamphlet published by the Brazilian Embassy in London the city is described as:

> '... a city of great buildings. The list is almost endless, but the student of architecture should not miss Niemeyer's Palacio da Alvorada, the President's residence... Brasilia has much to offer both its own population and the tourist. It has several art galleries and many museums as well as sixteen cinemas and a host of night-clubs and restaurants...'

In an article written by the freelance journalist Paul Forster the following comments were made about Brasilia:

> '... it is the wastelands between the buildings, the pedestrian tracks around the traffic interchanges and the general lack of municipal care and detail that really let the place down... there is a distinct shortage of the street-corner bars and markets that are such an important feature of Brazilian life elsewhere.'

Figure B The planned part of Brasilia, there are no favelas in sight

Figure C Contrast: a shanty town in Rio de Janeiro

1 Use your atlas to find Brasilia. How far inland from Rio de Janeiro is the new capital? (2 marks)

2 Why has the building of Brasilia been so successful for:
a) the urbanized coastal areas of Brazil
b) the inland areas of the country? (3 + 3 marks)

3 Why do the think the article published by the Brazilian Embassy is so full of praise for the new capital? (3 marks)

4 Describe in your own words what the freelance journalist is saying about the new capital city. (3 marks)

5 Like all Brazilian cities, Brasilia has its favelas, called 'satellite towns'.
a) What are these settlements like?
b) Why do they grow up? (2 + 2 marks)

6 You are very poor and have no job. You have just moved to Brasilia.
What will you do for a home?
a) Describe the way you would settle in a favela. (3 marks)
b) Describe what you would want to do to improve your way of life over the next few years. (4 marks)
Total 25 marks

Details for pupil profile sheets Unit 5

Knowledge and understanding

1 Urbanization
2 Squatter settlements
3 The homeless
4 Self-help city – favelas
5 Informal sector
6 Migration to the cities
7 Improvement cycle/poverty cycle
8 Urban growth in Rio and Brasilia
9 Ujamaa in Tanzania
10 City model

Skills

1 Interpreting various block graphs
2 Reading a picture map
3 Drawing line graphs
4 Describing photographs
5 Working out a mean

Values

1 Awareness of urban growth problems
2 Some people's problems are others' normal lives
3 Empathy work – identifying with a young migrating couple
4 People migrate to improve their lives
5 People work hard to improve their lives
6 Understanding that some people are trapped by poverty
7 Deciding on priorities for development
8 Realizing that rural improvement is an alternative to cities
9 Comparing images (of Brasilia)

6.1 Explaining population

Unit 6: Population trends

Look at Figure A. What do you think it shows? It is called a population *age-sex pyramid* and shows the number of boys and girls in a school. This school is in a large housing area on the outskirts of a town. To explain the shape of the graph we need more information. The number of pupils in Years One and Two is lower than that in Years Three, Four and Five because there are now less children between 11 and 13 years living in the housing area. The Sixth Year has more girls because some come from a nearby school to take a secretarial course.

Figure A (*right*) An age-sex pyramid

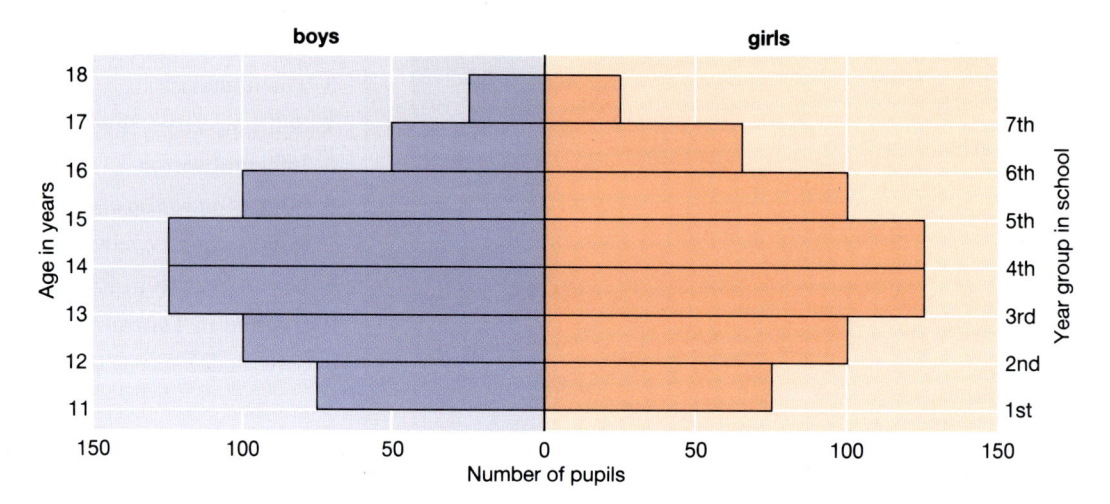

Figure B (*below*) Population change

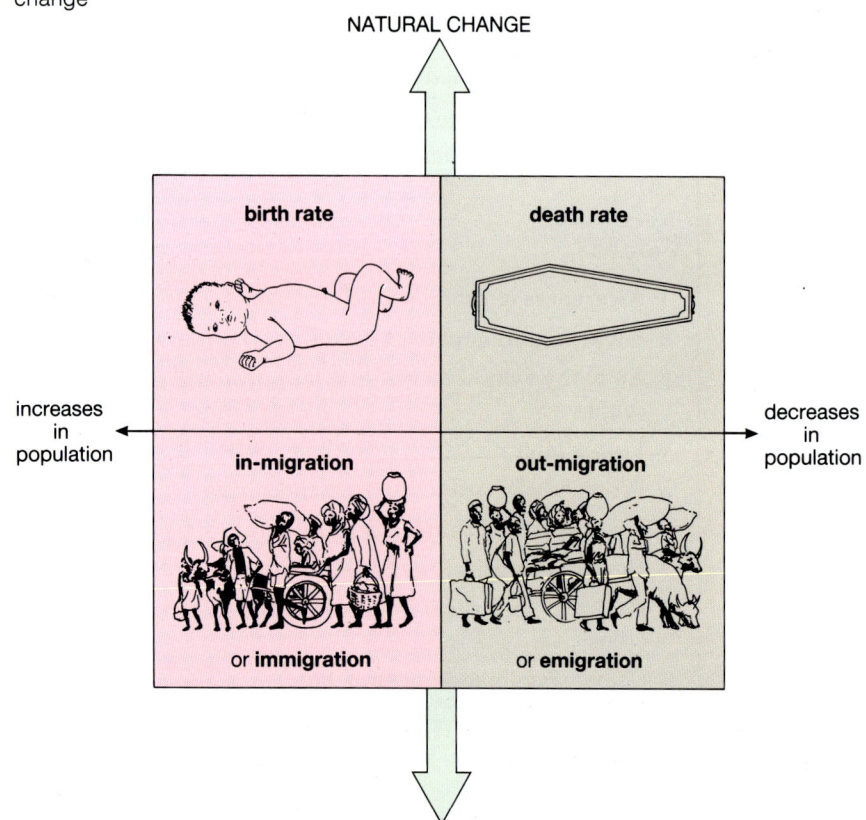

The two important features of *population change* are shown in this age-sex pyramid. They are:

1 natural change (fewer 11–13 year olds)
2 migration or movement (girls moving into the Sixth Year)

Age–sex pyramids can be drawn for schools, neighbourhoods, towns, regions or countries. Different shapes occur because of differences in natural change and net-migration. Figure B shows the relationships between the features of population change. Read through the definitions and look at the summary diagram on page 91 and then answer the questions.

Figure C (*facing page*) Summary definitions

90

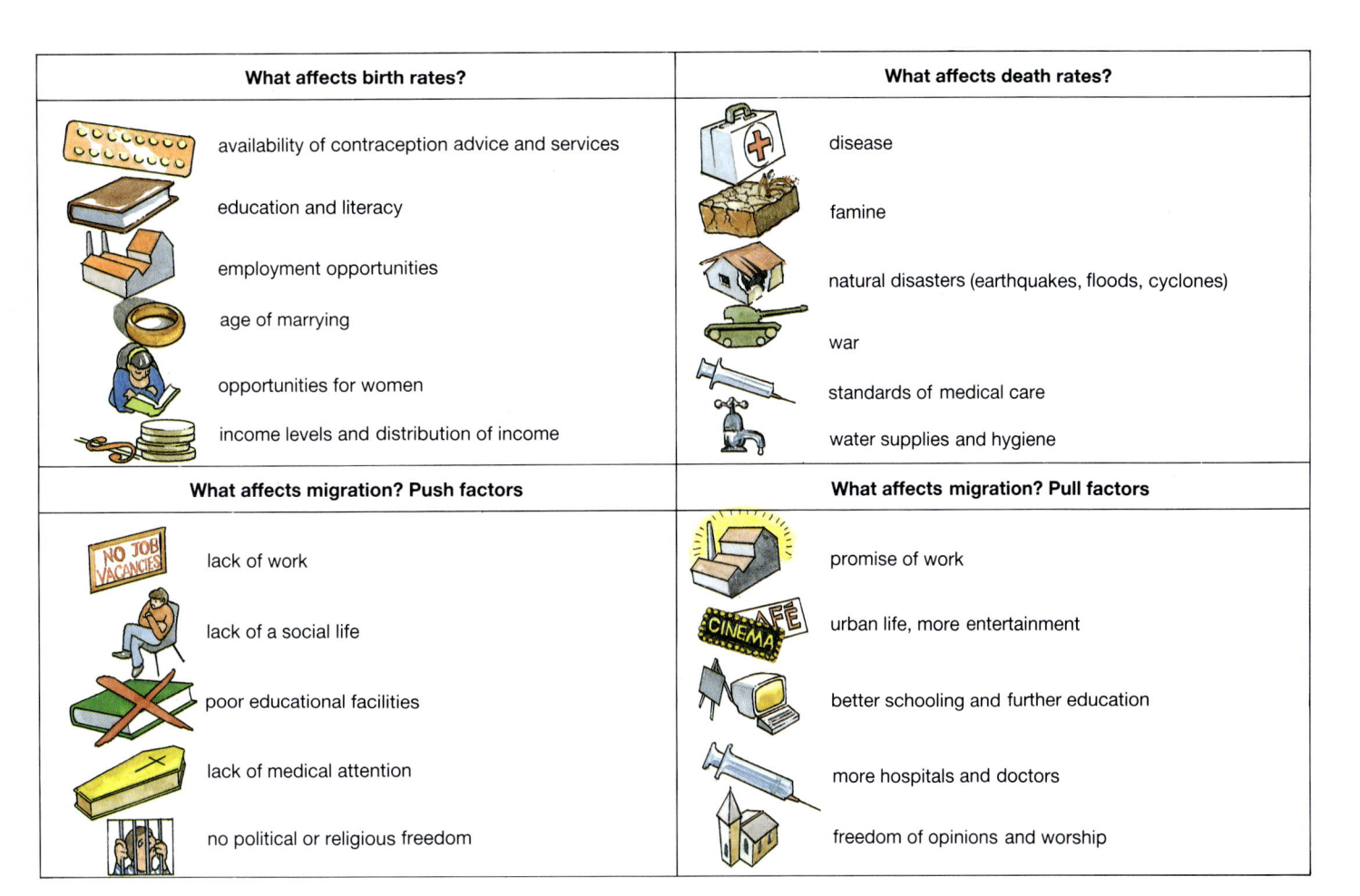

What affects birth rates?	What affects death rates?
availability of contraception advice and services	disease
education and literacy	famine
employment opportunities	natural disasters (earthquakes, floods, cyclones)
age of marrying	war
opportunities for women	standards of medical care
income levels and distribution of income	water supplies and hygiene

What affects migration? Push factors	What affects migration? Pull factors
lack of work	promise of work
lack of a social life	urban life, more entertainment
poor educational facilities	better schooling and further education
lack of medical attention	more hospitals and doctors
no political or religious freedom	freedom of opinions and worship

Definitions

Birth rate The number of babies born in a year for every 1000 people.
Death rate The number of deaths in a year for every 1000 people.
Natural change The difference between the birth rate and the death rate. It may be a natural increase or a natural decrease.
In-migration The number of people coming into an area.
Out-migration The number of people leaving or moving out of an area.
Net migration The difference between in-migration and out-migration. It may be a net migration increase or decrease.
But if migration is between different countries:
Immigration The number of people coming into a country from another.
Emigration The number of people leaving a country for another.
Net migration The difference between immigration and emigration. It may be a net migration increase or decrease.

QUESTIONS

1 Look at Figure A.
   a) How many pupils are there in the First Year?
   b) How many pupils are there in the Fourth Year?
   c) How many pupils are there in the school?

2 Fill in the gaps:

Country	Birth rate	Death rate	Natural increase
A	40	20	20
B	30	15	?
C	15	?	2

Region	In-migration	Out-migration	Net migration
A	600	800	− 200
B	1000	500	?
C	1000	?	− 500

3 Write about 'push' and 'pull' factors which might influence the following people to migrate:
   a) a rich family living in a large city like London
   b) a poor rural family living in a remote region of the UK
   c) an educated Indian family living in a large Indian city
   d) a poor Indian family living in a drought stricken area of central India

6.2 How long a life?

Population pyramids are being turned upside down!

You can see what this means. There are increasingly more old people and less young people.

In the UK about one fifth of the population is of pensionable age (over 65 years for men and women). It is a proportion that is increasing. People are living longer. The map (Figure C) shows that the *life expectancy at birth* is over 70 years in the developed world (North America, Europe, Australia/New Zealand and Japan). The people of the developing world do not have such a high life expectancy. It is lowest in parts of Africa and Asia.

Why do people live longer?

The average life expectancy in the rich developed world in 1950 was about 66 years. Now it is over 70 years. You probably know several people who are over 80 or 90 years old. In 1950 there were many fewer people of this age. There has been an improvement in health care, medicines and people's diets. The life expectancy in the poor developing world is increasing (Figure B).

Death rates were high because people were dying of diseases and ill health. Many health hazards are now being controlled. Malaria, cholera, typhoid, yellow fever, tetanus, measles and diarrhoea can be prevented (Figure D). But this does not mean that they no longer occur. Every year, five million children die of diarrhoea alone.

Infant mortality

This is the rate (per 1000 live births) at which children die before they are one year old. It is a tragedy when we hear of babies dying. In the developing world up to 170 per 1000 babies can die. The

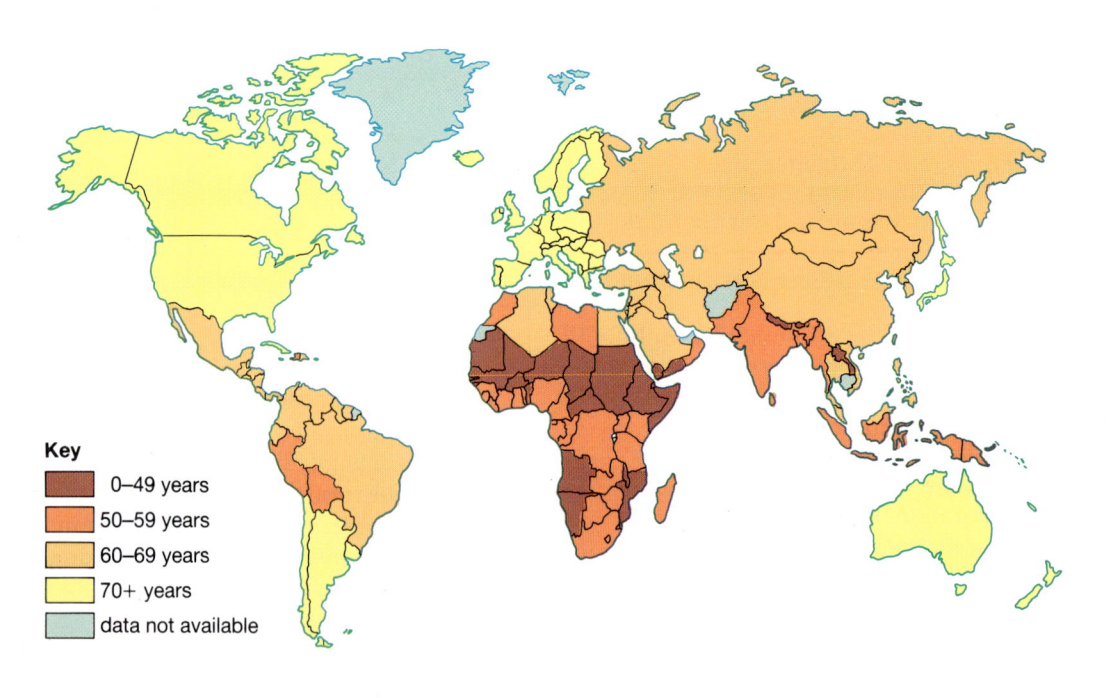

Figure A The future trend: more old people, less young people

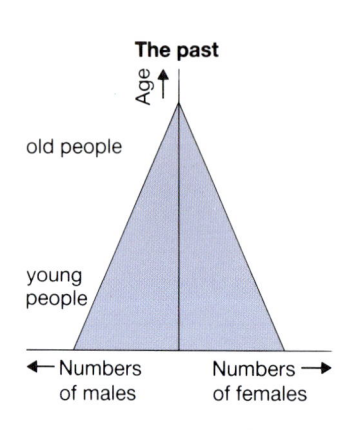

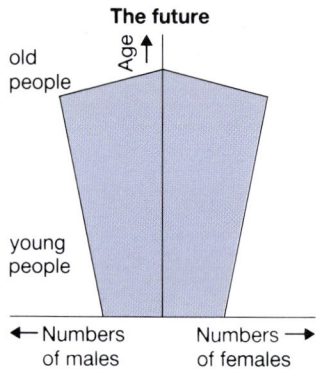

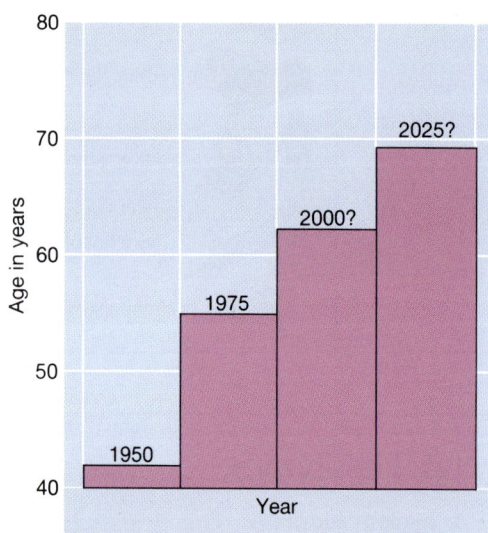

Figure B (*above*) People are living longer in developing countries

Figure C (*right*) Life expectancy at birth

Key
- 0–49 years
- 50–59 years
- 60–69 years
- 70+ years
- data not available

infant mortality rate is highest in the 32 poorest countries: many of these are in Africa, for example, Senegal and Mali (Figures E and F). In the rich countries infant mortality is very low – it is only 10 per 1000 in Scandinavia.

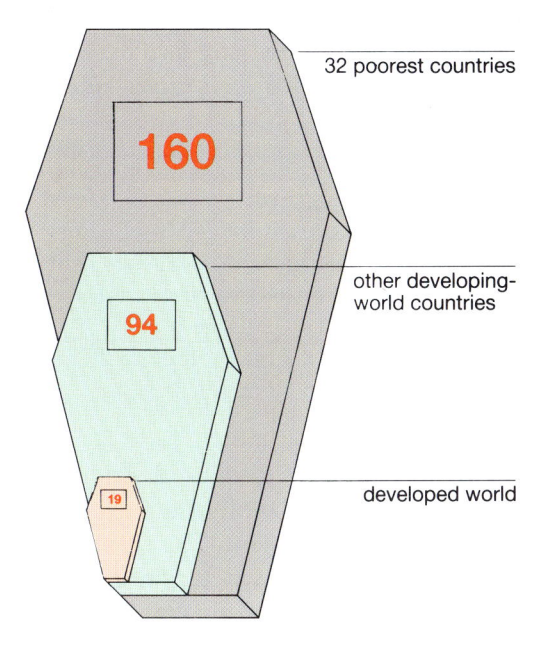

Figure E Comparison of infant mortality rates (per 1000 live births)

- 32 poorest countries: 160
- other developing-world countries: 94
- developed world: 19

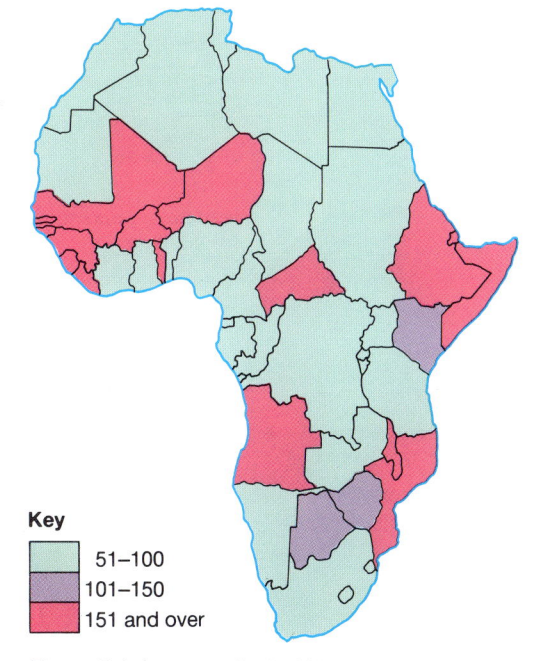

Figure F Infant mortality in Africa

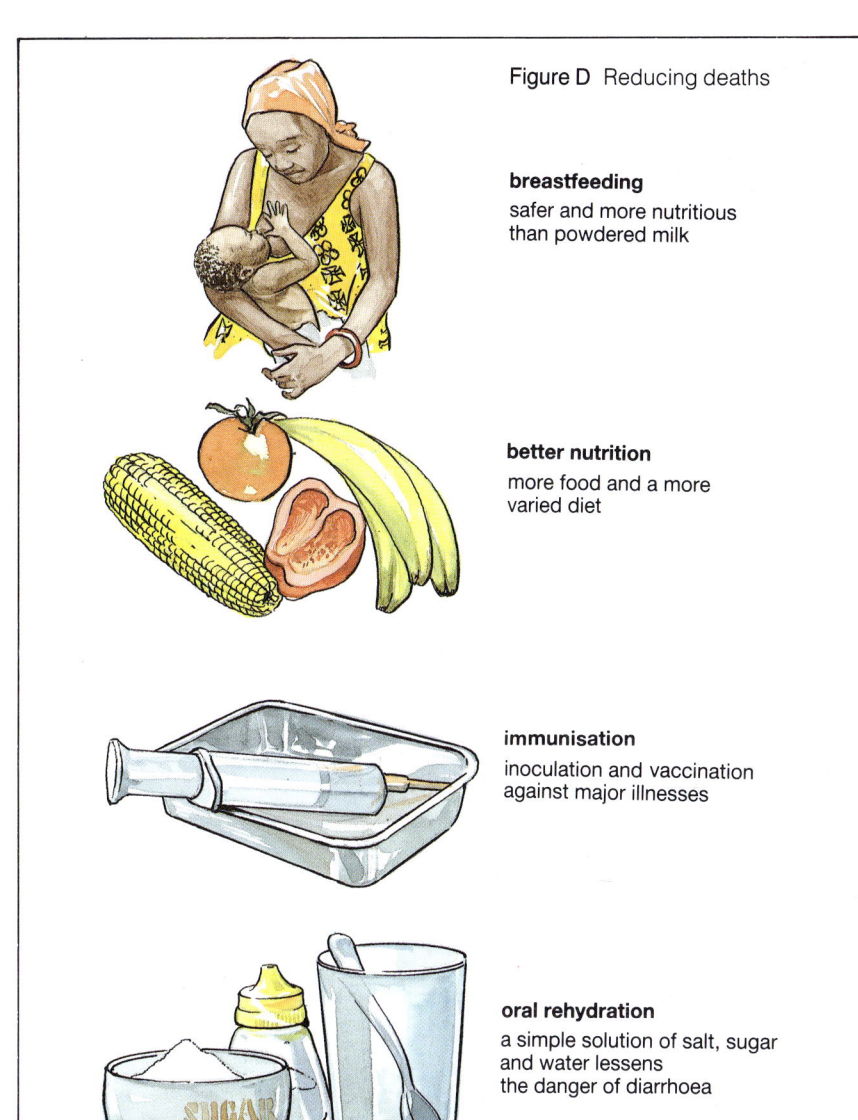

Key
- 51–100
- 101–150
- 151 and over

Figure D Reducing deaths

breastfeeding
safer and more nutritious than powdered milk

better nutrition
more food and a more varied diet

immunisation
inoculation and vaccination against major illnesses

oral rehydration
a simple solution of salt, sugar and water lessens the danger of diarrhoea

QUESTIONS

1. Explain what is meant by 'population pyramids being turned upside down'.
2. Why has the life expectancy been high in the rich world since the Second World War?
3. Why are people beginning to live longer in the developing world?
4. What exactly is infant mortality?
5. Use Figure F:
    a) Name five countries in Africa where infant mortality is over 150 per 1000.
    b) Which two countries in mainland Africa have the lowest infant mortality rates?
6. What are the reasons for infant mortality being so high in some African countries?
7. How do you think infant mortality can be reduced in the African continents?

6.3 World distribution of population

Figure A World population distribution

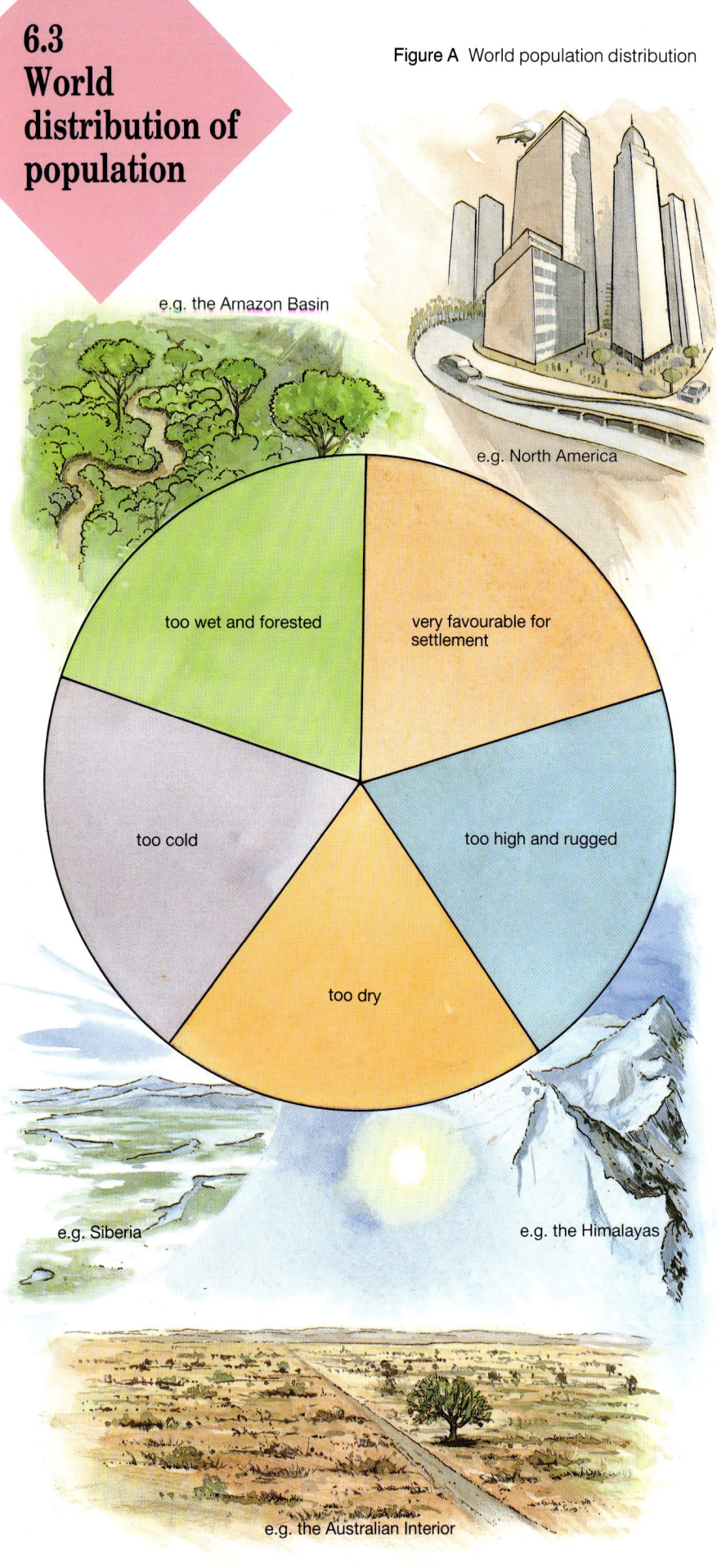

e.g. the Amazon Basin

e.g. North America

- too wet and forested
- very favourable for settlement
- too cold
- too high and rugged
- too dry

e.g. Siberia

e.g. the Himalayas

e.g. the Australian Interior

The distribution of population in the world is very uneven. The majority of the world's people live on only 20 per cent of the land (Figure A).

Comparing distributions

A good way of comparing two distributions is to place two *pie graphs* side by side.

> **Drawing a pie graph**
> A pie graph is a circle divided into sectors. Each sector in Figure A is 20 per cent. There are 360 degrees in a circle therefore each 20 per cent = 72 degrees.
> 1 per cent = 3.6 degrees therefore 20 per cent = 3.6 × 20 = 72 degrees.

Study the two pie graphs in Figure B which show the distribution of world population by continent. The second pie graph has been drawn larger because the total world population was larger in 1985. These are therefore *proportional pie graphs*.

Figure B Changing world population

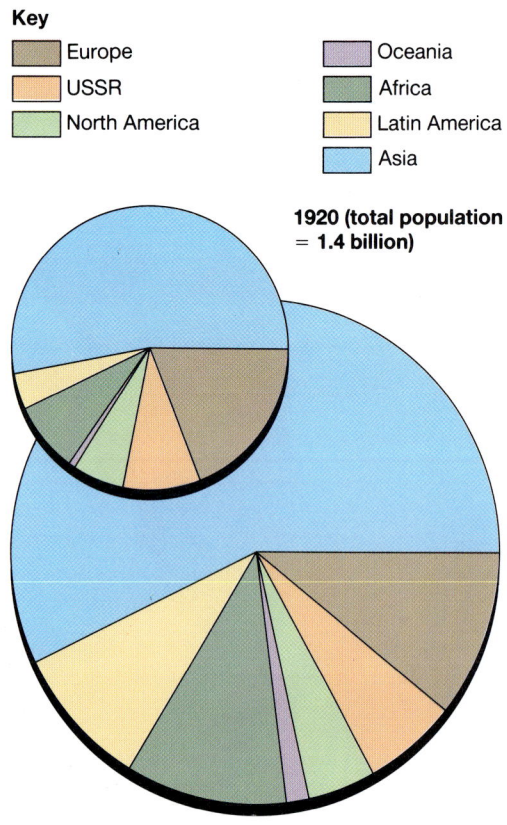

Key
- Europe
- USSR
- North America
- Oceania
- Africa
- Latin America
- Asia

1920 (total population = 1.4 billion)

1985 (total population = 4.4 billion)

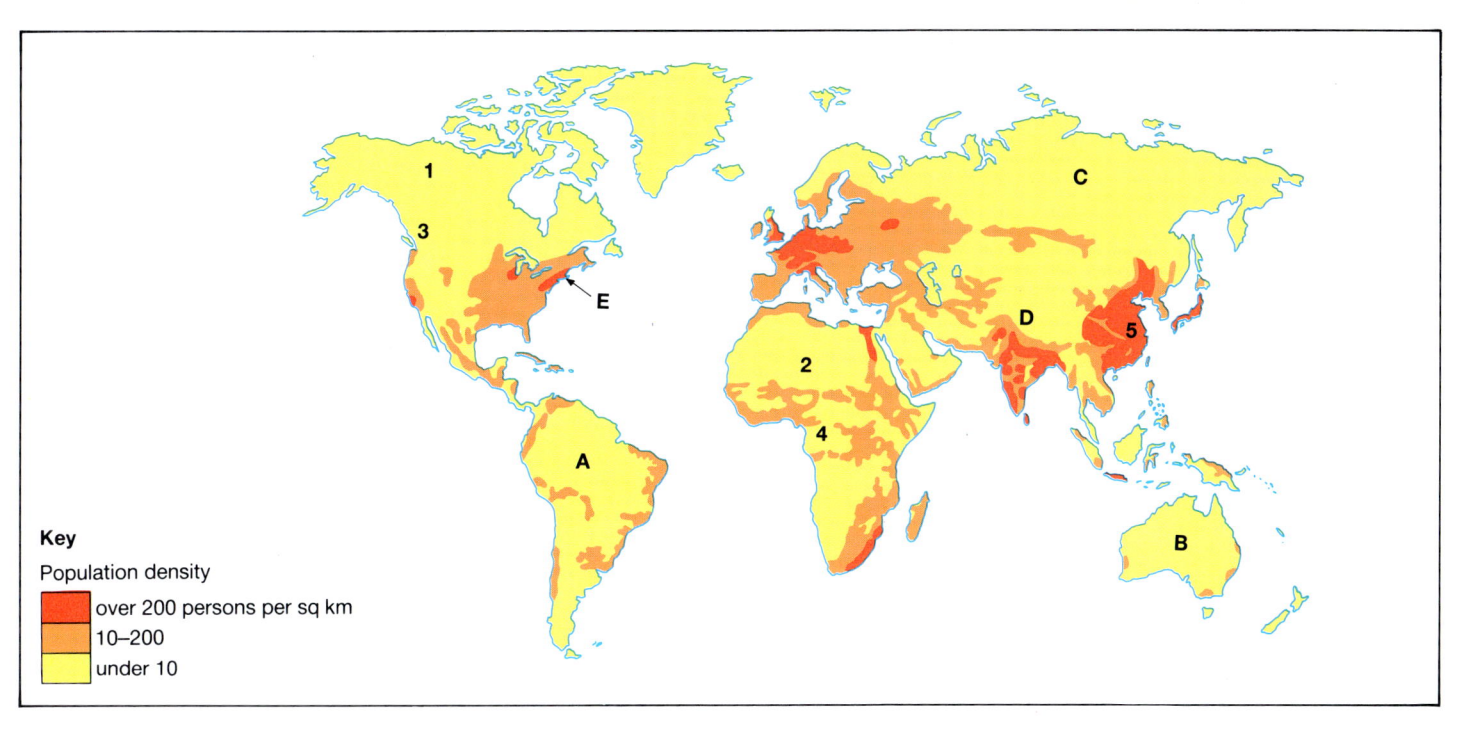

Figure C World population density

Figure D Urban/rural population distribution

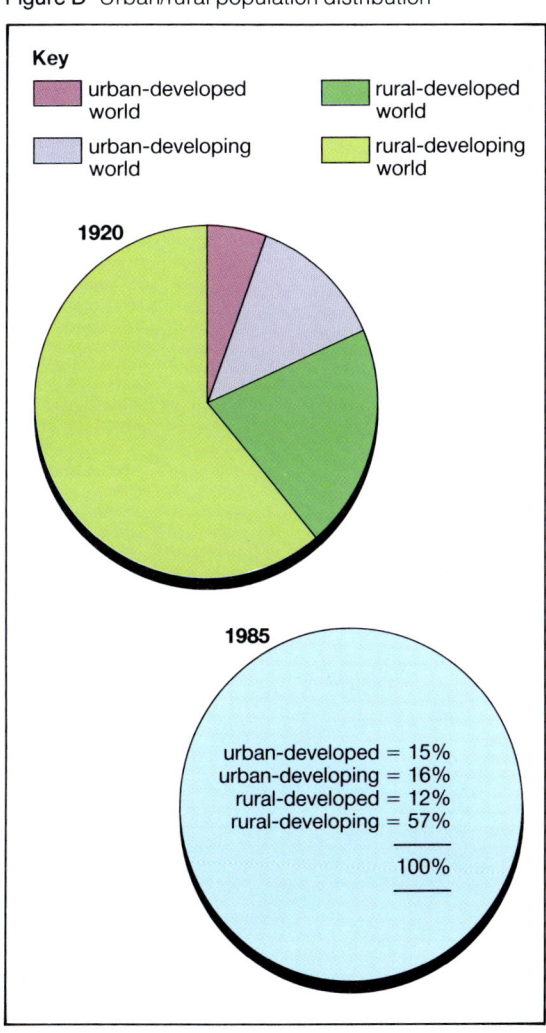

Key
- urban-developed world
- urban-developing world
- rural-developed world
- rural-developing world

1920

1985

urban-developed = 15%
urban-developing = 16%
rural-developed = 12%
rural-developing = 57%
100%

QUESTIONS

1. Identify each of the example regions on the pie graph (Figure A) with the letters A to E on the world map (Figure C).

2. Numbers 1 to 5 on the world map are other examples of regions like A to E.
   a) Which numbers are the following regions?

   The Sahara   Zaire Basin
   Canadian Northlands Eastern China
   Rocky Mountains

   b) How suitable is each area, 1–5, for people to live in?

3. Name the three largest world areas where population density is over 200 persons per square kilometre.

4. Name one European country where population density is under 10 persons per square kilometre.

5. Study the pie graphs, Figure B.
   a) How many more people lived in the world in 1985 than in 1920?
   b) Name two major continents which have increased their share of world population.
   c) Name two continents which have decreased their share of population.
   d) Approximately what percentage of the world's population lived in i) Asia in 1985 ii) Europe in 1985?

6. Study Figure D. Construct a pie graph for 1985 using the statistics provided. Start your graph with a vertical line. Use the key given.

7. Write about the differences between the two graphs (Figure D): 1920 and 1985.

6.4 Population patterns explained

About 70 per cent of the world's population lives in the developing world. This percentage is increasing – why? The *natural increase* of population, that is birth rate *minus* death rate, is higher in the developing world than in the developed world. The table below shows figures for some countries in the 1980s.

Doubling times

If a country has a natural increase the same as Brazil (24 per 1000) it will double its population in 30 years. A country which is growing at the rate of the USA (natural increase 7) will double its population in 100 years. The graph, Figure A, shows these growth rates.

Natural increase (rate per 1000 people)

Countries	Birth rate	Death rate	Natural increase
Developed			
UK	13	12	1
USA	16	9	7
USSR	20	10	10
Developing			
Brazil	32	8	24
Nigeria	49	17	32
India	34	14	20

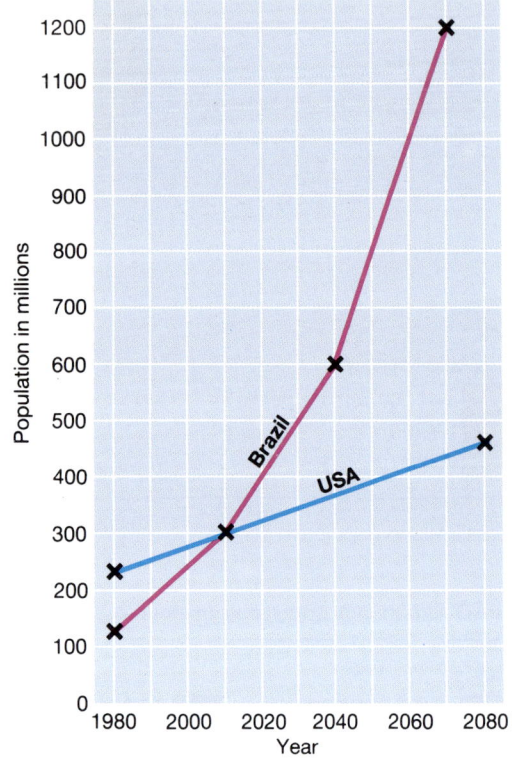

Figure A Population growth for USA and Brazil (if natural increases remain at 1980s levels)

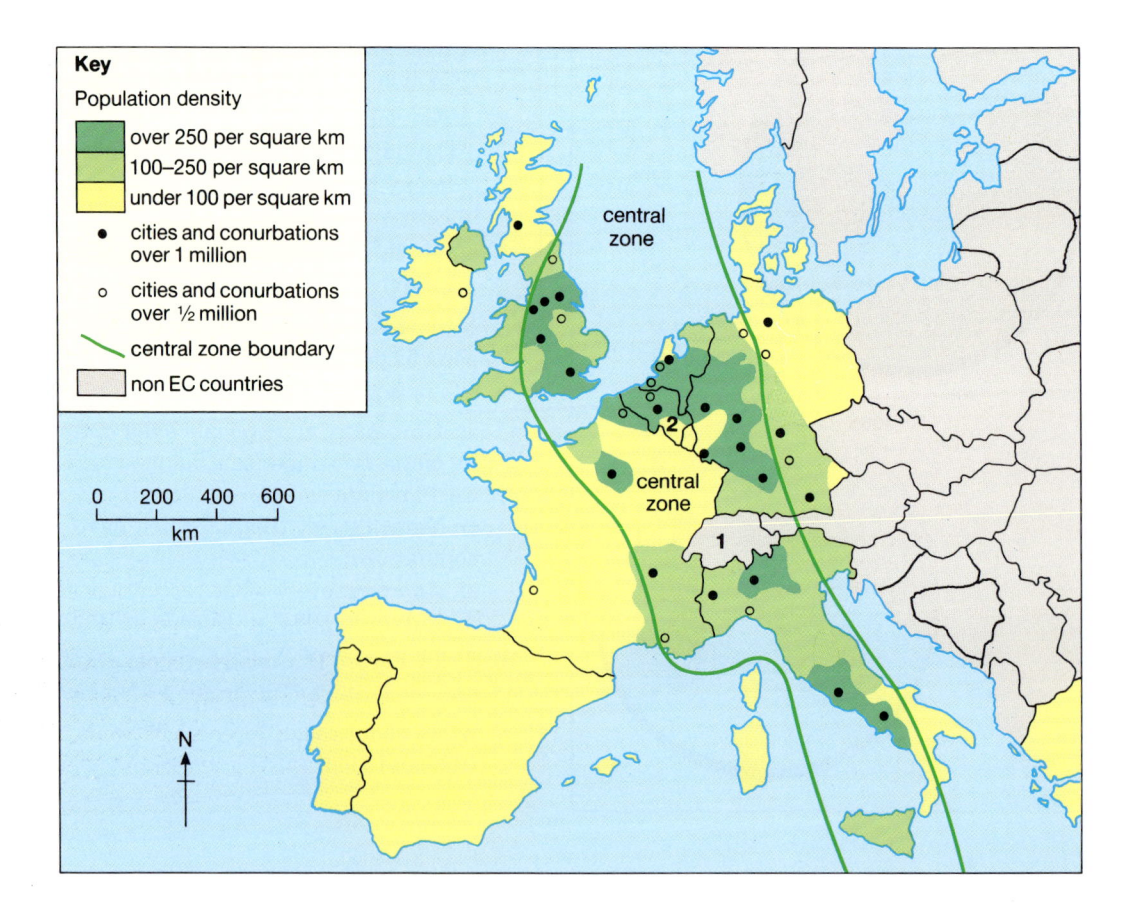

Figure B Population density in the Central Zone of the EC

Figure C Developed world cities: West Berlin (left) and Amsterdam (right)

The EC – where the people live

Seventy-five per cent of the EC population lives in only 50 per cent of the total area of the EC. Europe, like all other continents, has an uneven distribution of population.

In the central zone of the EC there are 22 *million* cities (cities with a population of one million or more). It is predominantly lowland and there is a variety of rocks and soil types. Farming is highly developed and a wide range of crops and fruit is grown. Sheep, beef and dairy farming are very successful. Europe's major coalfields and oil fields are within this central zone.

Some of the world's major industrial regions are in this area of Europe. There are large seaports and international airports. It is a very rich area, people have a high standard of living. It is one of the world's largest industrial and consumer markets. The European capitals are important financial and banking centres. Tourism is another significant sector of their economies.

QUESTIONS

1. a) Place the world population statistics shown below in rank order and use them to draw a bar graph.
   b) Colour the developing world in a strong colour to distinguish it from developed world (light colour). Is there a clear difference between the developing world and the developed world?
   c) How does the rank order of annual population increase compare with the rank order of population under 15 years old?

World population statistics

Continents	Annual % population increase	% population under 15 years old
Africa	2.9	45
North America	0.7	22
Latin America	2.4	39
Asia	1.8	37
Europe	0.3	22
Oceania	1.3	29
USSR	1.0	25

2. a) Copy the graph, Figure A.
   b) Plot the population growth rates of the following countries:
      i) Egypt – 43 million in 1980, doubling every 30 years
      ii) Japan – 118 million in 1980, doubling every 100 years.
   c) Write a summary of what your final graph shows.

Use your atlas to answer the remaining questions.

3. Name one million city from each of the following countries: England, France, Belguim, the Netherlands, West Germany, Italy.

4. i) Name the mountain areas (1 and 2 in Figure B) in the central zone of the EC.
   ii) What is the population density in these areas?
   iii) Why is the population density low in these areas?

5. Why has this part of Europe such a large population? Answer this using the following sub-headings – the Land, Farming, Resources, Industry, the Cities.

Unit 6 ASSESSMENT

The age-sex pyramid

1 State what an age-sex pyramid shows. (2 marks)
2 Study the age-sex pyramid (Figure A) which is for a large city in the developing world. Describe the following characteristics:
   a) the proportion of children under 15 years (2 marks)
   b) the proportion of males between 20 and 40 years (2 marks)
   c) the proportion of old people over 60 years. (2 marks)

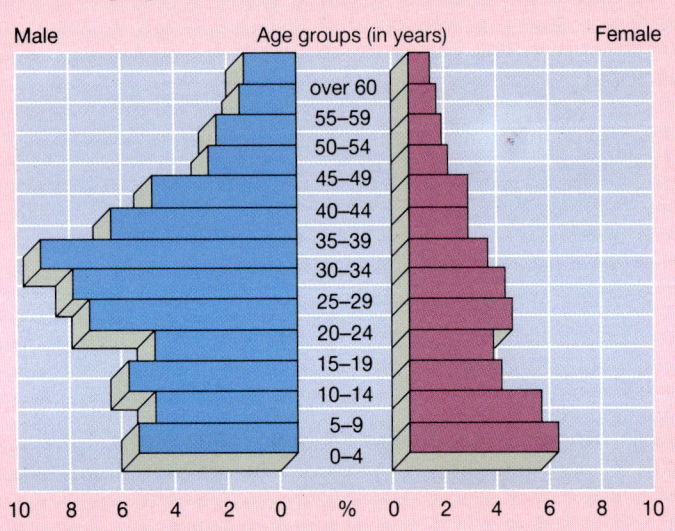

Figure A Large city age-sex distribution

3 a) Why is there a 'bulge' in the pyramid for males between 20 and 40 years? (2 marks)
  b) Why is there such a small percentage of old people? (2 marks)
4 a) What are the main characteristics of the three age-sex pyramids (Figure B)? (6 marks)
  b) For which type of countries or smaller areas would you be likely to find these pyramid shapes? (6 marks)

Total 24 marks

Figure B Three age-sex pyramids

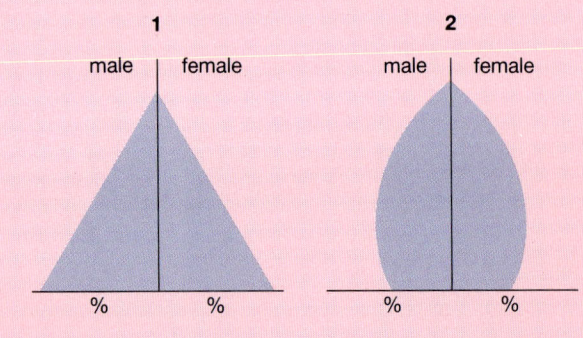

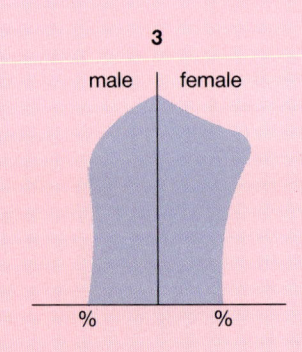

Mapping infant mortality

1 What exactly is infant mortality? (2 marks)
2 On a copy of Figure C shade in the countries that have been left blank. The figures for infant mortality are given. Use the key provided. Some countries have been named for you.

Infant mortality (per 1000 births)	
United Kingdom	0–20
Ireland	0–20
Netherlands	0–20
Denmark	0–20
Norway	0–20
Sweden	0–20
Finland	0–20
USSR	21–30
West Germany	0–20
East Germany	0–20
Portugal	31–50
Spain	0–20
Switzerland	0–20
Austria	0–20
Czechoslovakia	0–20
Hungary	21–30
Yugoslavia	31–50
Bulgaria	21–30
Turkey	100–150
Algeria	100–150
Morocco	100–150

(10 marks)

3 a) Describe the pattern of infant mortality shown on your map (6 marks)
  b) Try to explain the pattern. (6 marks)

Total 24 marks

Figure C Infant mortality rates in Europe

Key
- 0–20
- 21–30
- 31–50
- 51–100
- 101–150

Details for pupil profile sheets Unit 6

Knowledge and understanding

1. Age-sex pyramids
2. Population change – birth rate/death rate
3. In-migration/out-migration
4. Immigration/emigration
5. 'Push' and 'pull' factors
6. Life expectancy
7. Infant mortality
8. Distribution and density
9. Developed/developing world contrasts
10. EC population and cities

Skills

1. Calculating population statistics
2. Reading choropleth (shaded) maps
3. Drawing pie graphs
4. Completing population doubling graphs
5. Interpreting age-sex pyramids
6. Drawing a choropleth map

Values

1. Understanding attitudes that influence migration
2. Realizing that different attitudes affect population characteristics

7.1 Urban/rural population

Unit 7: Contrasts

The world has become more urbanized and a smaller proportion of people now live in the countryside (the rural areas). There are big differences in the way of life between urban and rural people. Only 22 per cent of British people live in rural areas.

In the developing world there are greater differences between rural and urban areas. People do not move from the towns to the countryside. The move is very much one way – from rural to urban areas (see spread 7.5).

Comparing two rural areas

The two photographs Figures A and B show two contrasting rural areas. Figure A is in a highly urbanized country, Canada (76% urban). Figure B is in a very rural country, China (21% urban). Life in these two rural areas is very different.

Figure A Rural Canada

Figure B Rural China

Rural China

- 79 per cent of people live in the rural areas
- The rural people are poorer than the urban people
- Rural areas have less developed roads and infrastructure than the urban areas
- There are many villages which provide all the services for the community

Rural Canada

- Only 24 per cent of people live in the rural areas
- The rural people have a high standard of living like the urban people
- Rural areas have well developed roads and services
- Children often travel to school and college in nearby towns. People use the nearby towns for their provisions.

QUESTIONS

Why do people live in the countryside in Britain?

1. Which type of people fit the following comments?
   a) 'My work is here in the country'
   b) 'We moved to the country when we reached 60 years of age'
   c) 'We moved out of the city to get away from it all'
   d) 'I have always lived in the country and commute to work in the city'

2. In a developed country like Britain some people have the opportunity to move out of the urban areas. Put yourself in the position of the people in b) and c).
   For each write why you decided to move away from the urban area.

3. Do you think that people who commute to a city from the countryside are really rural people? Explain your answer.

Rural Canada/rural China

4. Study the photographs of Canada and China. Compare what you see on the two photographs in two columns. Use the following sub-headings:
   fields
   types of farming
   communications
   types of settlement
   population density

5. How is the rural life of Canada so different from the rural life in China?

7.2 Mapping from the census

Every ten years since 1801 (except 1941) there has been a census. Statistics are collected from every household in Britain. Statistics from the most recent censuses are made available at several scales. On this spread there are statistics for counties and regions.

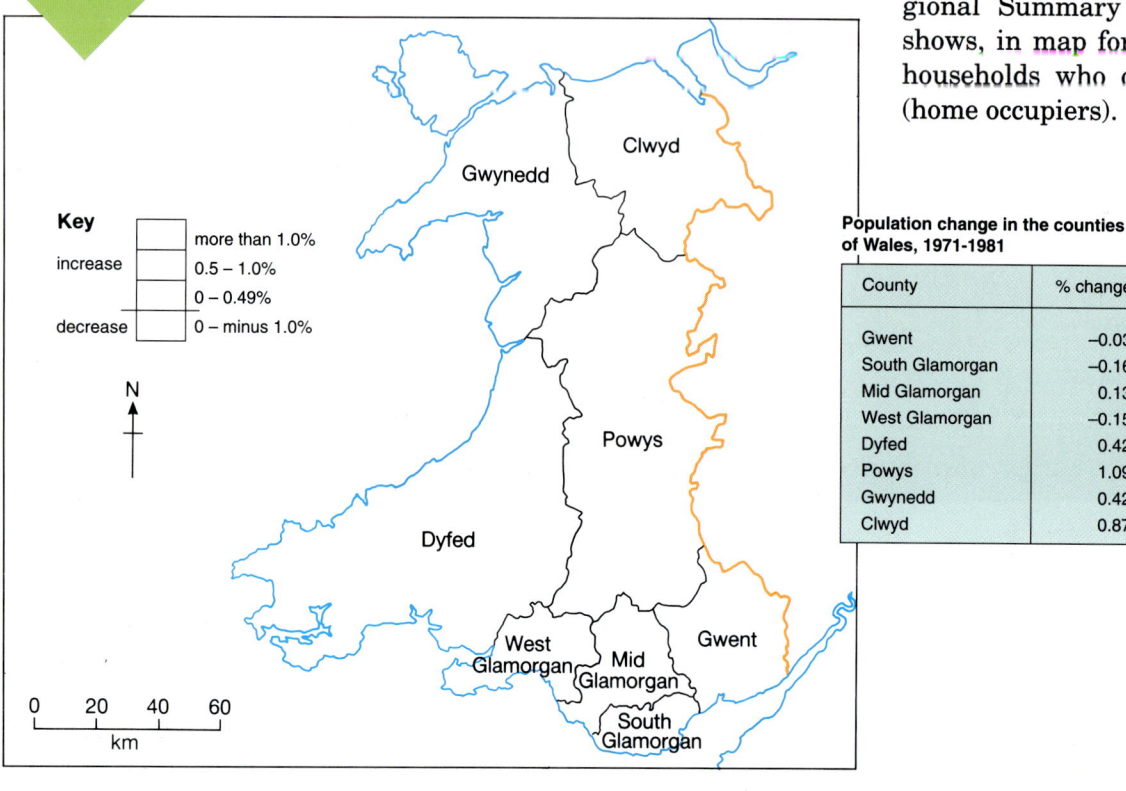

Mapping other census information

Quick comparisons of the whole of Britain can be made by using the census *regional summary* statistics. Figure C is an extract from the National and Regional Summary Table H. Figure D shows, in map form, the percentage of households who own their own home (home occupiers).

Key
- increase: more than 1.0%
- 0.5 – 1.0%
- 0 – 0.49%
- decrease: 0 – minus 1.0%

Population change in the counties of Wales, 1971-1981

County	% change
Gwent	–0.03
South Glamorgan	–0.16
Mid Glamorgan	0.13
West Glamorgan	–0.15
Dyfed	0.42
Powys	1.09
Gwynedd	0.42
Clwyd	0.87

Figure A (*above*) The county divisions of Wales and population change, 1971–1981

Population change 1971-1981

County	% change rural	towns
Gwent	+13	–3
South Glamorgan	+20	–4
Mid Glamorgan	+15	–2.5
West Glamorgan	+8	–3
Dyfed	+9	–2
Powys	+19	+7
Gwynedd	+9	+1
Clwyd	+10	+7

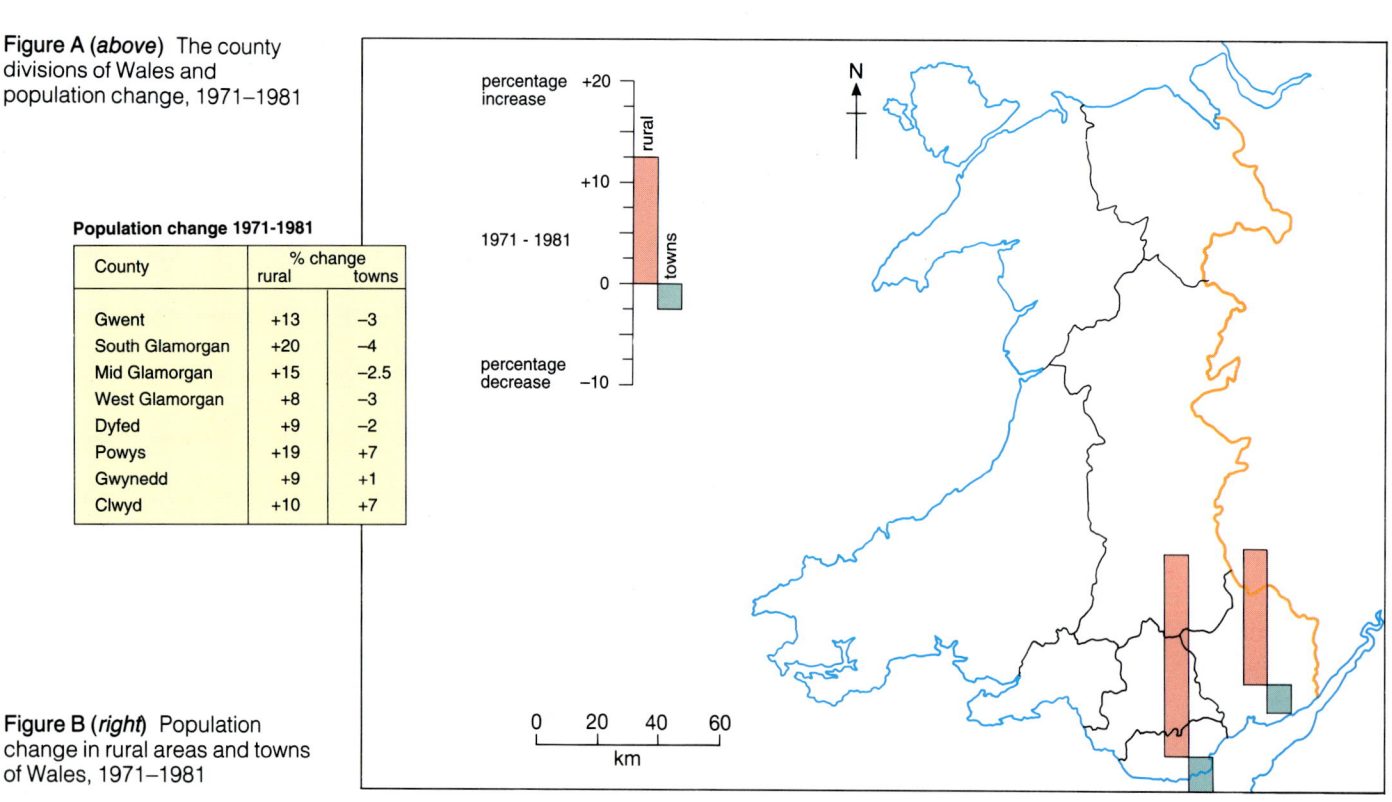

Figure B (*right*) Population change in rural areas and towns of Wales, 1971–1981

Figure C Table H from the Census: National and Regional Summary

Figure D Percentage owner-occupied housing in England and Wales

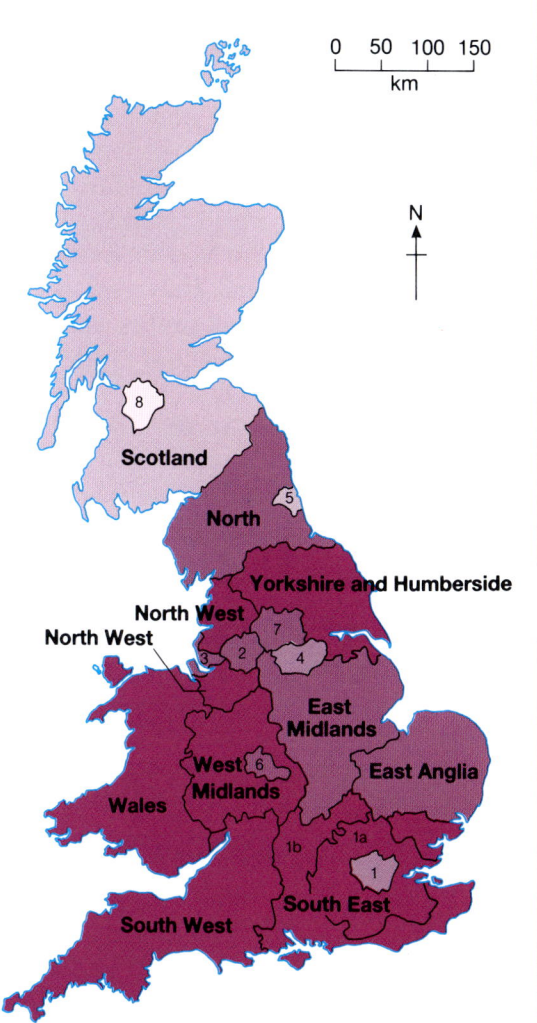

Table H Housing: tenure

Area	Total households	Owner occupied
		Private households with usual residents
GREAT BRITAIN	19,492,428	55.7
England and Wales	17,706,492	57.8
England	16,720,168	57.6
North	1,119,435	47.1
Tyne and Wear Met. County	423,624	38.7
Remainder	695,811	52.2
Yorkshire and Humberside	1,769,051	56.2
South Yorkshire Met. County	475,728	46.9
West Yorkshire Met. County	747,058	59.0
Remainder	546,265	60.3
East Midlands	1,372,401	59.6
East Anglia	678,623	58.4
South East	6,090,943	57.3
Greater London	2,507,656	48.6
Outer Metropolitan Area	1,882,003	63.4
Outer South East	1,701,284	63.4
South West	1,576,897	63.2
West Midlands	1,813,830	57.4
West Midlands Met. County	936,292	53.7
Remainder	877,538	61.2
North West	2,298,988	59.6
Greater Manchester Met. County	944,245	57.0
Merseyside Met. County	528,864	52.0
Remainder	825,879	67.4
Wales	986,324	60.5
Scotland	1,785,936	34.7
Central Clydeside Conurbation	588,904	29.3
Remainder	1,197,032	37.5

Key

1 Greater London
1a Outer Metropolitan Area
1b Outer South East
2 Greater Manchester
3 Merseyside
4 South Yorkshire
5 Tyne and Wear
6 West Midlands
7 West Yorkshire
8 Central Clydeside conurbation

Percentage owner occupied
- over 60
- 51–60
- 41–50
- 31–40
- 30 and under

QUESTIONS

1 Figure A shows the counties of Wales. Trace this map and use black and white shading to map the population change between 1971 and 1981. Complete the key.

2 Read the short account below about population change in Wales. Briefly explain the population change 1971–1981 in the following counties of Wales: i) Gwent ii) Clwyd.

> 'Between 1971 and 1981 population increased in mid-Wales and in the west and north. In the county of Clwyd the high increase in population can be explained by people moving into the county. The north coast is particularly attractive to retired people. South Wales is the only area of population decline. Here there has been industrial decline. Coalmines have closed and heavy industry has made people redundant. People have moved out of the region.'

3 Trace Figure B and complete the map to show how the population of the rural areas and the towns changed from 1971 to 1981. Try to place your graph blocks near the centre of the county.
   a) In which two counties did the rural area grow significantly?
   b) In which counties did towns grow?

4 Study the total household figures (Figure C). The statistics are given by region.
   a) Which is the biggest single region in Britain in terms of total number of households?
   b) What proportion of the total households of Great Britain live in this region?

5 Write a summary of the distribution of owner-occupied households in Britain in 1981 (Figure D).

7.3 Rich world vs poor world: farming

Study the diagram (Figure A) of a farm system. It shows that there are *inputs*, *processes*, and *outputs*. Then look at the two photographs (Figures B and D) which show two contrasting farm systems. Answer questions 1 to 6.

In answering the questions you will have noticed big differences between a rich world farm system and one in the poor world. Other types of farming in the rich and poor worlds would show similar patterns in the level of inputs and outputs.

Answer questions 7 and 8 and then think of the difficulties facing a poor country trying to improve its farming.

How can a poor world farming system increase its inputs? Where is the capital going to come from? How can better seeds be purchased if profits are low? How can improved breeds of animals be introduced?

It becomes easier to see how 70 per cent of the world's people remains poor. You can begin to realize why this 70 per cent of the world's population eats only 40 per cent of the world's food.

We can look at the poor world in terms of a *poverty cycle* similar to the ones shown in spread 5.4, page 82.

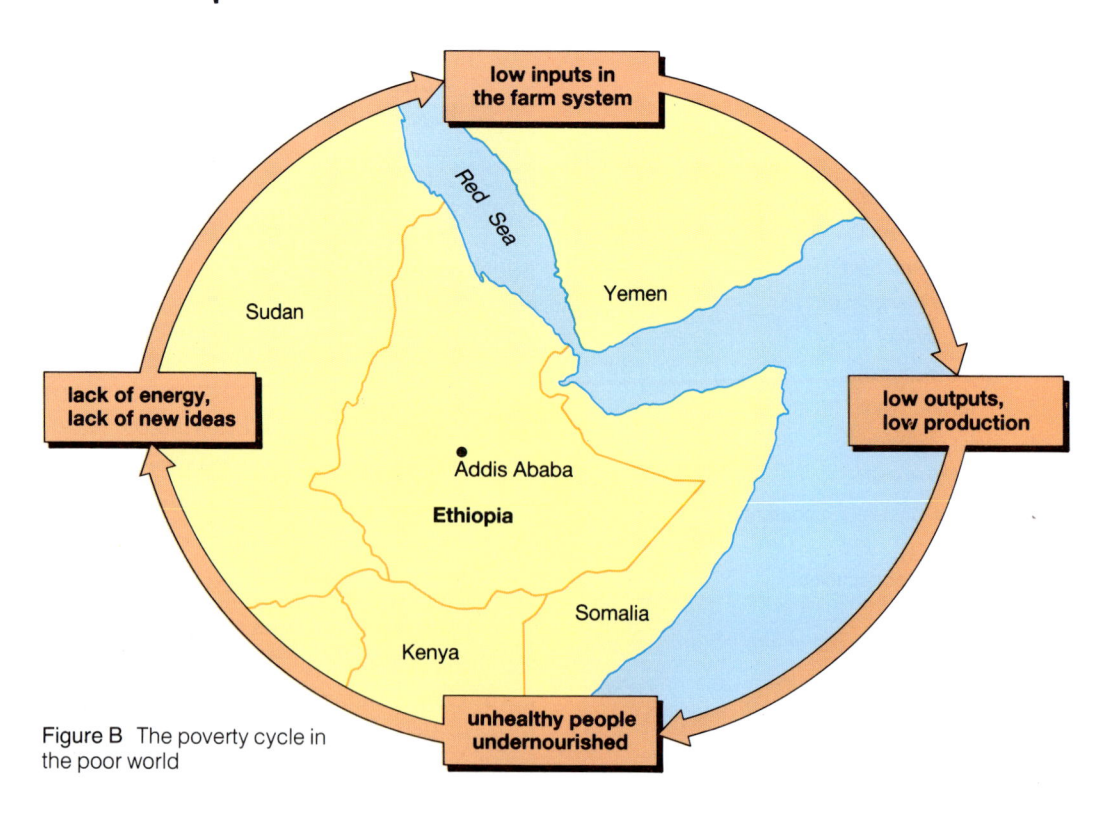

Figure A A farm system

Figure B The poverty cycle in the poor world

104

Figure C Intensive farming in the Netherlands

Figure D A shepherd in a dry area of Syria

QUESTIONS

1. a) For the farming systems shown in Figure C say why you think there are high inputs of labour and capital.
   b) Make a list of the processes (jobs) that would have to be done on the farm during a year.
2. Why should good profits be made on these farms?
3. How might the farmer use the profits to improve the farm?
4. For the system shown in Figure B, copy and complete the input and output diagram below. Use the words listed under the diagram.
5. Why are there small profits made with this farming system?

Rearing sheep

Inputs	Processes	Outputs

meat, poor soils, shearing, shepherd children, dry climate, skins, tending the animals, lambing, wool.

6. Why will small profits not help to improve the farm system?
7. Draw a similar cycle to Figure B for a farm system in the poor world.
8. How do you think farming in the poor world can be improved?
9. How can a poverty cycle be stopped?
10. Draw a *wealth cycle* for a rich world country. Base it on the opposite of the poverty cycle.
11. **Further work** Choose a type of farming that you have studied in a poor world country. Or find an example of one in another book.
    a) Draw a diagram of the farm system to show inputs, processes and outputs.
    b) Suggest ways of improving the inputs for the farm system, then draw a new diagram to show the increased inputs and outputs.

7.4 Measuring standards of living

On average, people in the rich, developed world are better off than people in the poor, developing world. In the United Kingdom the GDP per person is $6514 but in Brazil it is $2232 per person. These are average figures and you must remember that there are very poor people living in the United Kingdom and also very rich people living in Brazil. It is not sufficient to use just one measure or *indicator* when comparing countries. If several indicators of *standard of living* are used then a clearer picture of the differences can be seen.

Standards of living in the UK and Brazil

Indicator	UK	Brazil
Population per doctor	650	1632
Calorie intake per person per day	3210	2574
Percentage pupils at secondary school	100	32
Infant mortality per 1000 births	14	79
Life expectancy in years	74	63

Figure A (*below*) The contrast between house prices in the 'north' (top row) and in the 'south'

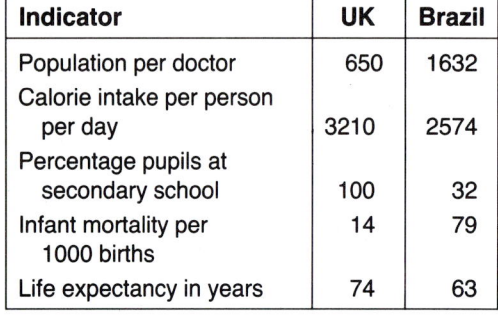

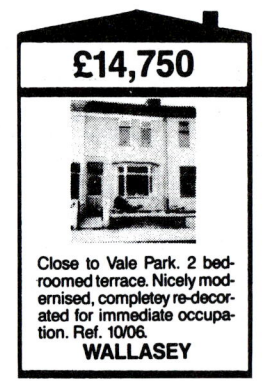

Standards of living in Britain

In the mid 1980s people began to talk about a divided Britain. The differences between the north and the south were becoming more marked. How can we measure differences in the standard of living between the north and the south? We could use the same indicators that compare Brazil with the UK. We could also use the statistics that are collected in the census, see pages 60/61, 62/63 and 102/103.

Figure B Ownership of home-computers (percentages)

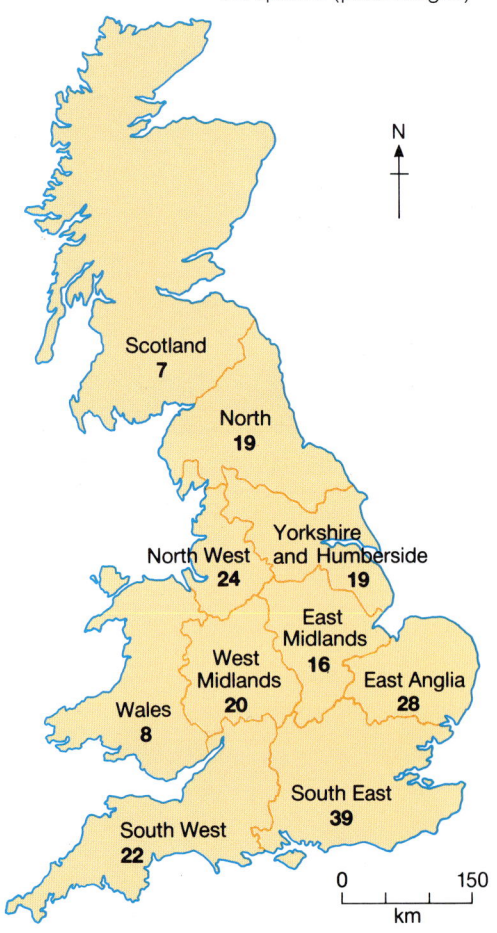

- Scotland 7
- North 19
- North West 24
- Yorkshire and Humberside 19
- West Midlands 20
- East Midlands 16
- East Anglia 28
- Wales 8
- South West 22
- South East 39

£14,750 — Close to Vale Park. 2 bedroomed terrace. Nicely modernised, completey re-decorated for immediate occupation. Ref. 10/06. WALLASEY

£24,950 — Attractive 3 bedroom semi, lounge with living flame gas fire, separate dining room, fitted kitchen, bathroom/shower, electric heating, garage, gardens, convenient all amenities. Ref. 14/03 PRENTON

£25,950 — 3 bedroom semi, lounge, dining room, burgundy bathroom suite/shower. Fitted kitchen, cooker, gas fires, wall heaters, large rear garden. All amenities. Ref 9/01. WALLASEY VILLAGE

LITTLEMORE — End of terrace 2 bedroom House set in a very quiet location siding onto playing fields. Separate garage, early viewing is recommended £79,000 sole agents

EAST OXFORD — A spacious 3 bedroom Victorian terrace Property £79,950 sole agents

TEMPLE COWLEY — A completely renovated 2 bedroom Victorian terrace House with many original features retained £74,950 sole agents

COWLEY — Larger than average 3 bedroom semi detached house which has been the subject of a large extension to the rear and fitted to a very high standard £96,000 sole agents

Unemployment

Unemployment figures are collected in the ten-yearly census. But monthly figures are available from the Department of the Environment.

Figure C Changes in unemployment, June 1979 – June 1986 (percentages)

Scotland −8
North −10
North West −12
Yorkshire and Humberside −6
East Midlands 0
West Midlands −7
East Anglia +13
Wales −13
South West −3
South East +2

One way of understanding the north and south divide better, is to compare two small areas. Sheffield and Luton are both urban areas that have grown up because of manufacturing industry. In Sheffield, now, the traditional steel and cutlery industries have declined. In Luton the motor car and aircraft industries have expanded. The graphs in Figure D show two indicators of the divide that exists between Sheffield and Luton. The gap between Sheffield and Luton has grown during the 1980s.

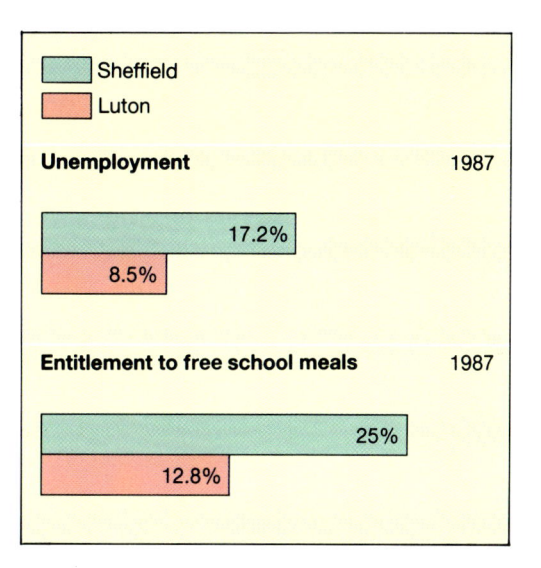

Figure D Unemployment in Sheffield and Luton

Unemployment 1987
- Sheffield: 17.2%
- Luton: 8.5%

Entitlement to free school meals 1987
- Sheffield: 25%
- Luton: 12.8%

QUESTIONS

1 On a copy of the map, Figure C, shade the regions which lost employment between June 1979 and June 1986 (all the minus figures).

2 Can you see a clear division between the north and the south of Britain?

3 Draw similar graphs (to Figure D) for Sheffield and Luton using the following statistics for 1984.

Unemployment in Sheffield and Luton

Indicators	Sheffield	Luton
Unemployed	14.5%	9%
Children entitled to free school meals	19%	12%

4 a) How big was the 'unemployment gap' between Sheffield and Luton in i) 1984 and ii) 1987? (Use your graph and Figure C.)
b) How would you describe the increase in the 'unemployment gap' between Sheffield and Luton? Has it doubled, has it increased by more than 50 per cent, has it increased by less than 50 per cent?

5 Study Figure B which shows the ownership of home computers in Britain in 1986.
a) How clear is the north/south divide in computer ownership?
b) What are the exceptions to the north/south divide?

6 Suggest some other possible indicators that could be used to measure differences in the standard of living between the north and south of Britain.

7 **Further work** a) Write down all the possible ways of measuring standards of living.
b) If you had to compare standards of living between the rich world and the poor world which five indicators would you choose to use from your list?
c) State why you chose your top five indicators.
d) Choose two countries that you have studied – one poor and one rich. Find out the statistics for your five indicators for both countries.

7.5 People moving: migration

In spread 5.3 you read the story of Pedro and Maria who had left their village and moved to the city of Rio de Janeiro. Why did they want to move? Why did they choose to move to a city? Their reasons were similar to millions of others who make the trek to the city. They were looking for a better way of life with a higher standard of living.

Every day between 70 000 and 80 000 people move to a town or city. Cities are like magnets, they attract people; they 'pull' people towards them. Figure A lists some of the 'pull' factors. It also shows some of the reasons why people leave the rural villages. These 'push' factors are present because rural areas are not as attractive as cities.

The mobile youth

Pedro and Maria were young when they left for Rio. They were like the majority of *migrants* who move to the cities. They had a longing for something better than their villages. They were attracted by the lights and glamour of city life, the city shops, the famous sports team and the faster life of Rio. They had energy, determination and a sense of adventure.

If it is the young who leave the rural areas, what happens to life in the village after they have left? What is a village like that has lost its young people?

The 'push' of the rural areas → **The 'pull' of the city**

The 'push' of the rural areas	The 'pull' of the city
few job opportunities	wide range of jobs
modern machinery means fewer workers needed on farms	new jobs in industry and services
low standard of living	more money, greater purchasing power
poor transport	good urban transport systems
lack of safe running water	more chance of a good water supply and drainage
poor health care	better health services
few good schools	wide range of education

Figure A The trek to the city

FELIX

Felix is 45 years old. He is married with six grown up children. He has lived in the village all his life. He works on a sugar cane farm but is very poor. Although he can not read or write he is a contented man. He always works hard and in the evenings he likes to sit outside the village bars. He has never thought of leaving the village.

Figure B The lives and prospects of four villagers

ISOBEL

Isobel is 30 years old. She is married with three children. She moved to the village from a small farm when she was 16 years old. She works in a village shop and sometimes behind a bar. With her husband's money from truck driving her family is quite well off. She thought of leaving the village a few years ago but is now settled.

MANUEL

Manuel is 19 years old. He is not married but he has a girl friend. He has part-time employment at sugar harvesting time. He has bought a Japanese moped with some money his uncle left him. He is bored in the village and would like to go to the city. He wants to enjoy modern life and there is not much of it in the village.

CHRISTINA

Christina is 20 years old. She is married but has no children. She and her husband want to earn some money before they have a family. She has worked in a new factory in the nearby market town but lost her job when new machines were introduced. She would like to work in a city shop or an office. At school she did well and continued her education until she was 14 years old.

Questions
Group role play

1 Choose one of the four village people illustrated on this spread and read through their character summary.

2 For your chosen village character write down or think through why you do or do not want to move to the city.

3 In small groups of four, listen to each other's views about leaving the village for the city.

4 Try to come to a decision about whether two of the people should leave the village. Give a summary of the reasons leading up to your decision.

5 **Further work** These pages have looked at migration from village to city in the developing world. Draw out a similar presentation to Figure A to show why people are moving away from cities in the developed world.

   Remember inner-city areas have many problems and are losing population. In this case the countryside is 'pulling' them: the city is 'pushing' them.

7.6 International migration

The Austin family left Slough in the 1970s and moved to California. Why did they move home? We can see some *push* and *pull* reasons for their move in the letter below, written from California in 1978.

The Austin family *emigrated* to California. The Americans call them *immigrants*.

> 10572, Trenton Avenue,
> Los Angeles,
> Calif 90060.
> USA
>
> 10/26/1978
>
> Dear Peter,
>
> Thank you for your letter asking how we are getting on. It certainly would be good to see you sometime out here. We are now at the end of our first long, hot summer. The weather is so reliable you can go to the beach and know it will be warm and sunny.
>
> Finding work was no problem at all for myself. My wife is well paid in a factory job with good working conditions. The schools for the children are very well equipped and have superb sports facilities. John will be leaving for College in two years and the one he is interested in sounds very exciting.
>
> Of course we miss Slough but as you know the coal business was not doing very well. Neither of us could earn as much as we wanted. Also my asthma problems were not going to improve in England. Here the drier atmosphere has helped a lot. We liked Slough and all our friends but it lacks the excitement of LA. Last week

Figure A (*above*) News from the Austins

Immigration into the USA

Where did the Americans come from? Originally the country was occupied by many different Indian tribes. Even the Indian people had moved into the continent from Asia thousands of years ago. The first Europeans arrived in the 1500s. Later they brought African people as *slaves* to work on their plantations. This movement of black Africans was *forced emigration*. Between 1880 and 1914 forty million Europeans emigrated to the USA. These included Irish, British, German, Scandinavians, and later, Italians, Spanish and Greeks.

In recent years many Mexicans have emigrated to the USA. Sometimes Mexicans arrive in the USA without official papers, crossing the border in remote places. They are called *illegal immigrants* and when caught are usually sent back. Since the Vietnam War some Vietnamese have moved to the USA. In the USA today there is a mix of different people with their own religions, languages and culture.

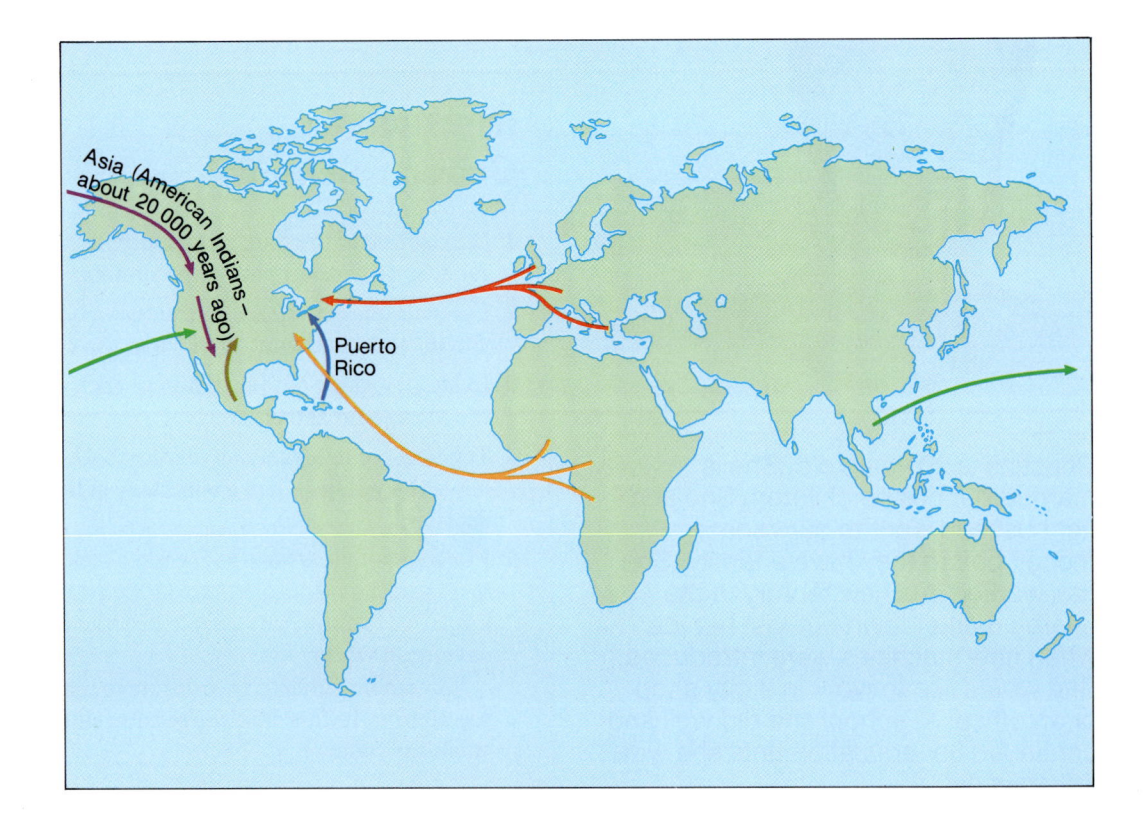

Figure B (*right*) The origins of North Americans

Culture clash

As we saw in Spread 4.2 immigrants face many problems when they move into a foreign country. In Britain, West Indian and Asian immigrants have suffered *racial disadvantage* and prejudice. It will always take a long time for people of different backgrounds and culture to live in harmony together. In the East End of London Jewish people were harassed in the 1930s. In the 1980s the Asian communities suffered from racial harassment (Figure C). Churches, synagogues, mosques and temples are close together in parts of East London. People with different cultures generally keep together, then they have security.

When Vietnamese fishermen moved to West Florida on the Gulf coast of the USA they quickly became successful fishermen. But many of their fishing methods upset the local American fishermen. The Vietnamese did not handle their boats like the Americans, they did not follow the established rules of right of way. They could not communicate with the Americans. Unfortunately they were seen by the Americans as a threat to their livelihood. They were seen to be overfishing the declining fish stocks. It was a case of culture clash. The immigrants were not immediately acceptable to the Americans.

Figure C Racist graffiti in Hackney, London

Figure D 'Little Saigon' in Los Angeles, USA

QUESTIONS

1. Divide your page into two columns. Label one column PULL factors and the other PUSH factors. List the reasons given in the letter why the Austin family emigrated to California.
2. John (the son) was 15 when the family emigrated.
   a) Write down some of the good points about his new life.
   b) Now note down some of the difficulties that faced John as an immigrant in a foreign country.
3. John now has two children. Are John's children immigrants?
4. On a copy of the world map (Figure B) label the arrows to show where the immigrants to the USA have come from. Two are already labelled to help you.
5. What is meant by forced emigration?
6. What is an illegal immigrant?
7. Why do you think the USA has often limited immigration into the country?

Further work A group of Africans from the drought region of the Sahel (Ethiopia and the Sudan) have moved into a small market town in Britain. They have been saved from death by famine and starvation. A new life awaits them.

At first the local community welcomes them and provides for them. As the months pass the Africans begin to learn English and settle into the British way of life. The initial welcome wears off and both the African and the British communities realize there is a culture clash.

Write about the difficulties faced by the Africans and their children as they start to settle down in the town. Your account should only be from the Africans' point of view. It should be less than 200 words long.

7.7 Fewer people: population planning

Family size

One hundred years ago British families were much larger than they are today. As Britain has industrialized and developed, family size has decreased. Women have been able to find work more easily, children are not the priority they used to be. British families plan to have fewer children and they use a wide range of *birth control (contraception)* methods. This situation is similar in the other developed countries.

In the developing continents, family size is bigger. Families plan to have more children even though birth control is far more available than it used to be.

Figure A An extended family in Southern Africa

Larger families
- more children to work and earn money
- more help around the home and in the fields
- children are able to look after the sick and old
- greater security and more activity in the family
- there will be a surviving son to pass the family farm on to

The *fertility rate* refers to the average number of children born to a woman in her lifetime. The European fertility rate is now only 1.8 children per woman. In Africa it is 6.4 children per woman.

Survival

Having more children means more will survive. Infant mortality rates are still high in developing countries but they are falling. As more children survive, couples will have less children. Contraceptive methods become more popular and accepted. The more developed a country becomes the less children are needed.

Small families
- fewer children means fewer mouths to feed
- fewer children means less work around the home – mother can go out to work
- children are not needed to look after the parents in old age – there are old people's homes and hospitals
- customs are different – handing on a farm or business is not essential
- security and activity is found outside the family

Population control

Some countries have tried to control their population increase. In India a programme of male sterilization (vasectomy) was followed. But it was difficult to encourage men to have this small operation. Now there is greater emphasis on education and the building of health centres. People will have fewer children voluntarily when they know that survival rates can be improved. Contraceptives are more readily available and people are learning more about them. The marriage age has been raised from 15 to 18 for women and from 18 to 21 for men. Later marriages mean less children in a lifetime.

One way of educating people that smaller families are an advantage is to advertise. Figure B is an example from India.

Figure B An Indian advertisement, in Hindi, which reads 'We are proud of our two children'

Figure C A one-child Chinese family

Family planning – the Peking way

In China there is a tax on people with more than two children. One child per family is encouraged and rewarded by:
- a certificate for the parents
- priority in school, medical care, and employment for the child
- a salary bonus for the parents
- better housing

This method of family planning seems to take away freedom of choice, but it is working.

QUESTIONS

1. Why is the average family larger in a developing country than in Europe?
2. a) What is the fertility rate?
   b) What will cause the fertility rate to fall in a developing country?
3. What are the advantages of having small families?
4. Why are the Indian sterilization programmes not totally successful?
5. What ways are now being used in India to slow the population increase?
6. How are the Chinese trying to reduce the population increase?
7. a) What are your views on the Chinese methods of family planning?
   b) Can you think of problems that may occur because of these population control policies?

7.8 Population patterns – employment

The *triangular graph*, Figure A, is probably a new type of graph for you. You read the three axes along the arrows as shown for Brazil. The countries furthest apart on the graph have the greatest differences. Compare Tanzania with the United Kingdom. In Tanzania 80 per cent of people are employed in primary industry, (farming, fishing and mining). In the UK, only 5 per cent are employed in this primary sector.

Figure A (*below*) A triangular graph

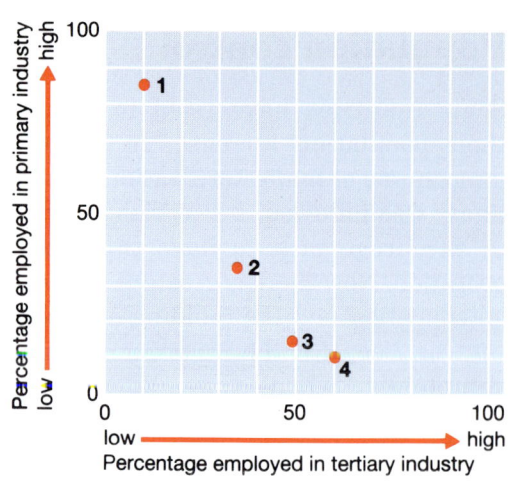

Figure B Employment in industry

Linking wealth and employment

You have compared the UK and Tanzania. One is a rich industrial and urban country, the other is a poor agricultural and rural country. If we plot the wealth per person (GDP) against the percentage of the population employed in primary industry we can see that the two statistics are closely linked (Figure C). *Gross Domestic Product* or GDP is the total amount of goods and services produced in a country.

Countries with a high GDP have a low percentage in primary industry. Countries with a low GDP have a high percentage in primary industry.

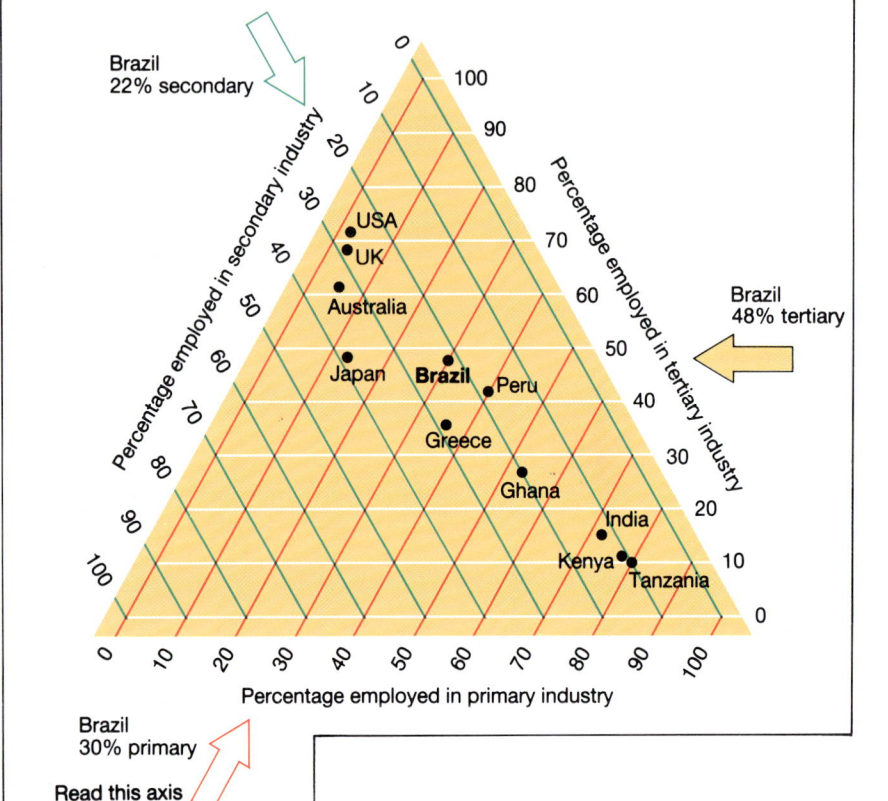

Primary industry:
farming, forestry, fishing, mining, quarrying

Secondary industry:
manufacturing (factory industry)

Tertiary industry:
services, communications, administration, professional

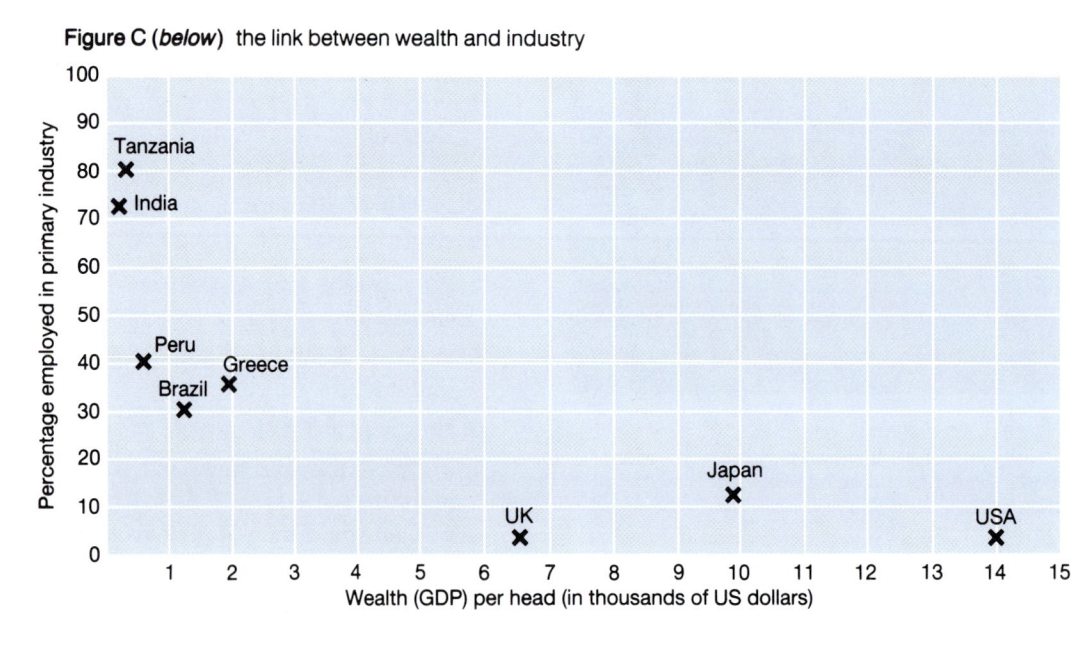

Figure C (*below*) the link between wealth and industry

Patterns of Unemployment in the UK

Unemployment varies in different parts of Britain. There is a higher level of unemployment in northern Britain than in London and the south of England. This is a result of the older industries in the north declining and not being replaced by newer industries. Patterns of unemployment also vary by ethnic groups and by age (see Figure D).

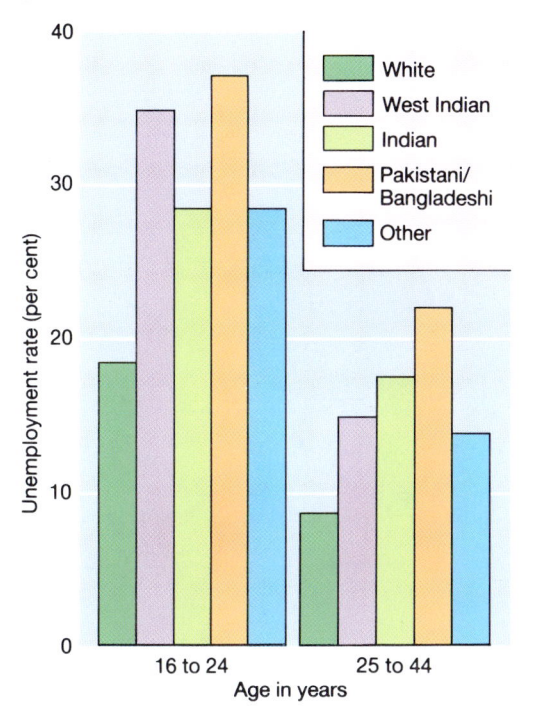

Figure D Patterns of unemployment by ethnic group and age of males

Figure E A London dole queue

QUESTIONS

1. Read the following information off the graph (Figure A):
   a) the percentage employed in primary industry in
      i) Brazil
      ii) Tanzania
      iii) United Kingdom
   b) the percentage employed in secondary industry in Japan
   c) the total employment situation in Tanzania

2. Give one example of a country for the circles marked 1, 2, 3 and 4 in Figure B.

3. Link up the following statements in each case with either Tanzania or the United Kingdom
      i) high primary employment, low primary employment
      ii) high percentage urban population, low percentage urban population (refer back to pages 100/101)
      iii) developed country, developing country

4. Why do you think that there is such a close link between GDP and the percentage employed in primary industry?

5. Do you think that there is a close link between life expectancy and percentage employed in primary industry?

6. Plot the life expectancy figures below against the percentage employed in primary industry (from Figure C).

   Life expectancy

Country	Life expectancy	Country	Life expectancy
Tanzania	51 years	UK	74 years
India	52	Greece	74
USA	74	Brazil	63
Peru	59	Japan	77

   a) Is there a close link between the two sets of statistics?
   b) Write an explanation of your results.

7. Look at Figures D and E.
   a) What is the approximate unemployment rate for:
   i) whites 16 to 24 years
   ii) whites 25 to 44?
   b) What is the approximate unemployment rate for:
   i) West Indians 16 to 24
   ii) West Indians 25 to 44?
   c) Which ethnic groups have the highest unemployment rate in both age groups?
   d) How do unemployment rates compare for all males between the two age groups?
   e) Can you suggest reasons for the varying unemployment rates between whites and ethnic groups? (Refer back to the sections on racism, pages 58/59.)

7.9 Population patterns: conflicts

Living in the developed world we have avoided a major war since 1945. But wars (the active engagement of a regular army in fighting) are on the increase.

Post Second World War conflicts

Decade	Wars per year
1950s	9
1960s	11
1970s	14

Where are today's wars? Figure A shows the current war zones. You can add the latest war areas to a map of your own. The shadings on the map show the number of war deaths since 1945. Over 16 million people have been killed in wars since 1945! Many of the countries that have had a recent war are now ruled by military governments.

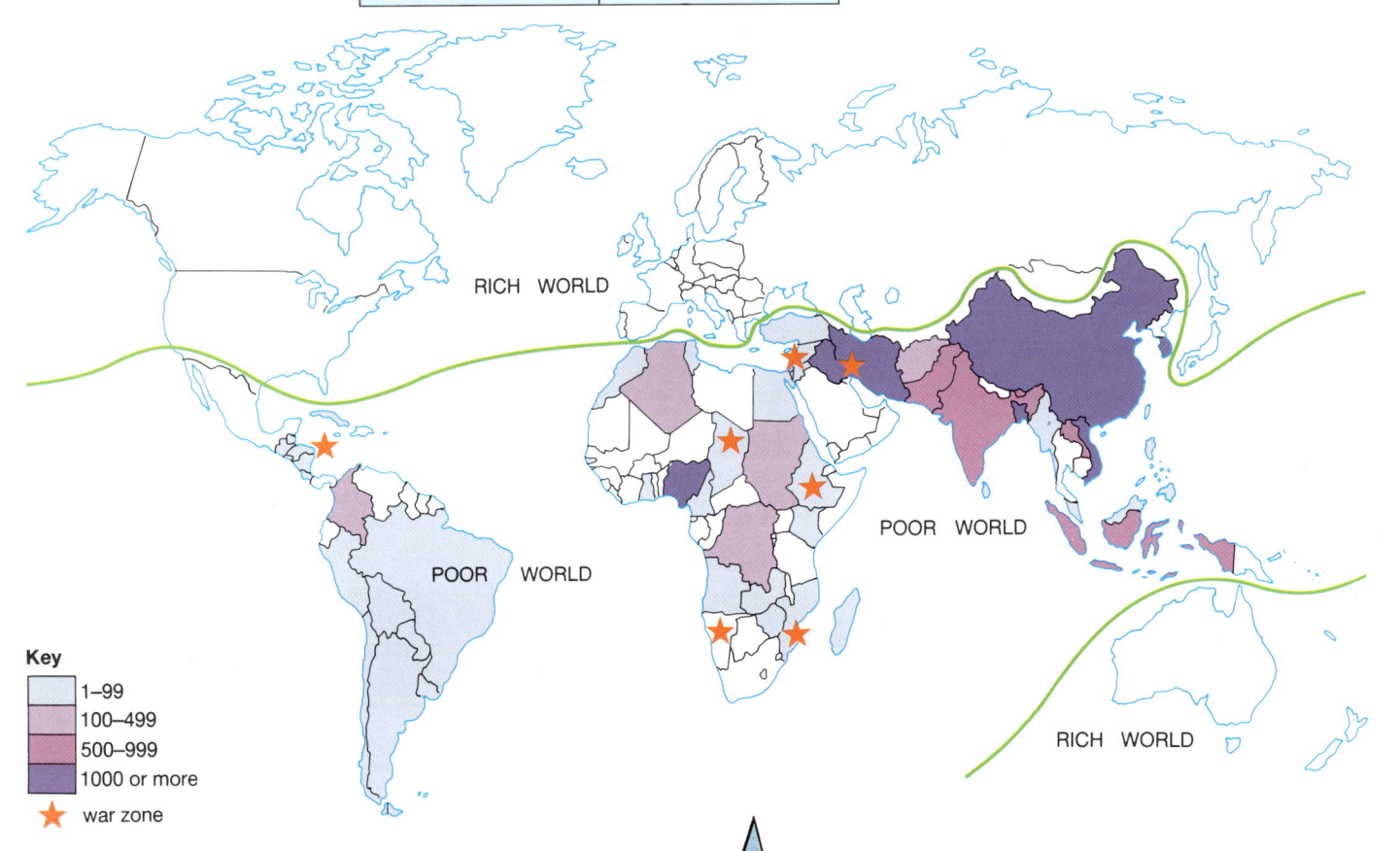

Key
- 1–99
- 100–499
- 500–999
- 1000 or more
- ★ war zone

Figure A (*above*) War zones and number of war deaths (in thousands) since 1945

The cost of conflict

Seventy per cent of the world's weapons come from the rich countries. But most of the world's conflicts are in the poor countries. The developed world is profiting from the developing world's conflicts. Could not the money spent on weapons be better spent on improving the standards of living in the poor countries?

Figure B (*left*) In developing countries three times more is spent on military equipment than on health care, clean water and sanitation

Refugees

Ten million people have left their own countries because of *threats* to their lives. They have been *persecuted* because of their race, religion, or political beliefs. In the case of the recent Ethiopian famine people left their country simply to flee famine and starvation. Figure C shows a *refugee* camp in Thailand. 300,000 refugees have fled to Thailand from the war-torn countries of Laos, Kampuchea and Vietnam.

Figure C A refugee camp in Thailand

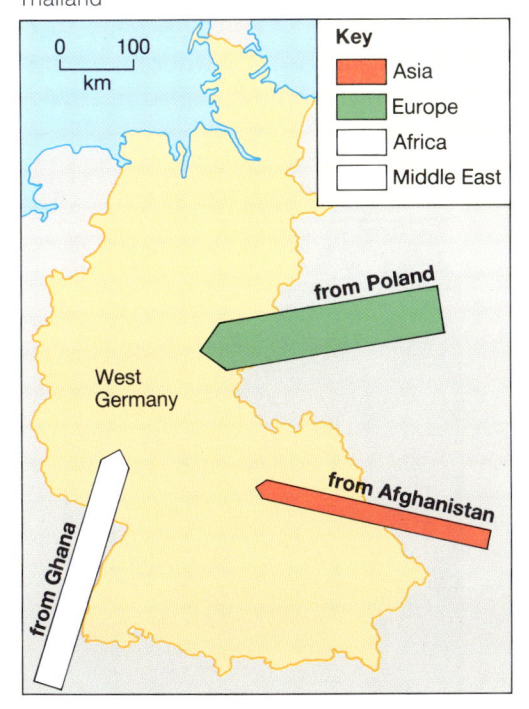

Figure D Origins of refugees in West Germany

QUESTIONS

1. Study Figure A.
   a) Make a list of the war zones in the world, add any other ones that you know of.
   b) Which countries have lost the most people in wars since 1945?
   c) How is the world divided in terms of war zones and war deaths?
   d) Can you suggest reasons for the pattern of conflict in the world since 1945?

2. Study Figure B. Divide your page into two columns. In the left column write down six types of military spending. In the right column write down six types of spending that the developing countries need to increase.

3. What is your opinion on military spending in the poor world today? Is it necessary?

4. What is a refugee?

5. Describe the refugee camp (Figure C).

6. Have you heard of any refugee problems recently? If so write down where the refugees have gone to. Why have these people had to move?

7. **Further work** In 1985, 70 000 people applied for *asylum* in West Germany. The table shows where the main groups came from.

Origins of refugees

Country of origin	Number of refugees
Europe	
Czechoslovakia	1 400
Poland	6 500
Africa	
Ethiopia	2 500
Ghana	4 000
Asia	
Afghanistan	2 500
India	4 500
Sri Lanka	17 000
Middle East	
Iran	9 000
Lebanon	4 500
Turkey (Kurds)	7 500

a) Make a copy of the map of West Germany (Figure D).
b) Show the flow of refugees to the country in 1985 by *flow lines*. The thickness of the lines indicates the number of refugees.
Afghanistan   2 500 = 2.5 mm
Poland   6 500 = 6.5 mm
Ghana   4 000 = 4mm
c) Make sure your map has a scale explaining the flow lines. It should also have a colour key eg. Asia – red, Europe – green, Africa – blue. (Use different colours for each of the continents.)

7.10 Population inequalities: South Africa

Some of the greatest population inequalities in the world today exist in South Africa. Since 1948 the country has been built on a system of *racial segregation* called *'apartheid'*. The land and the people are divided.

Figure A shows the divided land. Eighty seven per cent is owned by the minority white population. Thirteen per cent has been divided into *'homelands'* or *'bantustans'*. Some of these homelands contain the least fertile land with few natural resources.

Apartheid's 'principles'

There are seven basic ideas behind apartheid in South Africa:

- **Group Areas Act** People can only live in areas allotted to their own racial category.
- **African Homelands** All Africans are allotted a tribal homeland, which the Government then considers to be their only real home – even if they have never visited it. They are then only in 'white South Africa' to work.
- **Separate voters' roles** Black people vote only for people of their own racial category, for authorities which only have very limited powers. Africans still have no vote at all in national elections.
- **Separate education** Children go to schools designated for their own racial grouping.
- **Separate amenities** Public transport, places of entertainment etc. segregated. This is now not universally applied and depends upon decisions made by local authorities.
- **Mixed Marriages Act** Forbade marriage between people from different racial groups until it was repealed in 1985.
- **Immortality Act** Forbade sex between people from different racial groups until it was repealed in 1985.

Figure A (*below*) The ten 'homelands' of South Africa

Key
- Bophuthatswana (Tswana)
- KwaNdebele (Ndebele)
- Gazankulu (Tsonga, Shangana)
- KaNgwane (Swazi)
- Lebowa (North Sotho)
- Qwaqwa (South Sotho)
- KwaZulu (Zulu)
- Transkei (Xhosa)
- Ciskei (Xhosa)
- Venda (Venda)

Evidence of inequality in South Africa

Indicators	Blacks	Whites
Occupations (% employed)		
management	2	95
mining	91	8
service	68	19
Average monthly income (rand)	273	1 834
Health (numbers in one year)		
cholera	6 557	9
tuberculosis	42 470	660
Infant mortality (per 1000 births)	80	13

Figure B An Oxfam anti-apartheid poster

The Poverty of APARTHEID

— OXFAM'S CONCERN —

Breakdown of South African population (figures rounded up)

Racial category	Population (millions)	Percentage of total population
African – black people belonging to African tribes	24	74
Coloured – 'mixed race' people	3	9
Indian – people who originated from the Indian sub-continent	1	3
White – white people of mainly European origin (Dutch, British particularly)	5	15

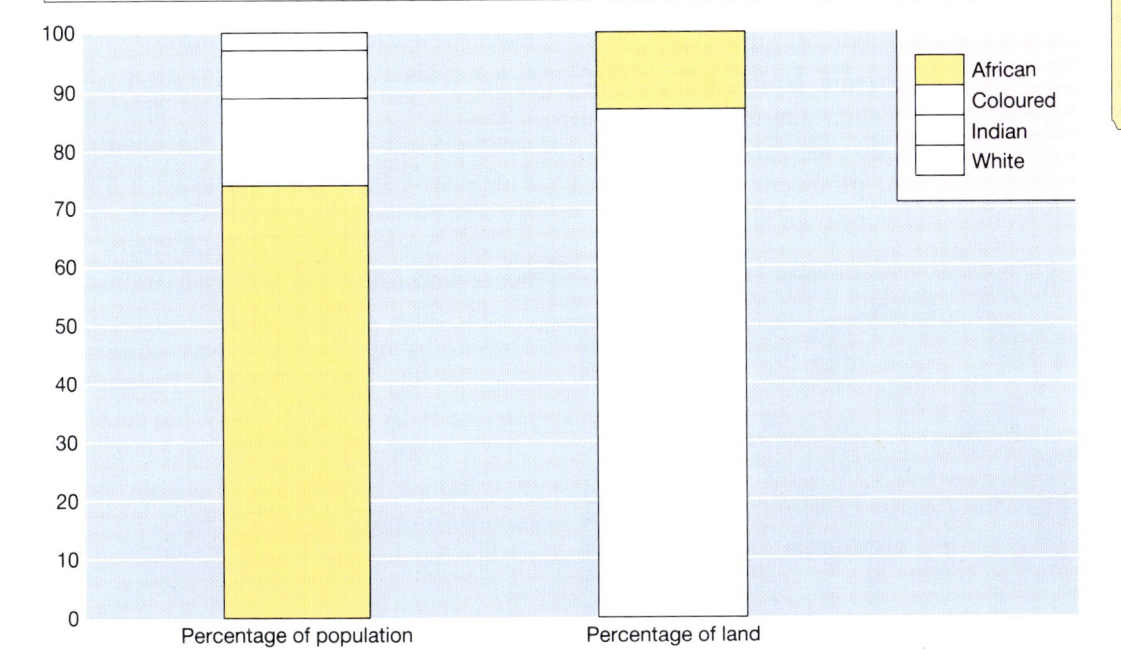

Figure C The table and graph show population and land divisions in South Africa (see question 1)

UPDATE...UPDATE...UPDATE

Changes have taken place in South Africa in the past few years. The apartheid system is gradually being discarded. South Africa has been accepted back into world sports competitions. But there is still a long way to go before there is equality for all South Africa's peoples.

August 1992

Legend: African, Coloured, Indian, White

Percentage of population | Percentage of land

Figure D Downtown Johannesburg

QUESTIONS

1. Study the statistics in Figure C. Copy out and complete the two graphs below the table to show the unequal divisions of land and people. Use the same colours on each graph.
2. Where did the white people in South Africa originate from?
3. What is a 'coloured person'?
4. Write in your own words what apartheid means.
5. Are blacks allowed to vote?
6. Write about the differences between the occupations of Africans and whites.
7. What is your opinion about the differences in wages earned by Africans and whites?
8. Choose two of more sets of statistics about inequality. Design a poster to illustrate the inequalities.
9. **Further work** Follow something about South Africa in the News. Look for the reasons behind the issues.

7.11 Towards a single world: sport and culture

In 1896 the Olympic Games were revived at Athens. Every four years athletes and sportspeople from all over the world meet to compete. The venues change:

    1968 – Mexico City
    1972 – Munich
    1976 – Montreal
    1980 – Moscow
    1984 – Los Angeles
    1988 – Seoul
    1992 – Barcelona

The events can be watched live on television by hundreds of millions of people in many countries. Satellites are used to make the television links. Videos are used to see the events again. The world seems to have shrunk. An event on the other side of the globe can be viewed in the comfort of your own front room.

Towards uniformity

Five hundred years ago, before the European powers had started colonizing, the world was divided into distinct religious areas. Racial types were still separated: no white or black people lived in the Americas. Black people in Europe were very uncommon although there is evidence from paintings and literature that some had moved to Europe.

At the end of the twentieth century there is much more uniformity. Different religions, cultures and people exist side by side. An Islamic Egyptian family can buy *Coca Cola* from their local shop. They can watch American soap operas on television. They listen to European pop music and can buy a Japanese car or moped like any European family.

The move towards uniformity has been dominated by the rich industrial world. The largest multi-national oil companies operate in many countries. You can buy ESSO petrol in Turkey and pay for it by VISA card. Wherever you buy a record it is likely to have been distributed by one of the five major record companies (Figure B).

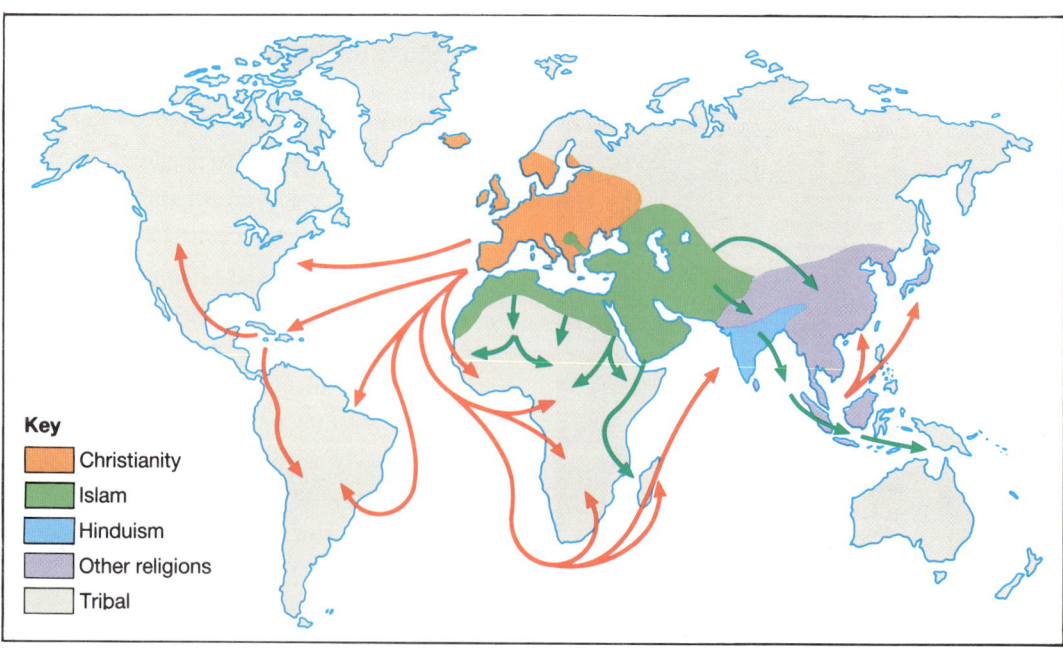

Figure A World religions 500 years ago and their spread

Key
- Christianity
- Islam
- Hinduism
- Other religions
- Tribal

Pop and rock

Over 60 per cent of records sold in the world are pop and rock. Again it is the rich world countries that dominate the music business. British pop groups earn money for videos which are used to advertise goods on Japanese television. In Japan, young people adopt British pop culture and dress like young Brits! (Figure C). The same Japanese kids will also be eating in the downtown Tokyo McDonalds.

It took a longer period of time for pop culture to reach South America. When the pop group *Queen* visited Argentina and Brazil in 1981 it was a breakthrough into a new area. 'We were really nervous . . . I don't think they had ever seen such an ambitious show', said Freddie Mercury. Half a million people came to see them in their first eight South American concerts!

The Live Aid concert on 13 July 1985 had the largest television audience the world has ever known. The rich and the poor throughout the world were aware of the Ethiopian famine. Bob Geldof had been to Ethiopia, he had seen a refugee camp for 27 000 people that had only fifteen bags of flour left. But he was not thinking about Africa as he sang at the concert. He said, 'today was about a single world'.

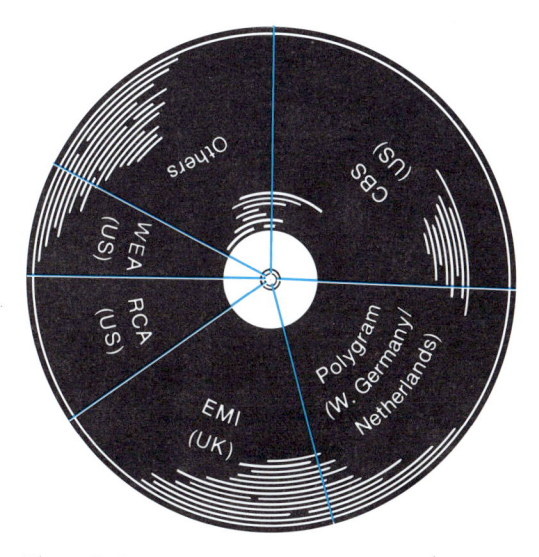

Figure C (*above*) Japanese punks

Figure D (*below*) The Band Aid concert

Figure B The world record industry, dominated by the rich world

QUESTIONS

1. a) List at least three world events that have happened recently in the area of sport and culture.
   b) How do you know about these events?
2. In this spread, television, sport and pop culture were given as examples of the world shrinking. What other examples can you think of that make the world seem smaller?
3. Why do you think sport and culture can bring different people closer together?
4. a) In what ways do you think we are moving towards a single world?
   b) In what ways do you think the world is becoming more divided and more separated?

Unit 7 ASSESSMENT

Rich world vs Poor world

For this assessment you have to compare the characteristics of two countries.

Country A is a typical rich European country.
Country B is a typical poor African country.

Compare the two countries in two columns. You can give typical figures for the characteristics or use single words or phrases. A few details are provided but you must provide 25 answers.

Indicators	Country A	Country B
Population 1980	50 million	20 million
Birth rate	19 per 1000	?
Death rate	?	?
Natural increase	7 per 1000	?
Doubling time	about 100 years	?
Infant mortality	?	110 per 1000
Population under 15 years	?%	?%
Fertility rate	?	?
Urban population	?%	?%
Rural population	?%	?%
Workforce in agriculture	?%	?%
Adults literate	?%	?%
Unemployed or underemployed	?%	?%
Access to safe water	?	?
Number of books published per million people	the highest in the world	?
Food intake	?	?

Total 25 marks

Limiting a country's population growth

You suggest the programme

You are the economic affairs minister in a developing country. You are convinced that your country can only advance if the population increase is reduced.

1 To convince the other government ministers of your ideas you prepare a short statement (up to 50 words). In it you state why you believe in a population policy. (5 marks)

2 You prepare three possible population policies. Each one is up to 50 words and sets out a simple programme with its *advantages*.
   A A programme of compulsory birth control
   B A programme of incentives for parents who only have one child
   C An expansion of rural health clinics and an increase in the training facilities for doctors and nurses.
   (3 × 5 marks)

Figure A The United Nations Family Planning Association

You receive opposition

There is significant opposition to the programmes. Some people think you have no right to limit family size. Other people are simply ignorant of your ideas.

3 Write three letters of opposition that you migh expect to receive. One letter for each programme, each up to 50 words. (3 × 5 marks)

You decide on a programme

After a lucrative offer of help from UNFPA (United Nations Fund for Population Activities) you decide to introduce Programme C. There will be aid for family planning, child health clinics and several aspects of medical care.

4 Write about the facilities that will be provided as part of your population programme. (5 marks)

You look ahead

5 Look thirty years into the future and list what your country will achieve in terms of
   a) population characteristics
   b) economic development (2 × 5 marks)
   Total 50 marks

Figure B Bushmen in Namibia

Figure C A rich world family

Details for pupil profile sheets Unit 7

Knowledge and understanding

1 Urban/rural contrasts
2 Rural Canada and China
3 Census statistics
4 Inputs/outputs – farming
5 Standards of living – indicators
6 UK North/South differences
7 Migration to the city
8 International migration
9 Culture clash
10 Employment/unemployment
11 Family planning
12 South Africa – apartheid
13 Wars and refugees

Skills

1 Comparison work (two areas)
2 Using and mapping census statistics
3 Choosing indicators
4 Group role play
5 Using a triangular graph
6 Linking sets of statistics

Values

1 Understanding attitudes towards migration
2 Understanding the link between poverty and undeveloped farming systems
3 Taking on roles
4 Identifying with migrants/immigrants
5 Realizing how much family size depends on different attitudes
6 Understanding apartheid and its inequalities
7 Realizing that sport and culture are uniting influences

Index

age-sex pyramid 90, 92, 98
age structure 60
apartheid 118
Asda 30
Birmingham 74
birth control 112, 122
birth rate 91, 96
Brasilia 88
Brazil 84, 106, 114
Canada 100
capital city 22, 40
car ownership 61
catchment area 38
census statistics 60–63, 102, 103
central business district (CBD) 32, 33, 64, 65, 86
central place 14
China 100, 113
choropleth map 60, 61
city 16
conurbation 16
costs – economic and social 46
death rate 91, 96
derelict land 66
desire lines 42
disadvantage 58, 111
Eastbourne 52, 53, 54
East Kilbride 70, 71, 72, 73
EC – European Community 97
Edinburgh 56, 57
enquiry route 18
expanded towns 70
favela 81, 88, 89
fertility rate 112
fieldwork 8, 12, 18, 25, 36, 41, 52
functions 14, 85
garden festivals 68
Grasmere 12
Gross Domestic Product 114
hamlet 6
hierarchy 22, 27
Hong Kong 78, 79
housing density 34, 66
housing quality 36
hypermarket 30

hypothesis 8, 18, 36, 61
industrial estate 52, 53, 54, 72, 74
industrial heritage 50
infant mortality 92, 93, 98, 99, 106
informal sector 81, 83
infrastructure 52
inner city 16, 66, 67, 68
inputs/outputs 104
land use 56, 64
life expectancy 92, 106
linear village 7
London 22, 40
Manchester 66, 67, 68, 69
market town 15
McDonald's 28
migration 91, 108, 110
million cities 84, 97
model 64, 86
motorways 47
neighbourhoods 38
Newcastle-upon-Tyne 75
New Towns 70, 71, 72, 73
  in Hong Kong 78, 79
nomadic people 4
nucleated village 7
overspill towns 70
patterns 24, 86
  population 96
  schools 38
pedestrian flow 28
pie graph 94, 95
place-names 6
planning 44, 68, 74
population
  change 12, 90
  density 95
  distribution 94, 95
  patterns 96
  planning 112, 122
poverty trap/cycle 82, 104
primary sources 8
primate city 85
proportional circles 94
push and pull factors 91, 108, 110
quality of environment 54

quality of housing 36
questionnaire 8, 19
racism 58, 111
refugees 117
regeneration 68
religion 120
Rio de Janeiro 84
room density 62
sampling 57
Sao Paulo 84, 85
scattergraph 8, 61
secondary industry 50
secondary sources 8
self-help 80
services 15, 24, 25
shanty town 80
Sheffield 30, 51, 107
shops 26, 27
site 2, 20
situation 11
social areas 74
social class 62
South Africa 118
sphere of influence 18, 31, 40
squatter settlements 77, 80, 88
standard of living 106, 108
superstore 19, 30
Swindon 60–63
Tanzania 86, 87
threshold 15
traffic flow 42
transect diagram 20
triangular graph 114
ujamaa 86, 87
underemployment 82, 83
unemployment 107, 115
urbanization 76
urban transect 32, 33
vandalism 58
viewpoints 17, 44, 45, 55
village 20, 21
villages – Tanzania 86, 87
war 116

Answers to question 1, page 33:
a = 7
b = 4
c = 6
d = 5
e = 2
f = 1
g = 8
h = 3

Acknowledgements

Aerofilms, pp. 57, 71; Aero-Industrial Photography, p. 47; Allsport, pp. 85 (*top*), 120; Asda, p. 30; British Airways, p. 49; Camera Press, p. 59 (*top*); Canada House, p. 64; Format Photos, pp. 5 (*bottom*), 82; Alastair Gray, p. 84, 89 (*bottom*); Susan Griggs, pp. 78, 80, 89 (*top*); Robert Harding, pp. 85 (*bottom*); 101, 123; Hutchison Library, pp. 5 (*top*), 83, 105 (*bottom*); IDG/Aerocamera Hofmeester, p. 105 (*top*); The Image Bank (Robert Ostroweki), front cover, p. 123; Kelham Museum, p. 51 (*both*); Rob Judges, p. 39; Macdonald's, p. 28; Magnum, pp. 97 (*both*), 111 (*bottom*), 119; Manchester City Council, p. 32 (*bottom right*); Marcus Moenda, p. 113; Network, pp. 58 (*both*), 111 (*top*); 112, 115; Rex Features, pp. 120, 121 (*top*); Salford City Council, p. 69; Frank Spooner, p. 117; The Stock Photo Library, p. 23 (*all*); Charlotte Ward-Perkins, pp. 9, 20, 25 (*all*), 32 (*top right*), 41; West Air Photography, pp. 6, 33 (*bottom*), 63, 72.

All other photos supplied by the author.
All illustrations by Oxford Illustrators

Oxford University Press, Walton St, Oxford OX2 6DP

Oxford New York Toronto
Delhi Bombay Calcutta Madras Karachi
Kuala Lumpur Singapore Hong Kong Tokyo
Nairobi Dar es Salaam Cape Town
Melbourne Auckland Madrid

and associated companies in
Berlin Ibadan

Oxford is a trademark of Oxford University Press

© Oxford University Press 1989
First published 1989
Reprinted 1993

ISBN 0 19 913327 1

All rights reserved. No part of this publication may be
reproduced, stored in a retrieval system, or transmitted,
in any form or by any means, without the prior
permission in writing of Oxford University Press.
Within the UK, exceptions are allowed in respect of any
fair dealing for the purpose of research or private study,
or criticism or review, as permitted under the
Copyright, Designs and Patents Act, 1988, or in the
case of reprographic reproduction in accordance with
the terms of licences issued by the Copyright Licensing
Agency. Enquiries concerning reproduction outside
those terms and in other countries should be sent to the
Rights Department, Oxford University Press, at the
address above.

Typeset by Pentacor PLC, High Wycombe, Bucks
Printed in Hong Kong

Pupil's Profile Sheet
Settlement and Population

Unit ☐

Pupil name _____

After completing this unit you should be able to do the following

KNOWLEDGE AND UNDERSTANDING
Understand and use the following terms and concepts:

		YES	NO
1	_____		
2	_____		
3	_____		
4	_____		
5	_____		
6	_____		
7	_____		
8	_____		
9	_____		
10	_____		

SKILLS
Understand and use the following skills:

1	_____		
2	_____		
3	_____		
4	_____		
5	_____		
6	_____		
7	_____		
8	_____		
9	_____		
10	_____		

VALUES

1	_____		
2	_____		
3	_____		